HARTFORD PUBLIC LIBRARY
500 MAIN STREET
HARTFORD, CT 06103
HPL

EASTERN WISDOM

THE PHILOSOPHIES AND RITUALS OF THE EAST

D1366927

THIS IS A CARLTON BOOK

First published in the USA by
Marlowe and Company
632 Broadway, 7th Floor
NY 10012
New York, New York

Text copyright © Michael Jordan
Design copyright © Carlton Books Limited

All rights reserved. No part of this book may be
reproduced, stored in a retrieval system, or transmitted
in any form or by means, electronic, mechanical,
photocopying, recording or otherwise, without the
prior permission of the copyright owner.

Library of Congress Cataloging-in-Publication Data available on request

ISBN 1-56924-732-3

Project Editor: Sarah Larter
Art Editor: Diane Klein
Design and Editorial: Andy Jones, Barry Sutcliffe and Deborah Martin
Picture Researcher: Rachel Leach
Production: Sarah Schuman

Printed in Dubai

EASTERN WISDOM

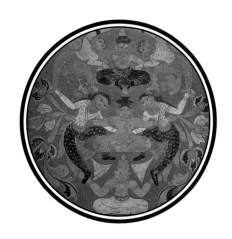

THE PHILOSOPHIES AND RITUALS OF THE EAST

MICHAEL JORDAN

Marlowe & Company

CONTENTS

6996

INTRODUCTION

The philosophies of the east have arisen, not unlike those of the occidental cultures, from a host of different influences and over a vast time-span that reaches back to the misty edge of prehistory. Beliefs of tremendous antiquity have been evidenced through archaeological discoveries spanning the regions of the globe from India to Japan. Some were clearly carried eastwards from the Cradle of Civilization in Mesopotamia whilst others can only have been derived independently, the product of more local minds and inspiration.

In each case it is possible to detect beliefs and understandings of the world around us that have been part of a common frame existing virtually everywhere on the planet. These beliefs are represented in the tribal shamanism of nomadic hunting cultures and the philosophy of animism from which it derives. They can be discerned in the Vedic scriptures which form the bedrock of Hinduism, in the ancient Bon religion of Tibet and the archaic Wu priesthood of China, as well as in aspects of primitive Shinto belief, strands of which are still evident in modern Japan.

Yet out of this common mould arose philosophies that are peculiar to the eastern mind and its attitude concerning life and death. It is almost inconceivable that a Gautama Buddha, a Lao Tzu, the founder of Chinese Taoism, a Confucius, or a Hui Neng, the sixth Chinese Patriarch who gave the oriental world

the concept of Zen, would have arisen in the western hemisphere.

Most of the philosophies of the east not only claim great antiquity but also exert dynamic influences on modern life. Hinduism and Buddhism are a veritable part of the everyday round of living and dying amongst vast millions in the Indian sub-continent and much of South-East Asia. In Japan and Korea religious observances are an essential prerequisite to many of the activities of the secular world. This was also true in China until such traditions were driven out by the impositions of Communism, but these deep-rooted instincts may yet stage their comeback as liberalization proceeds.

One of the keys to the success and remarkable tenacity of the eastern philosophies has been the ability to adapt, to compromise, and to meld comfortably with the beliefs of others. Many of the older faiths, whose appeal was in danger of becoming passé, embraced Buddhism and Confucianism, the great driving forces of missionary zeal in the eastern hemisphere. They achieved this symbiosis unfettered by the restraint that has too often punished Judaism, Christianity and Islam, the great bastions of monotheism.

It is these distinctions, in part, which stimulate us in the west with such a fascination and curiosity about the wisdom of the east, not so much alien as quintessentially exotic.

HINDUISM

*H*induism is among the oldest of the world's faiths. Yet, in spite of the fact that it first evolved more than five thousand years ago, Hinduism is also very much a living tradition, with a purpose and logic relevant to India and her needs and ways of thinking. Providing a religious meaning to all of life, it represents a powerful cohesive force among people who are otherwise vastly disparate in language, culture and social position. Today, Hinduism is practised by at least 400 million devotees in India. In addition there are some 100 million believers known as *harijans* (God's people), who are outside the Hindu caste system. Hinduism also attracts several millions of devotees in countries around the globe and is particularly strong in the United States. As a devotional system, Hinduism is distinctly different from religion in the western sense. It is not for occasional airings on Sundays or to be pulled out to celebrate births, marriages and deaths. In India, where the secular and non-secular merge almost indefinably, Hinduism is part of everyday activity.

Its purpose was, and still is, to provide an education and an inspiration to its adherents, to make lives that are often materially impoverished more meaningful, and to offer a spiritual goal of liberation and salvation. It represents a way of life.

Although Hinduism is the dominant faith in India, it rubs shoulders more or less amicably with other faiths. However, clashes of ideology do exist. An uneasy truce with Islam continues, with tension never far beneath the surface; Sikhs in the Punjab are demanding religious and cultural independence; Tamil separatists are in rebellion against the Buddhist majority in Sri Lanka.

The basis of Hinduism and its many traditions is a profound faith in the revelation contained in the *Veda*. This sacred 3000-year-old text provides the lynch-pin for everything which has come after. All Hindu commentaries, systems and schools derive from that ancient liturgy delivered to the first sages or *rishis* by divine authority. It is the *Veda*, above all, which distinguishes Hinduism from other religions and wisdoms of the east.

THE INDUS VALLEY CIVILIZATION

*T*he Indus river is born in the foothills of the Karakoram mountains and flows south-west through Pakistan, skirting the hills of Baluchistan and emptying into the Arabian Sea just south of modern Karachi.

In 1944 the newly appointed British Director of Archaeology in India, Sir Mortimer Wheeler, began excavations of a vast mound on the banks of the river, near the modern town of Sukkur. Beneath the accumulated layers of soil he discovered the foundations of an early Bronze Age city, built of fired bricks and arranged in a meticulous grid pattern with a perimeter of some three miles. Mortimer Wheeler established that the city was not less than 4000 years old. At about the same time his archaeological teams unearthed an equally impressive urban centre some 350 miles to the north-east.

These ruins represent the lost capital cities of the Indus valley civilization which existed before the Aryan hordes poured in from the north-west and stamped their culture, irrevocably, on the indigenous population of prehistoric India. To the south-west was Mohenjo-Daro, the so-called 'mound of the dead', and to the north-east was Harappa.

CLUES TO A LOST EPOCH

In terms of quality and style of life in these ancient cities, their peoples were organized on a class system in the upper echelons of which were successful traders who lived in some sophistication with well-built houses, municipal baths, economic complexes and comprehensive sewerage systems. Their downfall as urban centres, which seems to have begun in about 1900 BCE, may have been partly due to their topographical positioning since the Indus valley is subject to frequent flooding, although the exact reasons are unclear. We do, however, have gruesome evidence that Mohenjo-Daro came to a final violent demise. At some time around 1500 BCE invaders from Europe who probably entered the region through Persia (Iran) ransacked the city in a welter of bloodshed. These were cattle breeders, the so-called Aryan hordes, who fought from fast horse-drawn chariots. The skulls of many of the last native inhabitants, who met their deaths in their homes and in public places, display damage that suggests butchery beneath the sword and attests to the victory of the newcomers.

There are no clear indications of an organized religious hierarchy amongst the Indus peoples nor are there buildings which could be designated unmistakably as temples, although there is some argument that what has been described as a public bath may in fact have possessed a non-secular function as a place of ritual cleansing similar to the spiritual washing which is still practised amongst modern Hindus. There are also some indications that the cities may have been governed by god-kings comparable to those of the contemporary Sumerian city states to the west. Amongst the clues are a number of finely sculpted heads, carved from soapstone or steatite. Most of

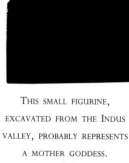

THIS SMALL FIGURINE, EXCAVATED FROM THE INDUS VALLEY, PROBABLY REPRESENTS A MOTHER GODDESS.

these depict bearded males, their hair neatly arranged and wearing similarly patterned styles of dress. The countenance is haughty and the assumption must be that these were rulers who possessed the aura and trappings of divinity. Also unearthed from the ruins are a number of small figurines which are believed to represent the oldest gods and goddesses of the Indus valley civilization although their precise identities are unclear.

The greatest problem with understanding these people and their culture is that, prior to the arrival of the Aryans, the limited material discovered to include inscriptions has, thus far, resisted deciphering. The Aryan invaders created a script known as Sanskrit and it was through this medium that the earliest-known myths, religious beliefs and practices were recorded. We have to assume that the Aryans amalgamated elements of the religion of the Indus valley civilization with their own and that, prior to their arrival, indigenous beliefs and philosophies relied on preservation by word of mouth.

THE CITADEL WITHIN THE RUINS OF MOHENJO-DARO, ONE OF THE LOST CITIES OF THE INDUS VALLEY CIVILIZATION.

A WARRIOR LEADER – HISTORICAL OR MYTHICAL?

From the tone of the ancient hymns it seems clear that the Aryans were 'led' by Indra. Whether he was an historical warrior leader or a purely mythical figure is impossible to determine but the indications are that he demolished the Indus valley cities with considerable violence and he became one of the most prominent of the early 'Vedic gods', so-called because they feature strongly in the most ancient of the Indo-European holy books, the *Veda*. Much of Indra's fighting was against a demonic horde led by the primeval personification of chaos, Vritra, whom Indra eventually slew with his magical weapon, the thunderbolt. Indra is also reported to have crushed a serpent-like ally of Vritra, called Dasa.

In one of the Vedic hymns Indra's mother, Aditi, cries:

With his great weapon my son killed Vritra and set these rivers free ... not for my sake did the shoulderless one [Vritra] wound you, generous Indra, and strike away your two jaws; though wounded, you overpowered him, and with your weapon you crushed the head of the Dasa.

The assumption must be that Vritra and Dasa, with their demonic retinue, represent the old warrior gods of the Indus whom the celestial champions of the invaders were obliged to crush. The hymn describes the release of waters when Vritra is killed which 'were screaming together like righteous women' and it may be that a mythology arose recording a great inundation of the Indus plain which coincided with the invasion and which came to represent some kind of divine 'ethnic cleansing' process.

There is also strong evidence that the Indus valley civilization worshipped a mother goddess. It would be surprising if an agricultural people did not recognize such a figure. Archaeology has unearthed small female figurines from Mohenjo-Daro, depicted naked and with their emphases on breasts and genitals, that are familiar in various forms throughout the ancient world.

It is probably safe to guess that the Indus valley possessed an ancient religion which included a pantheon of agricultural deities worshipped in seasonal rituals that involved sacrifice and other offerings of appeasement, and which was headed by priest kings who were revered as living divinities. Beyond this surmise we have little to go on. But it was from the fusion of this culture with that of the European invaders, resulting in the Indo-Aryan stock, that the great religions of Hinduism and, subsequently, Buddhism, were to be forged.

THE HINDU PANTHEON

*I*t is arguable that the many Hindu deities reflect aspects of the one but the pantheon which has evolved over thousands of years, in terms of names, images, attributes and responsibilities, is truly vast. Some of the most ancient members, the local protective goddesses of the village cults, are still evident. Under the influence of the BRAHMANA caste, however, many have been incorporated into the greater body of classical Brahmanic culture and tradition and in this respect names have changed as local deities have been 'Sanskritized' and given more august titles. On the larger national and international scale there are distinct 'regional' variations in the exact nature of deities worshipped and the scriptures in which they are detailed.

It all adds up to an extremely diverse picture made more complex by the fact that deities may also be worshipped in one or more aspects and varieties and that they may command substantial numbers of different names or epithets. The god Shiva claims more than a thousand such varieties by which he may be described in literature, inscriptions and art, some benevolent, others cruel and destructive. Principal male deities also possess *shaktis* or female aspects which often display the same characteristics as the principal god. This, in itself, can further complicate the picture because the *shakti* can also be said to represent the energy of a god. For example, the *shaktis* ascribed to Shiva include Parvati, Devi, Durga, Kali and others, each of which relates to Shiva in one of his different aspects.

It is possible, as with almost all other cultures, to group deities according to their activities. Hence there are creator

SARASVATI, THE GODDESS OF WISDOM, IS USUALLY DEPICTED PLAYING A STRINGED INSTRUMENT.

gods and goddesses, the most senior amongst whom are the *trimurti* (trinity) of Brahma, Vishnu and Shiva and their accompanying *shaktis*. Beneath this trio are deities concerned with natural phenomena — rivers, mountains, lakes, agriculture, war, disease, love, fertility, birth, marriage, death and many other aspects of life.

The early Indus valley civilization undoubtedly possessed its pantheon but we have very little detail of the personalities. It included a mother goddess and a fertility god who was associated with animals, possibly as a lord of the hunt. It appears that there was also a bull cult, which presumably involved a bull-like god. Beyond this scant detail the existence of specific deities is largely down to speculation. The Indus valley people probably followed a strongly animistic style of religion which included a profusion of spirits concerned with the natural world and its effect on the human population.

THE INDO-ARYAN DEITIES

The pantheon of the Indo-Aryan culture which succeeded it is more clearly defined because it is described in the collection of early sacred texts, the *Veda samhita*. In the *Rig Veda* the primordial male principle of creation is described as Daksa and beside him stands his female counterpart, Aditi, the archaic mother goddess, each of whom, paradoxically, has given birth to the other. Daksa may also be synonymous with another archetypal being named Prajapati since one of the great creation hymns, to an unnamed god, ends thus:

> *He who in his greatness looked over the waters, which were pregnant with Daksa, bringing forth the sacrifice, he who was the one god among all the gods — who is the god whom we should worship with the oblation?*
>
> *Let him not harm us, he who fathered the earth and created the sky, whose laws are true, who created the high, shining waters. Who is the god whom we should worship with the oblation?*
>
> *O Prajapati, lord of progeny, no one but you embraces all these creatures. Grant us the desires for which we offer you oblation. Let us be lords of riches. (Rig Veda, p.28)*

At the head of the pantheon is the god Indra who probably began his existence as a sun deity or a weather god but who is identified with an early bull cult that perhaps came from the Indus valley civilization. He suggests great strength and is also identified with fertility and war. In common with the peculiar birth mechanism of many other deities the world over, his mother, Aditi, keeps him in the womb for an abnormally long gestation period to protect him possibly from a jealous father named Tvashtri. Even after his birth, not as a vulnerable infant but as a man of giant stature, she hides him:

> *Why has she pushed him far away, whom she carried for a thousand months and many autumns? For there is no one his equal among those who are born and those who will be born.*
>
> *As if she thought he was flawed, his mother hid Indra though he abounded in manly strength. Then he stood up and put his garment on by himself; as he was born he filled the two world halves. (Rig Veda, p.142)*

A FIVE-HEADED IMAGE OF SHIVA FROM A MANDI INDIAN PAINTING, C.1730: AS THE DESTROYER, SHIVA WEARS A NECKLACE OF SKULLS AND HOLDS OBJECTS THAT SYMBOLIZE HIS POWERS.

Typical of the *shaktis* of such deities is the mother goddess Indrana, the consort of Indra, whose title changes to Aindri when she shares his more violent, warlike disposition.

Standing beside Indra is a storm god named Rudra, the father of a group of storm deities named the Maruts, whose *shakti* is Bhavani and who later becomes largely superseded by Shiva. Rudra shows a fierce, somewhat demonic character but he too is paradoxical in his conduct since he is able to cool fevers and heal but may also bring disease. Rudra is often invoked together with Vishnu who plays a minor role in the *Veda* as a sun god but who is destined to rise to prominence in the later Epic and Puranic texts.

Agni is the androgynous deity of fire and, since the two phenomena are inextricably linked in Hindu ritual, god of sacrifice. He is also closely associated with the intoxicating

IN THE VEDIC PERIOD INDRA WAS CHIEF AMONG THE GODS AND REPRESENTED STRENGTH AND FERTILITY.

sacrificial ambrosia of immortality, the *soma*. The circumstance of his birth is shrouded in mystery but it appears that he was coaxed, by the other gods, out of the primeval waters at the time of creation. There is an equal sense of mystery about his regular disappearance. Since fire is kindled and is extinguished it follows that the god must hide himself somewhere when he is not visible. Agni also represents one of the most important Vedic intercessors between humankind and gods since it is he who delivers the sacrificial offerings that ascend as smoke to the heavens.

The god Varuna takes a guardian role as the deity who oversees the proper operation of the systems, including water, which govern life on earth. He is the custodian of the sacred Vedic laws and, at the time of creation, was responsible for the separation of earth and heaven. He was originally a sky god and his name derives from the same Indo-Aryan root as Ouranos, the god of heaven in Greek mythology. Varuna is imagined to be a stern but fair master of human beings and typical of the invocations to him is the close of a Vedic hymn describing his deeds:

> *If we have committed an offence against a hospitable friend or a close friend or against one who has always been a comrade, or a brother, or a neighbour — one of our own or a stranger — loosen that offence from us, Varuna.*
>
> *If we have cheated like gamblers in a game, whether we know it or really do not know it, O God, cast all these offences away like loosened bonds. Let us be dear to you, Varuna.*
> (*Rig Veda*, p.211)

Amongst the other popular Vedic deities the sun god, Surya, controls the cosmic order and is also god of knowledge. Yama is the judge and god of death and his *shakti* is Yami. The pair also represent the first human beings. Yama is therefore the first man who experienced death and in whose footsteps we all follow. The demonic Vritra should also be included. He is envisaged as a great dragon which first created drought, a highly important factor in the life of India, and which is vanquished by Indra, in his role as a weather god, when he brings relief in the form of rain.

THE NEWER PANTHEON

Most of these Vedic deities found their way into the later Brahmanic, Epic and Puranic literature though not always with the same names or responsibilities. Hence there is a slow transition during which, for example, Rudra becomes sidelined in favour of Shiva or perhaps merges with him. Much of the newer pantheon is centred upon the three main gods, Brahma, Vishnu and Shiva, with their consorts or *shaktis*.

Sarasvati is the consort of Brahma and, like him, makes no appearance in the *Veda* other than as the deification of various sacred rivers including the Indus. She is also the goddess of wisdom and is the mother of Brahma's two children, Vac the goddess of speech, and Satarupa, both of whose names are also confusingly ascribed as epithets of Sarasvati. One tradition suggests that Satarupa is a true *shakti* in that she is formed from half of Brahma's own self, whilst in another myth she is the object of his incestuous desires. Brahma's second wife is Gayatri who may also be identical with Sarasvati. In some texts she is described as a milkmaid but no children are indicated from the union and *gayatri* is also the personification of a Hindu hymn composed in a certain characteristic arrangement of stanzas.

Lakshmi, who some texts indicate is a jealous rival of Sarasvati, is the consort of Vishnu although his *shaktis* vary in name and character to match his various human incarnations or *avataras*. Hence the goddesses Sita, Radha and Dharani become *avataras* of Lakshmi when she is partnered respectively with Rama, Krishna and Parasurama. Lakshmi is a fertility and mother goddess who is also believed to be the personification of the earth, and her children with Vishnu include Kamadeva the androgynous deity of carnal love. She is variously accounted in mythology as being the daughter of the primordial being, Prajapati, or to have sprung from foam when the ocean was churned, not unlike Aphrodite in Greek tradition. Aside from her role as *shakti* of Vishnu she is also described as consort to several other deities including Prajapati himself, Varuna and Ganesha.

Parvati stands as the chief consort of Shiva but amongst the most notorious of the goddess *shaktis* are those associated with Shiva in his destructive aspect, including the terrible forms, Kali and Durga. The more gentle and benevolent *shakti* is Parvati and amongst the offspring from Shiva and Parvati is one of the best loved of all Hindu deities, Ganesha, the god whose head is that of an elephant. The story of how he acquired his elephant head is both violent and bizarre. Parvati had yearned for a child from Shiva but he had constantly evaded fatherhood, preferring life as an ascetic. He once gave Parvati a rag doll as a baby-substitute but when it took life of its own as she held it to her breast he was seized with jealousy and decapitated it with a sweep of his hand. Parvati was immeasurably distraught and when Shiva realized her extreme grief he sent his bull-god lieutenant, Nandin, to find a replacement head which was to be removed from the first living creature he encountered facing towards the north. It happened to be an elephant and so Ganesha was restored but with a bizarre hybrid appearance.

These are just the more significant of the many thousands of deities and demons that make up the sprawling Hindu pantheon, the vast pyramid of which reaches down, ultimately, to humble local divinities whose names are recorded and observed only within individual village communities.

THE
GREAT
CREATOR
GODS

*H*induism, at first glance, appears to be indisputably polytheistic. It includes a pantheon of deities and their demonic counterparts that runs into thousands, a sizeable body of whom achieve major cult status throughout India and beyond, whilst many others represent little more than local household gods. Closer examination, however, reveals a situation that is somewhat different because many of the minor personalities which make up the pantheon are aspects of a major deity.

At the head of the Hindu pantheon reside three commanding figures, a trinity (*trimurti*) of gods who replaced the old Indo-Aryan creator deity Indra. Yet even this trio may be interpreted as being aspects of the one celestial power. It comprises Vishnu, Shiva and Brahma. Vishnu represents all that is positive and constructive in the universe. Shiva is his antithesis, reflecting the negative and destructive forces around us. Brahma stands as the balance between these two opposing principles. It might be imagined that these two 'force fields' and the buffer that stands between them are separate entities but that ignores a fundamental Hindu understanding of existence. It is not possible to create without first destroying, genesis cannot take place without dissolution, the ordered cosmos can evolve only if first there is chaos, construction is possible only if its bedfellow is destruction. These three deities at the apex of the modern Hindu pantheon are representations of abstract principles, more symbols than human likenesses. Therefore Vishnu, the preserver of the cosmos, is not possible without Shiva, the destroyer, and Shiva cannot exist alone without Vishnu.

VISHNU

It is probable that Vishnu originated in about 1700 BCE, or earlier, as a minor sun deity. His worship has continued to evolve to the present time when, as the highest creator god of the *trimurti*, he commands one of the major cults of Hinduism. He appears in the Vedic hymns but only briefly in his aspect as the Trivikrama, the minor cosmic deity who becomes a colossus in order to create the universe in three giant strides. His true claim to fame emerges only through the *Brahmanas, Upanishads* and later literature, particularly the epic of *Mahabharata* where he appears as Krishna and addresses his great morality lecture to the hero Arjuna in the *Bhagavad Gita*. In the sister epic of *Ramayana* he goes under the synonym of Narayana. It is through these scriptures that many of his incarnations emerge, the *avataras* of Vishnu, in order to protect mankind.

Vishnu is said to have been born from the left side of the primordial creator force and he is linked closely with the needs of humanity as the preserver, through *karma,* of morality and civilized order. Narayana, who is frequently regarded as an incarnate *avatara* of Vishnu, means literally 'son of Nara, the original, eternal man' but it can also be taken to mean the 'universal abode of man'. In his worship he is sometimes described as the 'Right Hand God' because of a characteristic gesture of *abhayamudra*. With the right hand raised, elbow

THE *TRIMURTI* OR TRIO OF CREATOR GODS — BRAHMA, VISHNU AND SHIVA — DEPICTED IN AN ENGRAVING FROM
THE ILLUSTRATED GLOBE ENCYCLOPAEDIA OF UNIVERSAL KNOWLEDGE, PUBLISHED IN 1882.

bent, and the palm facing outwards this actually means fearlessness but symbolizes his role as 'the preserver'.

Vishnu's chief adversary is Yama, the god of the dead. His most frequent consort is the goddess of fortune, Lakshmi, and the pair are often depicted together standing or seated on a lotus. Vishnu is also linked with sacred water or *nara* and is therefore a spiritual presence which pervades the holy river Ganges. He sleeps for four months of the year, resting on the coils of a great guardian serpent named Ananta or Sesanaga, and is awakened by a special annual ritual. His sacred animal and vehicle is Garuda, a bird-like human hybrid which devours demons, and he is usually depicted with four arms, several heads, a characteristic tuft of hair on his chest and he may hold an assortment of attributes including a conch, a prayer wheel or *cakra*, a mace and a lotus.

SHIVA

The opposite to Vishnu, Shiva is conceived as the Annihilator and the Destroyer. In terms of gender, he symbolizes masculine aspects of the cosmos that are destructive and unpredictable, whilst Vishnu stands as the embodiment of female stability and generative capacity. Yet Shiva is something of an enigma since he is also a generative power. He provides an ambivalence encompassing the extremes of ascetic denial and sexual eroticism and to his worshippers he embodies

Creator, Preserver and Destroyer, manifesting himself as a gracious *anugrahamurti* or destructive *ugramurti* character depending on mood and intent. His consort or *shakti* may also display a corresponding range of character and so she is variously drawn as Mahadevi, the great goddess, in her most dynamic form; as Parvati, the daughter of the Himalayas, and as Gauri, Sati and Uma when she is in her benign aspect; and as the terrible goddesses Kali and Durga when in her destructive capacity. The spiritual home of Shiva, the contemplative ascetic and *yogi*, lies on Mount Kailasha in the Himalayas.

He may have arisen in the mould of the Vedic storm god, Rudra, but others claim that he emerged before the Indo-Aryan period since seals, discovered at the archaeological site of Mohenjo-Daro and dating from the period of the Indus valley civilization, show attributes associated with Shiva. These include a *trisula* or trident and a *damaru* or small double-headed drum shaped like an hourglass and representing the rhythm of creation, both magical devices linked with primitive shamanism. A noose or *pasa* which fetters the soul refers to his life spent as the ascetic wandering in the Himalayas and probably stems, again, from his Indus valley beginnings. Other attributes, symbolizing Shiva's destructive power, include a bow or *dhanus* and a club or *gada* to which is attached a skull. He also holds the *linga* stone which represents a phallus and refers to his contrasting creative capacity as 'the giver of seed'.

Shiva is known by more than a thousand epithets which makes precise identification in texts difficult though his names

An Indian miniature shows Shiva and Parvati with their offspring, Ganesha.

generally include the appendage *murti*. In addition, he is usually depicted with four arms and with a blue throat which refers to the creation myth during which he holds the primeval poison *halahala* in his throat so as to save mankind from its terrible effect. In his appearance he also has the matted hair of the ascetic pilgrim and sometimes is drawn with water cascading from his head to symbolize his part in bringing the waters of the sacred Ganges down from the heavens. Less severe is his role as Nataraja, the Lord of the Dance or the dancer who controls the rhythm of the cosmos, surrounded by a ring of fire, and he is often shown thus in bronzes, particularly those originating from southern India. His sacred animal is a bull, Nandin, which is his vehicle and guardian and which represents an additional symbol of fertility.

BRAHMA

Although the senior deity of the trio, Brahma is the most remote and is the only member to whom no cult is addressed. Tradition has it that he emerged from the right side of the primordial creator force, whilst another suggests that he created himself through the power of his own mind, engendering a seed placed inside a golden egg floating on the primeval waters. When he emerged he used the broken halves to create earth and sky. The lifespan of Brahma is reckoned as 100 heavenly years, each of 360 days and nights, of which one day or *kalpa* is equal to 4,320 million earthly years. He has lived for 51 of these heavenly years and on each of his birthdays has destroyed and rebuilt the universe.

Brahma is the god of all knowledge, frequently carrying the sacred *Veda*. He has four arms and four heads facing in different directions generated, according to tradition, when his

THE ELEPHANT-HEADED DEITY, GANESHA, SON OF SHIVA AND PARVATI, AS SHOWN IN A POPULAR STREET POSTER IN BOMBAY.

daughter, Satarupa, circled around him in a fruitless attempt to escape his incestuous desire. His consort is generally Sarasvati, goddess of wisdom, though he is also associated with Vach, the goddess of speech, and with a milkmaid named Gayatri.

THE
AVATARAS
OF VISHNU

As a creator god, one of whose prime concerns is towards the well-being of humankind and the earth, Vishnu has contrived to intercede in worldly affairs when great danger or evil has threatened and tradition has it that he is destined to do so again in the future.

As Vishnu declares in the *Bhagavad Gita*: 'Whenever dharma declines and the purpose of life is forgotten, I manifest myself on earth. I am born in every age to protect the good, to destroy evil, and to re-establish the *dharma*.' He therefore adopts a messianic role that is not dissimilar in purpose to that of Jesus of Nazareth in the Christian faith. His intercession is carried out in the form, not necessarily human, of incarnations or *avataras*.

Hindu belief differs from the Christian faith in that the 'comings' of Vishnu have occurred on a number of occasions but, when Vishnu does appear in human guise, like the Christian Messiah, he experiences a normal birth from mortal parents although in his subsequent childhood he quickly demonstrates that he is something more than human. One of the most beautiful and moving passages from the *Bhagavata Purana* comes when Yasoda, the foster-mother of the baby Krishna, the eighth *avatara* of Vishnu, chastises him for allegedly eating dirt and demands to see inside his mouth:

> *Then she saw in his mouth the whole eternal universe, and heaven, and the regions of the sky, and the orb of the earth with its mountains, islands, and oceans; she saw the wind, and lightning, and the moon and stars, and the zodiac; and water, and fire, and air, and space itself; she saw the vacillating senses, the mind, the elements, and the three strands of matter. She saw, within the body of her son, in his gaping mouth, the*

whole universe in all its variety, with all the forms of life and time and nature and action and hopes, and her own village, and herself. (See *Hindu Myths*, p.220)

Some of the animals which are identified as incarnations were not originally regarded as Vishnu *avataras*. Matsya the fish and Varaha the boar appear first in *Brahmana* mythology unrelated to traditions of Vishnu. In the *Veda* the boar is actually identified with the creator being, Prajapati, who rescues the earth from demons. Only later is it linked with Vishnu who once assisted Indra in the rescue of a sacrificial boar.

Although they are referred to in various parts of the sacred literature of Hinduism, the early *avataras* are largely concerned with deeds involving the primeval ocean, the representation of primordial chaos, and their presence emphasizes the Hindu philosophy that an orderly cosmos can be achieved only through the instrument of chaos.

MATSYA (THE FISH)

The first *avatara*, introduced in the *Brahmanas*, emerges at the time of the primeval flood. The deluge is an experience shared by many cultures around the world but it may have been a distinct reality in northern India when the ice receded at the end of the last glaciation and large quantities of melt water from the Himalayas inundated the plains and river valleys. Similar fish gods are known in the Sumerian mythology of Mesopotamia and there is a suggestion that a common deluge tradition may have grown up between Sumer and the contemporary Dravidian stock in India. Vishnu appears with a human torso surmounted on a fish body and for his first remedial action attaches himself to a ship carrying the first man and law-giver, Manu, and tows it to safety. Later he engages in a ferocious battle with the demon Hayagriva who has stolen the *Veda* from Brahma whilst he sleeps.

MATSYA THE FISH, THE FIRST *AVATARA* OF VISHNU, TAKEN FROM AN
EIGHTEENTH-CENTURY EUROPEAN PUBLICATION.

KURMA
(THE TORTOISE)

This second *avatara* is described in the epic mythology of the
Mahabharata. It also emerges at the time when the primeval
ocean forms the focus of activity, although the event is placed
after the deluge since one of Vishnu's purposes is to recover
some of the possessions he lost at the time of the flood. It is
the intention of the gods to generate the ambrosia of
immortality from the primordial 'sea of milk' in order that they
may gain superiority over the demonic forces of chaos who
constantly threaten them and challenge their authority. This is
the classic imagery of chaos, symbolized by the restless waters,
being transformed into creation. Vishnu appears in the guise of
a huge tortoise which acts as a pivot for Mount Mandara, the
mountain that the gods use as a churning stick in order to stir
up the ingredients of the sea. They also employ Vasuki, the
seven-headed king of the snakes, as a rope which is passed
around the mountain in order to achieve the churning action.

VARAHA
(THE BOAR)

The third *avatara* is first described in the Brahmanic texts and
the mythological focus remains on the primeval ocean. Vishnu
incarnates himself as a giant boar in order to rescue the earth
after demons under the direction of their leader, Hiranyaksa,
have abducted it to the ocean bed. The boar is an appropriate
animal to perform this task since it appears strongly
amphibious. There are also fertility connotations in the
manifestation of the boar since it is an animal that roots in the
earth. Varaha dives down into the depths, kills Hiranyaksa, and
rescues the earth in the guise of a young woman. A complex
philosophy underlies this action since the primordial being with
whom the boar was first associated, Prajapati, also *distilled* the
earth from the ocean. Hindu belief argues that matter cannot
increase but can only be reorganized; it follows, therefore, that
whatever is 'created' or 'recreated' must already exist, albeit
in a different form. The stirring of the ocean, the birth of the
earth, its loss and subsequent restoration, are all to be
envisaged as chemical syntheses taking place in the closed
reactor vessel of the universe to which nothing is added and
nothing taken away.

NARASINHA
(THE LION)

As the fourth *avatara*, Vishnu once more incarnates himself to
save the earth from the tribulations brought by a demon. On
this occasion it is a brother of Hiranyaksa named Hiranyakasipu
who is said to be an incarnation of the demon king of Sri
Lanka, Ravana, known from the *Ramayana* epic. Hiranyakasipu
can be slain by neither man nor beast and in order to overcome
this invulnerability Vishnu adopts the guise of a man-lion
hybrid. Narasinha, epitomizing fierceness and bravery, goes to
the palace of Hiranyakasipu at dusk and conceals himself inside
a pillar by the entrance, from which he then springs to slay the
unwitting demon, ripping out his entrails. The incident is a
popular one in Hindu religious art which often depicts
Hiranyakasipu flung across the knees of Narasinha with the
claws of the man-lion plunged into his body.

VAMANA – TRIVIKRAMA
(THE DWARF – COLOSSUS)

This fifth *avatara* is the only one to be discussed in the *Veda,*
the most ancient of the Hindu texts. Vishnu appears first in the
dwarfish guise of Vamana, symbolizing the puny state of
humankind, in order to trick the demon Bali who is described
as a great-grandson of Hiranyakasipu. It is said that the prestige

of Bali had begun to overshadow that of the great god Indra and that it was necessary to restore a proper balance in the universe.

Vamana requests from Bali a plot of land no more than three paces wide on which he may rest and meditate. Examining the diminutive stature of Vamana, Bali accedes, condescendingly, to the request whereupon Vishnu transforms into a colossus, the Trivikrama, which means 'he who takes three strides'. His first step claims the heavens, his second the earth. His third pace encompasses the underworld but he declines to claim this realm and offers it instead as the dominion over which Bali shall rule. Conceding that he has been outclassed, Bali accepts.

The imagery of this act may link back to the more ancient Vedic role of Vishnu as a sun god since the three steps also, arguably, represent the three outer points of 'orbit' of the sun – the east, the zenith and the west.

PARASURAMA (RAMA WITH THE AXE)

In the sixth incarnation Vishnu appears in strictly human guise but his purpose remains to save the world from evil. This character is sometimes identified with Rama, whilst at others Rama is drawn as Parasurama's more famous brother. Parasurama is a brilliant archer who, in gratitude for his archery skills, adopts a contemplative life in the Himalayas as a Shaivite disciple. A number of references to Parasurama appear in the Epic and Puranic texts, offering differing reasons for Vishnu adopting this form but, generally, the context has changed from superhuman to human and to matters of political strife with which early Indian history was plagued. In a world dominated by a royal warrior class, the kshatriyas, who have become despotic tyrants, Parasurama appears as a fearless champion. He rids the earth of its oppressors and is rewarded by Shiva with the gift of an axe. As Parasurama he is born the son of mortal parents, Jamadagni and Renuka, and his consort is Dharani who is herself an avatara of the goddess Lakshmi. Parasurama is depicted holding a small axe or hatchet and is generally equipped with other warlike attributes including a sword, bow, arrows and knife.

AN EIGHTEENTH-CENTURY PAINTING FROM THE JAIPUR AREA, DEPICTING VISHNU IN THE CENTRE, SURROUNDED BY HIS TEN MAJOR AVATARAS.

RAMA

The most famous of the avataras are those of the epic myths, the Mahabharata and Ramayana. The incarnation of Rama has been variously identified as Parasurama before Shiva gave him his axe and as Parasurama's brother. Generally Rama is seen as a separate character, a minor incarnation who achieved immense popularity through the story of a hero setting out to kill a demon king, Ravana, who had abducted his wife, Sita. She is identified as an avatara of Lakshmi and is also known from the Veda but as a distinct deity who is worshipped as an agricultural mother goddess.

The Rama of the epic tale was born to Dasaratha and Kausalya, the royal family of the north Indian capital of Ayodhya, and became the embodiment of *dharma*, the principle of law and justice. Rama represents manhood and honour *par excellence* although he also succumbs to human weakness in the treatment of his wife. Rama's chief weapon is a bow and this also identifies him with Parasurama, the Shaivite devotee, who once tried to uphold the honour of Shiva by fighting Rama when the latter had broken Shiva's bow in a contest of strength. The weapon, henceforth, became the substance of Rama's armoury.

⋈

KRISHNA

Though Rama is the hero of the *Ramayana* it is Krishna, the eighth *avatara*, who steals the limelight in the *Mahabharata* and who is undoubtedly the most important incarnation of Vishnu. He seems, however, to have originated as a local pastoral god and only became associated with Vishnu in literature composed after the time of the *Mahabharata* epic. Like Rama he appears in human form but is born at Mathura to semi-divine princely parents, Vasudeva and Devaki, and is merely fostered by an ordinary mortal couple, Nanda and Yasoda. As a baby, known as Balakrishna, he lives with a brother, Balarama, and when he reaches adulthood he weds Rukmini. Like Sita she is an *avatara* of Lakshmi, but Krishna is also identified with many other female companions including Radha and Rati. Rukmini, nonetheless, is his first wife and always stands at his right side. Before he gained his popularity as the mentor of the hero Arjuna in the *Bhagavad Gita*, he is alleged to have been incarnated in Mathura in order to rid the world of a tyrannical despot named Kansa, his mother's cousin.

BUDDHA

The ninth and tenth *avataras* only properly emerge in the late Hindu texts, the *Puranas*. Paradoxically the ninth incarnation is not an attempt to assimilate the teachings of Buddhism but reveals strong anti-Buddhist sentiment since Vishnu incarnates as the *buddha* in order to rid the earth of an evil doctrine that is being evangelized by demons. In Hindu dogma the term 'demons' frequently refers to followers of alien religions, including Buddhism and Jainism. Vishnu agrees to impersonate the *buddha* so as to deceive the demons. In this guise he persuades them to abandon the path of the *Veda*, the single element which conveniently protects them from harm by the Hindu gods, and so renders them susceptible to slaughter.

⋈

KALKIN

The tenth and final incarnation is a futuristic one that has yet to appear and in this there are strong parallels with the Christian *Book of Revelation*. The coming of Kalkin, the avenger, will mark the end of the corrupt and evil present age of the goddess Kali and will usher in the new, golden age of Krita. In the *Vishnu Purana*, Kalkin will come riding upon a white horse much as does the 'pale rider' of *Revelation*. The human race will be annihilated, having resorted for many years to foraging for roots and berries in the mountains and having been abused by a succession of greedy and tyrannical rulers. But all will be re-established with its own renewed *dharma*. This is in line with a basic tenet of Hindu philosophy whereby chaos and dissolution must always precede rebirth and the renewal of creation.

KURMA THE TORTOISE PORTRAYED IN THE FACADE OF A HINDU TEMPLE IN SINGAPORE.

THE SECTS OF VISHNU AND SHIVA

Over the centuries Hinduism has developed a wide range of branches and sects, each devoting itself to a particular deity or aspects of a deity. But the Vaishnava and Shaivite movements, worshipping the two main creator gods, are probably the largest and most universal.

⊰⊱

THE VAISHNAVA DOCTRINE

Vaishnava-dharma is followed by the worshippers of Vishnu who identify him as the supreme being or *brahman* and also regard his *avatara* as Rama to represent the epitome of manhood and human aspiration. Vaishnavi refers to the female aspect or *shakti* of Vishnu who in the scriptures is identified as the goddess Lakshmi. The central scripture of the Vaishnavite sect is the *Vishnu Purana*. Vaishnava traditions are followed all over India though the sect is concentrated mainly in northern and central parts of the sub-continent where worship of Rama and Krishna, two of Vishnu's most celebrated *avataras* or incarnations, has been popular. These include the Hindi-speaking states of north-east India such as Manipur. There is also a strong but distinct Vaishnavite movement in the Tamil-speaking south and the sect dominates in the state

MAHATMA GANDHI,
A DEVOTEE OF THE
VAISHNAVA DOCTRINE.

of Gujarat. One of the most celebrated Vaishnava devotees was the assassinated leader Mahatma Gandhi, who came from Gujarat and who is reported to have uttered the words 'Eh! Ram!' with his dying breath.

The most important related sect, particularly in southern India, is that of *bhakti*, meaning 'devotion', which involves a mystical doctrine based on the belief that by means of total, uncompromising devotion, union may be attained with Vishnu through the intermediary of his mortal *avatara*, Krishna. The latter is sometimes referred to, confusingly, as Vasudeva, who is actually the father of Krishna, but the epithet Vasudeva-Vishnu is popularly used by Vaishnava worshippers to symbolize the underlying identity of Krishna. The holiest scriptures of the Bhakti movement include the *Bhagavata Purana* which was composed in about the ninth century CE and was derived from the *Bhagavad Gita*, the famous moral discourse between Krishna and the heroic prince Arjuna which forms the jewel of the *Mahabharata* epic.

The religious practices of Vaishnavites include *bhajan*, a style of sung or chanted expression of adoration which contains quotations from holy scriptures and frequently constitutes an important part of local village devotion.

The movement has strong links with the Buddhist tantric school of Sahajayana, founded by the Vaishnava poet and sage, Krishnacarya.

THE SHAIVITE DOCTRINE

This has to some extent become syncretized with that of Vaishnava but is followed by worshippers of Shiva known as *shaivabhaktas*, amongst whose sacred texts is the *Linga Purana*. The most revered of these *shaivabhakta* from the past include 63 canonized Shaivite saints, the most celebrated of whom are considered to be Appar, Manikkavacakar, Sundara-Nayanar and Tirujnana-Sambandha.

Shiva is strongly linked with fertility and Shaivite temples include a stone or metal sculpture known as the *linga* which represents a phallus. Symbolizing Shiva's function as the 'giver of seed' or *bijavan*, models of the *linga* stone are generally to be found in the homes of *shaivabhaktas* where they offer a focus of worship. Frequently the *linga* is decorated with offerings of white jasmine and the red leaves of the *bilva* tree, both of which are linked with the god. The *linga* may be incorporated in a *yoni*, its female counterpart, in a style of symbolic sexual fusion although some Shaivites claim that the *yoni* offers no sexual connotation and is only a receptacle for collecting holy water with which the *linga* is ritually bathed. It may additionally be embraced by a snake or *naga* which also represents a symbol of fertility. During Shaivite festivals phallic cakes are prepared and eaten as a further devotion to Shiva's sexual attributes.

One of the offshoots of the Shaivite sect follows a doctrine known as *Shaiva-siddhanta*, according to which Shiva is the absolute and eternal subject of all understanding and perception and is also the effective cause of everything that takes place in the universe. The system follows three cardinal principles: recognition of *pati*, the supreme being; *pacu*, which represents the individual soul or spirit; and *pacam*, the fetter or obstacle which prevents the soul from finding release through union with Shiva.

SHAKTISM

The tradition of Shaktism focuses devotion on the female aspects of the major deities, such as the goddess Devi who epitomizes the active feminine principle of the divine. She is seen very much as an abstract principle but nonetheless encompassing all the functions of Vishnu and Shiva and one who will respond to the prayers of her worshippers. Her most notable achievement in myth was probably the slaying of Mahisa. He is described as a demonic adversary of humankind who takes the form of a buffalo but who can also change into other animal guises. Devi is reputed to have killed him with his own sword and was thereafter also known as Mahisasuramardina, the Slayer of the Buffalo Demon.

Devi can be traced back to the ancient Indus valley civilization images of the mother goddess, but she made the successful transition into Indo-Aryan culture to the extent that the *Devi-bhagavata Purana* is devoted to her and contains a vast number of goddess myths and invocations. Today her popularity remains intact and most Hindu homes possess a Devi image. Devotion to her is especially strong in rural village communities where she is regularly invoked by Shaktas to ensure fertility of stock, ripening of harvests and protection from disease.

STONE SCULPTURE OF A *LINGA* — A SHAIVITE SYMBOL — WITH *YONI* IN A TEMPLE COURTYARD IN BHUDANESVAR, ORISSA.

HINDUKUSH RELIGION

*U*ntil we manage to decipher more of the Indus civilization scripts we may never gain a better idea about the nature of its ancient beliefs and wisdom. There are, however, some indicators to be found, not in the Indus valley but by journeying north from India, through Pakistan, into the fastness of the mountain range to the west of the Himalayas and known as the Hindukush. There, in remote and inaccessible valleys which were, until recently, in extreme physical isolation from outside influence, live a number of primitive tribes including the Kafirs, Chitralis and the Dards. Technically, these are not so much tribes as confederations of villages, each more or less confined to its own valley and linked to adjacent valleys only by hazardous mountain tracks.

The peoples of the Hindukush have been affected by the modern spread of Islam and much of their culture is in decline but enough remains to draw a reasonably clear picture of the ancient tribal religion. The indications are that beliefs among the Hindukush clans have remained little altered since prehistoric times. Although their language is not directly related to either of their nearer neighbours, India or Iran, the names of their deities bear some similarity to those listed in the *Veda* and they conduct sacrificial rites that may trace back, in part, to the style and purpose of those of the pre-Aryan Indus civilization.

THE LANDSCAPE'S SPIRITUAL DIMENSION

The religion differs significantly from that of the Indus valley in at least one obvious respect. The mountainous landscape is a dominating influence and features strongly in the beliefs, providing a mixed blessing in that the mountains are a protective barrier against intrusion but also restrict movement between valleys. They are seen to be places of great danger where death can come suddenly on a path made hazardous by mist or

THE LANDSCAPE OF THE HINDUKUSH IS DOMINATED BY IMPOSING MOUNTAIN RANGES WHOSE MYSTICAL AURA HAS PERMEATED THE PEOPLE'S RELIGIOUS BELIEF.

tumbling water, where an avalanche can descend unannounced and where lightning may strike at will. The mountains are overwhelmingly near yet their heights are equally inaccessible and so they have gained a mystical aura as places of the gods, with each valley having its own sacred peak and with the mountain itself often being seen as a sleeping divinity. This is true animism, the earliest known form of religious understanding at work, where nothing is guaranteed to be as it seems and where every object in nature has a hidden spiritual dimension. A vast boulder that has tumbled to the valley floor is the nose or the penis of some gigantic numinary whilst the high peaks, wreathed in clouds and apparently suspended in the air, are the fortresses of gods and giants, restrained from floating off into the heavens by magical and invisible chains.

People imagine an upper world either represented by the icy summits or consisting of seven heavens, one above the other and cemented together by the stars. Beneath is the middle world, a flat disc on which people and animals live, whilst below is an underworld of demons and, sometimes, of gods.

A KAFIR WOMAN IN THE BUMBURET VALLEY OF NORTHERN PAKISTAN.

The gods once lived amongst the human population but have since largely returned to their own worlds leaving people to get on with life as best they can and visiting the inhabited places merely to conduct their personal godly affairs.

DEITIES AND THEIR IMAGES

The Vedic god Indra is represented by a deity called Indr whose influence seems to have been largely lost in the Hindukush. Other deities are less easy to relate by name. The creator of the pantheon, Imra, probably compares with Prajapati of the *Veda* and the heroic weather god, Mandi, has clear affinities with both Rudra and Shiva. The mother goddess, Disani, may be linked with Aditi although she is also a consort of Mandi and there are stronger hints in her behaviour that she equates with the Shiva *shaktis*. A war god, Gish, seems to parallel Skanda and Maramalik, the god of the underworld, may be the Kafir version of Yama.

Divinities are often represented by crude and almost abstract lumps of stone which reflect the ineffability and ambiguity of the god or goddess and are sometimes sprinkled with offerings of blood and maize flour. These altar images, often seated several in a row, are placed in small sanctuaries close to the edge of villages. The shrines are not buildings in which devotees can gather but merely resting places of gods whilst sacrifices are made on verandas in front of the shrines at the climax of ceremonial dances. This tallies with the wooden models and sacrificial altars which it is believed stood as early temples in Vedic India.

The high priest is known as the *uta* who carries out the blood sacrifices and who performs certain ceremonial dances alone when he is allowed to approach the holiest of the shrines. This individual lives in a high state of spiritual purity and must observe many taboos including avoidance of places of the dead. The sacrifices mostly consist of goats and cattle and, once a year, a horse, all of which are slain by throat-cutting or by decapitation with an axe. The blood is then collected, sprinkled over the altar and finally thrown into a sacrificial fire to ascend to the gods as smoke. The element of fire, which became embedded in Hindu ritual, is essential because of its purity and the belief in its sacred nature.

At death, the soul of a man becomes a shadow known as the *partir* which leaves the body to travel to the underground realm of the dead. This place includes both heaven and hell and whilst it is controlled by a god, Maramalik, who lets no one return, there appears to be no real sense of judgement of the souls of the dead. The choice of paradise or torment is dependent on virtue during life. Although the dead remain in the underworld there is some suggestion of reincarnation in that the Kafirs follow an ancestral name-donor rite. It is thought that the characteristics of the dead donor are reborn in the child and that, perhaps, the ancestral spirit is thus reborn. Here, perhaps, is a hint of the earliest form of the principles of *karma* and *atman* which were to evolve and rest at the very heart of Hinduism.

THE
VEDA

The earliest known sacred texts of Hinduism, composed in the Indo-European language of Sanskrit, are collectively known as the VEDA, a word which translates literally as 'knowledge' although in this context it implies collections or SAMHITA of sacred knowledge. The dates of written composition have been estimated to lie between 1200 and 900 BCE although the oral traditions on which the texts are based may go back hundreds or perhaps thousands of years earlier.

These compositions, largely in the form of poetry or rhythmic prose, are believed to have been gained from divine origin and were originally designed to be spoken and listened to. They are, however, not particularly accessible in as much as they are composed with great economy of expression which suggests that there is more to be read between than within the lines. Many, particularly those contained in the *Rig Veda*, are obscure or paradoxical in their meaning and purpose, so they are placed in a category known as *shruti* or 'hearing' as distinct from some of the later, and more easily taught, religious texts which are classed as *smriti* or 'remembering'. Nor, apart from the *Rig Veda*, are these early works generally available in English translation.

THE IMPORTANCE
OF THE VEDA

The Vedic texts do not merely constitute the oldest sacred books of Hinduism, they are also the most revered of the scriptures and form the fundamental canon of Hinduism. Some indication of the level of veneration may be gained from the fact that Brahma and Vishnu often hold a book or *pustaka* in one or all of their hands which is considered to contain the *Veda*. The texts are characterized by the depth of their spiritual content but also by their mood. There is a lack of pessimism or negative soul-searching that is found in some of the later Hindu literature. These works are wholly positive in their view of life

and death and in their recognition of the cosmic and moral law (*rita*) which includes acknowledgement of the ultimate values in the universe – goodness, beauty and truth (*satya*). One of the prayers of the *Rig Veda* includes the plea: 'O Indra, lead us on the path of *rita*, on the path over all evils', and all of the deities who make their appearance can be said to embody the two principles of *rita* and *satya*.

There is something of a paradox in that female divinities feature hardly at all in the early works yet, at a mortal level, the text appears lyrical about the beauty of womanhood, the value of tender love between man and wife and the sanctity of motherhood.

Above all, and surprisingly in view of the multiplicity of names which appear in the Hindu religion, the *Veda* recognizes a single supreme power which reveals itself in many forms. All the Vedic gods are therefore aspects of the one divine entity. The old gods of nature who evolved amongst the Indus valley people, and who were joined by the deities of the Aryans, become manifestations of *ekadeva*, the Unity of the Godhead described as Prajapati (Lord of Creatures) or Visvakarman (Maker of the World). The *Yajur Veda* declares: 'Agni is That, Vayu is That, Chandramas is That, Light is That, Brahman is That, Waters are Those, Prajapati is He'. Similarly, *Atharva Veda* encapsulates the principle: 'He is the One, the One alone, In Him all Deities become One alone'. The *Veda* in general describes this ultimate and all-pervading power as representing the beauty and light of the natural world and also all the goodness and nobility of which the human spirit is capable.

THE PRINCIPAL VEDAS

There are four major Vedic works: the *Rig Veda*, the *Sama Veda* and the *Yajur Veda*, written down in about 1200 BCE, and the somewhat later *Atharva Veda* written in about 900 BCE. The *Rig Veda* includes hymns of praise used when the ancient priesthood offered sacrifices to the gods, whilst the *Sama Veda* contains a small number of original verses or *mantras* but otherwise reflects much of the *Rig Veda* material in a rearranged version set to music. The *Yajur Veda* or Sacrificial Veda differs in that it includes mainly the details of the rituals performed by the Vedic

SANSKRIT, THE LANGUAGE OF THE HINDU SCRIPTURES, ORIGINATED SEVERAL THOUSAND YEARS AGO, YET IS STILL USED IN INDIA TODAY.

priests in making their sacrifices but it also elaborates on the attributes of various musical requirements. Hence it indicates: 'for sound, the beater of the kettle-drum; for sublimity, the vina-player'. The *Atharva Veda* is distinctly magical in tone and details collections of spells, charms and other occult invocations. It is suggested that this material, though written down later than the other *Veda* collections, may claim the oldest origins dating back to the cults of the Indus valley peoples before the arrival of the Aryan invaders. The *Atharva Veda* belongs exclusively to the priesthood and was not designed for public recitation.

The best known of the *Veda* collections is the *Rig Veda*, which includes 1028 hymns, each of about ten verses or *mantras*, which constitute an anthology of material whose components are able to stand alone as complete works. The hymns are not in any fixed order but they follow a common theme of ancient and divine wisdom concerning creation and the activities of the Vedic gods. They also refer to the ritual of sacrifice and the use of *soma*, an amber liquid offered to the gods and drunk by Brahmins attending Vedic sacrifice, as well as a number of mystic incantations distinct from those recorded in the *Atharva Veda*. The hymns, though couched in simple language, include some highly complicated philosophical ideas that leave more questions than answers, perhaps because the

meanings have been obscured or lost through the passage of time. Riddles aside, they are also offerings of great beauty and artistry, even after suffering the ordeal of translation from the Sanskrit.

The creation hymn known as the *Nasadiya* proclaims the riddles of origins and leaves its questions hanging, offering none of the tidy answers that one finds in Mesopotamian or Egyptian creation theories.

There was neither non-existence nor existence then; there was neither the realm of space nor the sky which is beyond. What stirred? Where? In whose protection? Was there water, bottomlessly deep?

There was neither death nor immortality then. There was no distinguishing sign of night nor of day. That one breathed, windless, by its own impulse. Other than that there was nothing beyond.

It has been said that the *Veda*, this earliest recorded expression of Indo-Aryan faith, has never been matched in its profundity; that it represents not only the dawn of Hinduism but also the zenith of Indian philosophy and of human wisdom encompassing the whole process of evolution from its beginning to its completion.

THE BRAHMANAS, ARANYAKAS AND UPANISHADS

Out of the VEDA SAMHITA evolved at least two other significant groups of Hindu scripture which are usually regarded under the heading of Vedic texts and which have contributed much to the development of Hindu faith and practice. The original VEDA SAMHITA was composed by the priestly class of Brahmins, living in northern India, as their devotional scripture, but it also acts as their working reference manual. The Brahmin becomes affiliated to one of the four main Vedic SAMHITAS but, in addition, tends to join a specialist 'school' focusing on different aspects of thought and ritual, each of which finds its expression in different 'branches' of the VEDA.

Aspects of these disciplinary 'branches' are found in all the *samhitas* and so each has provided a foundation for its own accompanying *Brahmanas, Upanishads* and, sometimes, texts known as *Aranyakas,* all of which provide learned discussions of the *Veda* liturgy appropriate to particular schools. Thus, the *Rig Veda* is coupled with the *Aitareya Brahmana,* the *Aitareya Aranyaka* and the *Aitareya Upanishad* and others, whilst the *Atharva Veda* has the *Gopatha Brahmana* and the *Mundaka Upanishad* amongst its associated texts.

The writing of the *Brahmanas* and the *Aranyakas* started at about the time of the compilation of the *Atharva Veda* in about 900 BCE and continued for some two hundred years, whilst the *Upanishads* date from the end of the period in about 700 BCE until about 500 BCE.

THE BRAHMANAS

In common with the *Upanishads,* the earliest, the *Brahmanas,* are not hymns or *mantras* in the sense of the Vedic texts but rather commentaries which explain the meaning of the liturgical verses of the *Veda.* They concentrate largely on the important rituals carried out by the Brahmin priests and elaborate on the limited technical details of ritual contained in the Vedic liturgy. They also include a number of story narratives which suggest that the clearly defined deities of the earlier Vedic texts – those to whom sacrifice was to be addressed as individuals – were losing status against the omnipotent but wholly ethereal presence of the divine. This greater and all-pervading presence is *brahman,* the universal soul that infuses itself throughout the cosmos as the true and total reality. It is to *brahman* that sacrifice is principally to be made. It has also been suggested that, at the time when the *Brahmanas* became significant, the prosperity of India was being threatened as a result of dwindling natural resources, and the priesthood envisaged a more sophisticated and abstract sacrificial ritual as a means of responding to the problem.

By this stage the creator principle was also identified by name, Prajapati, and the writers were much more willing to

A BRONZE STATUE OF BRAHMA, SENIOR AMONGST THE HINDU CREATOR GODS.

provide answers as opposed to questions. The *Satapatha Brahmana* is typical of the newly found confidence about creation theories and origins:

> In the beginning Prajapati existed alone. He reflected, 'How may I produce progeny?' He exhausted himself practising asceticism, and he generated Agni [the god of fire] *from his mouth. Since he generated him from his mouth, Agni is therefore an eater of food ... Prajapati then reflected, 'I have created from myself a food-eater, Agni, but there is no food here other than me, whom he would not eat.' Now the earth was bald at that time; there were no plants nor any trees. And this was in his mind ...*

The account goes on to describe how Prajapati ejaculates his seed into Agni, in a form of sacrifice in order to appease his hunger (see p.13). However, the overall sense that is gained from the piece is that the brahmanic priests had found solutions to many of the puzzles articulated by their Vedic forebears.

In the *Brahmanas* there is also a discernible move to balance

A SEVENTEENTH-CENTURY INDIAN PAINTING OF THE RAJASTHANI SCHOOL, SHOWING KRISHNA WITH TRADITIONAL MUSICIANS.

out the sexual equation of the largely male pantheon which characterizes the early *Veda*. The trend is towards re-emergence of a number of mother goddess figures and, furthermore, some of the earlier Vedic gods, such as the old weather god Rudra, have lost popularity and undergone character changes. By the era of the *Brahmanas* Rudra has taken on much of the dark, malevolent colouring of Shiva with whom he is ultimately destined to be assimilated, whilst female deities such as Sarasvati and Aditi have come more into the limelight. Other deities have effectively undergone name changes. Hence the name of the old sun god, Surya, has become replaced in popularity by Vivasvan (the Shining One), who is also interpreted as one of a 'younger generation' of deities.

THE UPANISHADS

The *Upanishads* represent a further development of the thinking in the *Brahmanas* and are also mystical, their teachings partly explanatory, partly esoteric. The *Aitareya Upanishad* begins by offering an explanation of the creation hymn of the *Rig Veda*, the *Nasadiya*:

> In the beginning this world was the self [atman] one alone, and there was no other being at all that blinked an eye. He thought to himself: 'Let me create these worlds.' So he created these worlds – the flood, the glittering specks, the mortal, the waters. Now, the flood is up there beyond the sky, and its foundation is the sky. The glittering specks are the intermediate world. The mortal is the earth, and what is underneath are the waters.

Typical of the more esoteric teaching on ritual, in this instance also openly critical of some of the more traditional Vedic practices, is the *Mundaka Upanishad*:

> When the flame flickers after the fire is lit, let him then make his offerings, between the two pourings of ghee [sacrificial butter]. A man's daily fire sacrifice that remains without the new moon, the full moon and the four month sacrifice; and without offerings to guests; that is performed without an offering to all the gods, or without the following rules, will rob him of his worlds up to the very seventh. (*Upanishads*, p. 271)

The *Upanishads* in general are permeated by the concept of *brahmavidya*, the 'supreme science' which seeks knowledge, not of the external world but of the hidden reality which underpins it. This knowledge was kept by the Brahmin priesthood over centuries as a product of memory and so what proportion was lost and how much eventually found its way into written texts is unknown. Some of the larger *Upanishads* appear to be anthologies of material which must have begun as scattered fragments of text that were only later drawn together by the editors. Some of the individual texts appear in more than one *Upanishad*, suggesting that the editors may, in part, have relied on a common 'pool' of oral teachings.

A strong message of all the texts, but particularly of the *Upanishads*, is that *atman*, the individual soul of each person, is identical with the universal soul, *brahman* (see p.42). The message is emphasized in one of the most popular and widely read of the *Upanishads*, the *Bhagavad Gita*. This text is unusual in that it does not relate specifically to one or other of the *Veda samhita* but takes the form of a moral and philosophical discussion directed by the Vishnu *avatara*, Krishna, in his guise as a charioteer, to the hero Arjuna at the outset of the Battle of Kurukshetra. The battle constitutes the climax of the *Mahabharata* epic and, by convention, the *Gita* became incorporated into the heart of the *Mahabharata*. Nevertheless it does not rest comfortably as an integral part of the story and it is likely to have been composed separately, perhaps by the author of the *Mahabharata*, and then inserted into the epic at an appropriate place.

At the core of the *Bhagavad Gita* is a timeless teaching about what must be achieved to realize spiritual freedom and become one with God. The solution it proposes is the renunciation, not of material things, but of selfish desires and attachments. It discusses various paths that the disciple may take but it repeatedly advocates selfless action through the discipline of *karma yoga* whereby the individual identifies with the entirety of life and loses his separate aspects of body and mind, not by the route of isolated and passive asceticism but by active dedication to the service of others. As Krishna declares: *It is not those who lack energy or refrain from action, but those who work without expectation of reward who attain the goal of meditation. Theirs is the true renunciation. Therefore, Arjuna, you should understand that renunciation and the performance of selfless service are the same. Those who cannot renounce attachment to the results of their work are far from the path.* (*Bhagavad Gita*, p.104)

The texts attached to the *Veda* also include the so-called *Aranyakas* or 'forest treatises'. The distinction between these and the *Upanishads* is rather vague because both involve mysticism. The *Aranyakas*, however, include formulae for rituals practised amongst the more reclusive of the religious elite and are known as forest rituals since they were intended for recitation in the privacy of the woodlands away from the eyes of the village community.

Because the *Upanishads* are considered to represent the ultimate stage in the evolution of philosophy about *brahman*, the germ of which arose from the early Vedic texts, they tend to have become detached from any specific school of thought and adopted as standard teachings by all Brahmins. They are sometimes referred to as the *Vedanta*, meaning the 'end of the *Veda*'.

THE
EPICS

The religious writings of Hinduism reached their peak of historical development with two great epic sagas, the MAHABHARATA and the RAMAYANA, both of which have been described as the Collective Unconscious of India sending their own idiosyncratic yet universal message to humankind. Almost every culture possesses stories of epic proportions — some that actually took place as part of recorded history, some that are wholly fictitious and others, like these, which rest between the two — which form an essential part of the mythological repertoire. The Hindu sagas are neither strictly historical nor geographical, since the writers have taken liberties on both counts, but they are integral to popular and accessible Hindu philosophy, religious belief and culture.

There is a drawback to dating the texts accurately in that their writers avoided inclusion of reference to historical events that would conveniently allow a date to be placed on them. The constituent parts of the Epics were probably being circulated, piecemeal, as an oral tradition told and retold over several thousands of years by the priestly *brahmana* caste, before they were committed to Sanskrit prose. The best that can be established is that the *Mahabharata* was written down as a complete manuscript some time between 300 BCE and 300 CE and it has been attributed to the scribe named Ganapati who penned it at the behest of the sage or *rishi* Vyasa to whom the compilation of the *Veda* is also accredited. The *Ramayana* was written in about the same period by a scribe named Valmiki, though the possible 'window' is thought to lie between 200 BCE and 200 CE. During a long period of oral transmission the stories were probably revised and updated constantly and even after being established in manuscript form it seems clear that the material was regularly added to. The Epics in many ways

THE DEITY HANUMAN, WHOSE FORM IS THAT OF A MONKEY, FEATURES IN THE *RAMAYANA* AS AN ALLY OF RAMA.

represent a classic national archive into which other fragments of legend, political ideologies and philosophies were incorporated. Strands of opinion that arose and were considered worthy of a place over some thirty centuries found their way into the framework of one or other.

THE MAHABHARATA

The name translates as 'The Great [Epic of the] Bharatas', a not unreasonable description since it consists of no less than 90,000 stanzas. 'Bharata' means literally 'to be maintained' and refers, in this context, to the heroic ancestral race of the ancient kingdom of Hastinapura in northern India. According to tradition, they were descended from a king known as Santanu who was wedded both to the goddess of the Ganges and to a mortal wife, Satyavati. The goddess bore him a son, Devavrata, who became popularly known as Bhishma, 'one who undertakes a terrible vow', because he was sworn to chastity and Bhishma appears as the paterfamilias throughout much of the epic. The focus rests on the Battle of Kurukshetra, between two branches of the Bharatas, the Kauravas and the Pandavas. The Kauravas were led by Bhishma and the Pandavas by one of five princely brothers, a hero named Arjuna who, in the final moments of battle fatally wounded Bhishma. The conflict is said to have been triggered by jealous internecine feuding and to have taken place over a period of nine days on the plain of the upper Ganges.

There is much emphasis throughout the Epic on the righteous and moral conduct, or *dharma*, of the aristocratic military order known as *kshatriya* although the principles of *dharma* can be applied to all of humanity. The keynote element, known as the *Bhagavad Gita,* is a moral lecture delivered to the Pandava hero, Arjuna, by Krishna, the most significant *avatara* or incarnation of the god Vishnu. He appears to Arjuna in the guise of his charioteer and tells him that he must do his duty in a dispassionate way even though some of those he may shortly be slaughtering are his own kinsfolk. In the text the *Gita* is described as a gospel of devotion to duty, without attachment or desire for reward, that has shown the way of life for all men, rich or poor, learned or ignorant, who have sought for light in the dark problems of life. It remains hugely popular throughout the world as a moral discussion in its own right.

The scope of the Epic is far broader than a canvas of life on the battlefield. Throughout the story there is a close interplay between gods and mortals, the former guiding and advising the latter, and the *Mahabharata* ranges over the whole gamut of values that were held up as a 'benchmark' of excellence in ancient Hindu society. It contains the living past of India but

A MANUSCRIPT ILLUSTRATION OF THE BATTLE OF KURUKSHETRA, FOUGHT BETWEEN THE KAURAVAS AND THE PANDAVAS, RECORDED IN THE *MAHABHARATA* EPIC.

its timeless message also speaks to the present and the future. Between its pages is reflected the code of life and the ethical and social philosophy that sustains modern Hinduism. It lays bare all the triumphs and tribulations, strengths and weaknesses, that beset humanity irrespective of time and place.

Not surprisingly, the Epic as a whole is still immensely popular both in India and beyond. In most Indian homes it is taught, as it has been since time immemorial, to children at their mother's knee and it has been said that, 'He who knows it not, knows not the heights and depths of the soul; he misses the trials and tragedy and the beauty and grandeur of life'. These are sentiments which define the quintessence of the *Mahabharata*.

The importance of *dharma* is maintained to the final pages. Towards the end of the saga, one of the heroic survivors of the princely Pandava family, Yudhisthira, is exhorted by his mother, 'May your mind ever stand steady on *dharma*' and he remembers this to his dying moment. Weary of battle and slaughter, the princes have become pilgrims, questing for salvation in the snowy fastness of the Himalayas. Of five valiant brothers, most are to die, emptied of the will to live and only Yudhisthira remains until he too is approached by the god Indra. But Yudhisthira is accompanied by a dog which, unbeknown to him, embodies *dharma* and he refuses the invitation to paradise unless the dog may come too. Indra is pleased at Yudhisthira's loyalty and the dog disappears. Yudhisthira finds himself, not in heaven, but passing through a place of dark anguish where he sees his kinsmen suffering the tortures of hell. Again he refuses to leave them and, having tested Yudhisthira's devotion once more, Indra and Yama, the god of *dharma*, stand before him to roll away the darkness and dismiss suffering.

Yama declares, 'Wisest of men, I have tested you again and you have chosen to remain in hell for the sake of your brethren. It is inevitable that kings and rulers must go through hell if only for a while. This has been no more than an illusion designed to test you, for this is not hell but paradise.'

Whereupon Yudhisthira and his brothers attain immortality and become gods, finding peace and happiness. So ends the *Mahabharata,* a testimony to the futility of war and the strength of honourable conduct.

THE RAMAYANA

The *Mahabharata* is an epic tale which extols the virtues of unswerving loyalty, honourable conduct and the rewards of such exemplary behaviour. The *Ramayana* echoes much of what the *Mahabharata* has to offer in that it presents a timeless canvas of the principles and purpose of Hindu society in India. By contrast, however, it also reveals the tragic consequences which may follow when the same exemplary standards with

which the heroes of the *Mahabharata* kept faith to the last are abused. In comparing these two massive tales it is clear that both aim to create entertaining and adventuresome dramas in which all that is good in Hindu culture and philosophy is applauded and rewarded whilst the converse is ultimately punished. The *Ramayana* is a somewhat shorter work of about 24,000 stanzas and its author, the poet and sage or *rishi* Valmiki, may perhaps have examined the human character with a more candid eye than did his contemporary.

The focus of the *Ramayana*, in common with its sister work, rests on conflict and it is strongly political, revealing a strategic tale that contains much jingoism. This is not, however, an account of internecine feuding between branches of a family but of war on a national scale as the eponymous

SITA IS PLAYED BY AN ACTRESS IN *RAM LEELA*, THE STAGE PLAY INTERPRETATION OF THE GREAT *RAMAYANA* EPIC.

hero, Rama, takes on his arch-enemy Ravana, the demonic king of Sri Lanka (Ceylon). Like the *Mahabharata*, in its function and moral themes, it serves to unite a vast and fragmented people in a common focus, irrespective of caste and language, but the subject matter defines the historical schism between the Hindu culture of India and the Sinhalese, largely Buddhist, stock of Sri Lanka. The latter nation is portrayed as being in the grip of alien gods and disreputable forms of worship.

For some two thousand years Rama has been accepted as the physical incarnation of a god and he is recorded as the seventh incarnation or *avatara* of the creator god Vishnu, but prior to his heroic association with the *Ramayana* he featured in Hindu mythology only as a minor figure. It is through the writing of Valmiki that he emerges as the great champion and becomes a cult figure in his native region of India. In the *Ramayana* he is portrayed as an heroic but essentially mortal prince who is endowed with both divine and human qualities. Rama was born to Dasharatha, the king of the ancient northern kingdom of Ayodhya (now part of the modern state of Uttar Pradesh), and his wife Kaushalya, and his existence has been tentatively dated to the eighth or seventh century BCE, though there is no historical evidence from contemporary literature to support the possibility. If he existed it was only as a local prince whose biography remained inconspicuous for several hundred years other than amongst the poets of his locality. There are also conflicting arguments about whether Rama knew he was a divinity from the outset or whether this only became revealed to him in the final analysis.

It is through the character of Rama that two deeper messages of the Epic are conveyed. This seventh incarnation of Vishnu follows the pattern of the previous manifestations in that the god generates *avataras* of himself only when the world faces great evil. Here the malignancy rests in the character of the demonic Ravana. The second thrust of the *Ramayana* lies in the fact that Rama is drawn as the true and

THE DEMON RAVANA, KING OF SRI LANKA, FEATURES IN THE PLAY AS RAMA'S CHIEF ADVERSARY.

original incarnation of *dharma*. He and his consort, Sita, are born as human beings who experience all the pain and sorrow, strengths and failings, of mortal existence so that the gods may establish *dharma* amongst mankind.

RAMA, HERO OF THE *RAMAYANA* EPIC, IS SHOWN WITH HIS WIFE, SITA, HIS BROTHER, LAKSHMANA, AND HIS DEVOTEE, HANUMAN.

Rama and Sita lived together in Ayodhya but now the Lord and his consort in their human form learned at first hand the hardships, sorrows and conflicts of life on earth. In this aspect of the myth it may be possible to detect certain parallels with the Christian tradition but the Hindu message is accountably different in that Rama epitomizes the ideal of heroic manhood and manly behaviour whilst Sita is the female counterpart, chaste and loyal to the death.

Rama is provided with a number of allies. Through the early chapters of the epic he and his younger brother, Lakshmana, engage in various adventures, including the slaying of a monster, a familiar device which establishes Rama in the classic mould of the hero the world over. His marriage to the princess Sita is followed by an uneventful period of domesticity but, just as Rama is due to be crowned king by his dying father, the germ of disaster is born. Dasharatha has been married to three wives, each of whom has given him sons and, on his deathbed, he is duped into passing his inheritance to another sibling. These jealous machinations force Rama and Sita into exile and it is from there, deep in the forests, that Sita is abducted by Ravana.

After this traumatic episode the most significant of Rama's allies appears in the form of Hanuman, a god in the shape of a monkey. He may seem, at first glance, an odd character to be associated with such a hero but monkeys in India are considered to be sacred, half-human creatures, and the personality of Hanuman, meaning 'he of the large jaws', is elaborated to encompass the ultimate qualities of loyalty and devotion between comrades in arms. Hanuman's is a role model that has been emulated by many a young Hindu warrior.

It is in the climax that the real twist of the Epic comes for Rama, the incarnation of the god, for he is to succumb to human failings at a terrible cost. Ravana is defeated, his demonic horde routed, the Hindu way of life secured, and the imprisoned wife is restored to her husband. One might believe this the recipe for a happy-ever-after ending but it is not to be. Rama's conduct towards Sita becomes that of an arrogant male for whom public appearance is more important than the personal happiness of his liberated wife. Distrust becomes the assassin of loyalty. The finale of the story presents deep moral lessons and confronts a paradox of human behaviour that is familiar the world over, although here it carries an especially eastern tone.

Freed at last from Ravana's grasp Sita, her eyes downcast, walked towards her husband. 'My beloved and noble Lord,' she cried. Yet Rama was cold towards her. 'I have defeated the demons and recovered you. I have performed my duty to my caste. My vow is properly fulfilled.' As he spoke thus, his face

IN THE *RAMAYANA*, CLAY LAMPS OR *DEEPA* GREETED THE VICTORIOUS RAMA AT HIS HOMECOMING. DIWALI, THE FESTIVAL OF LIGHTS, RECALLS THIS MOMENT AND REMAINS ONE OF THE MOST POPULAR CELEBRATIONS IN HINDUISM.

darkened. 'It was not in mere devotion to you that I waged this terrible battle against Ravana but in the discharge of my duty. It brings me no joy to have you back for doubt is upon you like a sombre cloud. You must live alone and elsewhere under the protection of kinsfolk. I cannot take back a woman who has been defiled in the house of the enemy. (Adapted from *Ramayana*, pp.306–307)

Sita commands a funeral pyre and immolates herself. Only now does Rama question his own true purpose and identity and he cries in anguish to Brahma, 'Who am I?' The truth is revealed as the god provides the awful answer. He is Vishnu and Sita is the incarnation of the goddess Lakshmi. In the moment of revelation comes absolution and Rama returns to immortality and his beloved consort.

This is a popular version of the close of the myth that provides at least some comfort, but a more sombre outcome is recorded in an older rendering of the Epic. The revelation of his godhead and knowledge of his mortal weakness destine Rama to an eternity of remorse through which he and Sita are for ever apart.

PURANAS

The most extensive but also the most haphazardly compiled of all the Hindu religious texts include the PURANAS, which represent the more popular spectrum of religious belief. They were committed to writing mainly in the period from about 450–1000 CE after the composition of the great Epics but although they were written down between these approximate dates, the spoken tradition from which the PURANAS took substance extends back much further in time.

No one really knows when the *Puranas* first came into circulation but Puranic traditionalists claim that they were uttered by Brahma even before he communicated the *Veda*. Among the earliest, in terms of time of written composition, is the *Vayu Purana* dated to about 350 CE; one of the comparatively late works is the *Bhagavata Purana,* written down in about 950 CE; while others, like the *Kalki Purana,* were compiled as recently as the turn of the eighteenth century.

The *Puranas* constitute little less than religious encyclopedias and include eighteen known 'major' works or *Mahapuranas* with innumerable 'minor' tracts. A clear explanation of their ideological message is made difficult not least because they include considerable amounts of sectarian lore and because, over a long period of time, various authors have added and interpolated fresh material to the original texts without any strict rules or proper regard for uniformity.

Some experts claim that there existed, perhaps more than two thousand years ago, an 'official' *Purana samhita,* or collection, which became hopelessly adulterated as different individuals and sects added their own bits and pieces of authorship, theory and interpretation. This process has gone on until very recent times, evidenced by the fact that there are references in some of the Puranic writings to the British Empire occupation of India during the last century. Often there are in existence several manuscript editions claiming authority for the same *Purana* but with variations in ideology and without the benefit of an 'orthodox' or widely recognized version.

MYTHS AND LEGENDS

The term *Purana* simply means 'old' and therefore describes an ancient myth or legend that remains part of popular religious tradition. The *Puranas* have become accepted as sacred works and are chiefly concerned with the activities of gods and goddesses. Generally they are dedicated to specific deities and hence go under such titles as the *Vishnu Purana*, the *Shiva Purana* or the *Skanda Purana*. They may also be focused on particular dynasties in Indian religious history as is the case with the *Bhagavata Purana*. The true or 'classic' *Purana* is supposed to include five distinct sections or topics – creation (*sarga*), dissolution (*pratisarga*), world ages (*manvantara*), genealogies (*vamsa*) and dynasties (*vamsanucarita*). In practice, however, it may also cover various other areas of discussion such as spirituality and the aims and rules of life as well as details of shrines and religious practices.

Typical of the level of romanticized elaboration is the account of the birth of the *Veda* in the *Brahmavaivarta Purana*:

When Brahma had fashioned all this universe, he placed his seed in Savitri, his best wife, as a man full of desire places his seed in a woman full of desire. For a hundred celestial years she held the embryo, which was difficult to bear, and then when she was ready to give birth she bore the four enchanting books of the Veda, the various branches of knowledge such as logic and grammar, the thirty-six celestial Raginis [a variation of the Raga] that capture the heart and the six beautiful Ragas [a basic style of music] with their various rhythms.

THE WAR GOD SKANDA SHOWN WITH A PEACOCK IN A SIXTH-CENTURY PUNJABI SCULPTURE.

Genealogies frequently begin with the conception of a deity. The *Shiva Purana* contains tales of the circumstances in which several deities are engendered, including the war god Skanda, all drawn in colourful terms designed to provide popular entertainment – the seed of Shiva is so fiery that it burns all who receive it and it is passed from god to god, then to a succession of women who leave it in the icy heights of the Himalayas. But the mountain cannot stand its heat and hurls it into the sacred waters of the Ganges. Even the river is obliged to eject it on to a bank of reeds where it becomes the infant Skanda and is suckled at the breast of Shiva's consort, Parvati, in a tale rounded off to leave the listener happy that 'all's well that ends well'.

CREATION MYTHOLOGY

The subject of world ages and dissolution is discussed, again in an accessible fashion, towards the end of the *Vishnu Purana* in scenes that carry a powerful parallel with the Christian *Book of Revelation*. The scene is set where earthly rulers have become irreparably corrupt, draining the resources of a world in which religion and *dharma* have gone into terminal decline and ordinary humanity lives out a brief subsistence lifespan. But then the final *avatara* of Vishnu, known as Kalkin, will come riding upon a white horse:

Brahman will become incarnate as Kalkin, and his power and glory will be without end, and he will destroy the barbarians and the unbelievers and men of evil thought and deed, and he will re-establish everything, each with its own dharma. The Age of Kali will dissolve and the minds of people will become pure as flawless crystal and they will be as if awakened at the end of the night.

In their view of creation mythology, the *Puranas* elaborate on anything that appears in the *Veda* and *Brahmanas,* and deities such as Vishnu and Shiva, associated as they are with the more prominent sects, play a more significant role. Their theories of origins are also considerably embellished with descriptions of a whole plethora of heavens and hells that extend above and below the original scheme of a three-part universe. The *Puranas* give further colourful attention to the nature of the world

IN THE *VISHNU PURANA*, KALKIN – THE FINAL *AVATARA* OF VISHNU – RIDES IN APOCALYPTICALLY ON A WHITE HORSE.

aeons or *kalpas* created and destroyed by Brahma up to and including the present Age of Kali and the future Age of Kalkin, topics which are discussed in the *Vishnu Purana.*

Often found attached to the Puranic text is a eulogy or endorsement extolling the merits of the relevant work, known as a *Mahatmya* or 'Praise to the Greatness' of the *Purana.* These *Mahatmyas* typically include homilies about the importance to a household, as an aid to better and healthier living, of keeping a copy of this or that *Purana* and of reciting its stories on a regular basis.

ATMAN
AND
BRAHMAN

*T*he two closely interwoven philosophical concepts of 'self' and 'totality', ATMAN and BRAHMAN, rest at the very heart of Hinduism, yet their meaning is difficult for a westerner to understand and, indeed, the meaning is by no means fully agreed within Hinduism. The interpretations which are generally followed, however, are those contained in the conclusions or VEDANTA of the Vedic liturgy, the UPANISHADS.

In the *Chandogya Upanishad*, a father teaches his son, Shvetaketu, the nature of *atman* in simple everyday terms, amongst which is an analogy with a banyan fruit which he tells the boy to cut in half. Inside, the boy discovers tiny seeds and the father instructs him to take a single seed and cut it in two. When asked what he sees, the boy shakes his head and replies 'nothing'. The father explains to him that this 'nothing' is the essence from which a vast banyan tree has grown. The essence is invisible and this is how he must imagine self or *atman*.

By using a different analogy of bees and their honey, the father explains that *atman* is the self of the whole world. The bees prepare honey by gathering nectar from a variety of trees and by reducing it to an homogenous whole so that the nectar from each different tree is no longer able to differentiate its source. In the same way, when all creatures merge into the existent they are not aware that they are doing so. No matter whether a tiger, a lion, a wolf, a boar, a worm, a moth, a gnat, a mosquito, or Shvetaketu himself – they all merge into the essence that constitutes the self of the universe; that is truth, that is self (*atman*).

The first analogy would appear to suggest that *atman* is somehow distinct from *brahman*, whilst the second implies that the two are identical and that there is but one reality.

Tantalizingly, the question of whether the two ultimates of *atman* and *brahman*, separately named, represent a single principle or a multiplicity is never conclusively answered, but the message which runs through the core of the *Upanishads* is that both *atman* and *brahman* are parts of the same ultimate reality which come together in the highest level of consciousness. In this extreme state of bliss the immanent self of the individual, the *atman,* is at one with the transcendent divinity of the universe, *brahman*, the godhead.

The composer of the *Brhadaranyaka Upanishad* uses another honey analogy to make the point that *atman* and *brahman* are no more or less than parts of the One:

> *The earth is the honey of all beings, and all beings are the honey of this earth. The radiant and immortal person in the earth and, in the case of the body* [atman]*, the radiant and immortal person residing in the physical body – they are both one's self* [atman]. *It is immortal; it is brahman; it is the whole.* (*Upanishads*, p.30)

This message of uniqueness is probably the more persistent one in the *Upanishads*, which indicate that all objects can, through self-discipline and spiritual discovery, be progressively reduced to the One and then still further to a non-material or ethereal essence.

Atman and *brahman* have no real equivalent in western philosophy and are therefore often misinterpreted through the familiar Judeo-Christian images of the human soul and the separate entity of a singular supreme being. There is, however, a strong parallel with Christian belief, irrespective of precise distinctions. Through the understanding of the spiritual essence of *atman* and *brahman* Hindu philosophy reconciles the death of the mortal body and mind, the vital but ephemeral force, with the indestructibility of the soul, *atman*, since the latter is independent of the body and eternal. As the ultimate reality of pure consciousness of self, *atman* was never born because it has always existed, and therefore it cannot die but can only return to union with *brahman,* the source and breath of all that exists.

A SHRINE BUILT AROUND THE BASE OF A BANYAN TREE BESIDE THE HOOGHLY RIVER NEAR CALCUTTA: IN THE *UPANISHADS* THE BANYAN TREE'S FRUIT
IS AMONGST MANY EXAMPLES USED TO ILLUSTRATE THE CONCEPT OF *ATMAN* OR SELF.

According to *Upanishad* teaching, *atman* exists, unaltered, in three states of human consciousness – waking, dreaming and the sleep that is so deep as to be dreamless. After death of the body it journeys to another transcendental state, the quality of which is determined according to past actions or *karma*, where the original nature of self is discoverable. But, from this transcendental state, the *atman* may return to the material world if it has not yet achieved the ultimate reality of *ananda* or bliss.

Irrespective of state, *atman* includes five spheres of reality which correspond to an equal number of realities of *brahman*, each sphere being revealed within the one enveloping it by stripping away the layers until one reaches the ultimate core. Moving inwards from the vital to the increasingly mystical, the spheres include food (*annarasamaya*), breath (*atma pranamaya*), mind (*atma manomaya*) and understanding (*atma vijnanamaya*). At the core of understanding, and accessible only by peeling back the innermost curtain, lies the state of bliss (*atma anandamaya*).

If *atman* is the consciousness of the individual, *brahman*, the godhead, is the source of everything. The *Svetasvatar Upanishad*, depicting *brahman* in terms of a vast wheel, stresses the singularity of the saviour as *eka*, the One alone, and explains that parallel hindrances must be overcome, layers peeled away, in order to know its universal reality:

Within the wheel of brahman there are three parts – self, the foundation, and the imperishable. When those who know brahman have come to know the distinction between them, they become absorbed in and totally intent on brahman and are freed from the womb. This whole world is the perishable and the imperishable, the manifest and the unmanifest joined together – and the Lord bears it, while the self [atman], who is not the Lord, remains bound, because he is the enjoyer. When he comes to know God all the fetters fall off; by the eradication of the blemishes, birth and death come to an end; by meditating on him one obtains, at the dissolution of the body, sovereignty over all; and in the absolute one's desires are fulfilled. This can be known, for it abides always within one's body [atman]. Higher than that there is nothing to be known. When the enjoyer discerns the object of enjoyment and the impeller – everything has been taught. That is the threefold brahman. (Upanishads, pp.253–4)

The *Upanishads* provide the main source of understanding about *atman* and *brahman* and yet their message is often hard to fathom and different authorities argue the unanswerable question of whether self is or is not the same reality as the absolute One. Perhaps we may be permitted to know the answer only when we are stripped of all vitality and led into the transcendental state of true understanding.

KARMA

To a Hindu Brahmanic believer KARMA, or action, is a key component in the machinery which governs the cycle of death and physical rebirth, the Wheel of Existence, from which the soul, ATMAN, strives to escape. Much of the understanding of KARMA is contained in the UPANISHADS, in which KARMA is recognized in more than one form but is at its most significant as the law of SANCHITA KARMA. This is the sum total of a human being's conduct and actions, accumulated in a present life, which will then be evaluated to determine his or her destiny in the next existence. By similar token our present fate on earth has always been determined by the KARMA of our past lives.

It is accepted that the journey of the soul from one bodily state to another after death is deeply influenced by *karma* and that *karma* provides an explanation of why individuals differ in their fate, be this in terms of birth into high or low estate, material benefit or loss, fortune or misfortune. The causes of such, sometimes inexplicable, differences are summed up in simple terms in the *Chandogya Upanishad*:

> *People here [on earth] whose behaviour [karma] is pleasant can expect to enter a pleasant womb, like that of a woman of the Brahmin, the Kshatriya or the Vaishya class. But people of foul behaviour can expect to enter a foul womb, like that of a dog, a pig, or an outcaste woman.*
>
> *Then there are those proceeding on neither of these two paths — they become the tiny creatures revolving here ceaselessly. 'Be born! Die!' — that is the third state.*
>
> *As a result, that world up there is not filled up.*
>
> *A man should seek to protect himself from that. On this point there is this verse:*
>
> *"A man who steals gold, drinks liquor,*
> *and kills a Brahman;*
> *A man who fornicates with this teacher's wife —*
> *These four will fall.*
> *As also the fifth — he who consorts with them."*

A man who knows these five fires in this way, however, is not tainted with evil even if he associates with such people. Anyone who knows this becomes pure and clean and attains a good world.
(Upanishads, p.142)

This principle of *karma* also means that we reap that which we sow and that our fate lies in our own hands. It is not, therefore the fate that is accepted in the Classical Greek sense of the *Moirai*, the group of goddesses, Klotho, Lachesis and

PILGRIMS COME TO BENARES TO BATHE IN THE HOLY RIVER GANGES. THERE IS A BELIEF THAT IF A DYING PERSON SIPS THE WATER OF THE GANGES THE SOUL WILL BE LIBERATED FROM THE CYCLE OF DEATH AND REBIRTH.

Atropos, who determine the lot of human life, since that fate cannot be influenced or altered by us: it is predetermined from above. *Karma*, on the other hand, is entirely within our personal control. If we conduct ourselves well and observe good moral values then we become virtuous. Conversely, it is impossible for the *atman* to be tainted with evil unless we first perform evil deeds.

It follows that *karma* is the fundamental cause of rebirth since *karma*, whilst able to exert an influence on the destiny of *atman*, is associated with the body not with the self. If one is able to cut loose from *karma* then *atman* is also freed from the obligation to continue on the repetitive treadmill of life and death, life and death. It is *karma* which keeps in motion the vicious circle of bodily conduct, work performed, reward, desire, new activity. The *Brhadaranyaka Upanishad* explains:

> A man who is attached goes with
>   his action,
> to that very place to which
> his mind and character cling.
> Reaching the end of his action,
> of whatever he has done in this world —
> from that world he returns
> back to this world, back to action.
> (*Upanishads*, p.65)

Atman, however, has the innate ability to be free from such human failings. The *Chandogya Upanishad* also makes this clear:

> The self [atman] *that is free from evils, free from old age and death, free from sorrow, free from hunger and thirst; the self whose desires and intentions are real — that is the self that you should try to discover, that is the self that you should seek to perceive. When someone discovers that self and perceives it, he obtains all the worlds and all his desires are fulfilled.*
> (*Upanishads*, p.171)

The exit road, graphically described in the *Brhadaranyaka Upanishad* is achieved, little by little, life by life, as the bonds with desire are broken, and the soul moves from the yoke of mortality towards eternal freedom.

> When they are all banished,
> Those desires lurking in one's heart;
> Then a mortal becomes immortal,
> and attains brahman in this world.
> (*Upanishads*, p.66)

A SEVENTEENTH-CENTURY PORTRAYAL OF AN ASCETIC STRIVING TO OBTAIN RELEASE FROM *KARMA*.

It is in order to transcend and obtain release from *karma* that the whole process of asceticism and the life of the strict Hindu Brahmin is dedicated, to take the right upward path, first to obtain a good rebirth and then, ultimately, to depart. This is the promise of the *Upanishads* when a man correctly performs the holy rites and follows the true paths:

> Then, as sunbeams, these paths carry him to the place where the king of gods resides, the only place to reside ... through the doorway of the sun he goes, spotless, to where that immortal person is, the one immutable atman.
> (Words adapted from *Upanishads*, p.270)

SYMBOLS
AND
ATTRIBUTES

The vast pantheon of Hindu gods, goddesses and demons can be reduced, in theory, to a trinity or three-headed TRIMURTI, and then still further to a single divine principle, but in practice Hindu faith remains strongly polytheistic. This polytheism becomes more exaggerated by the fact that its throng of deities may also be known by an assortment of names which can change according to authors and local traditions.

At shrines in southern India one can discover images of the war god, Skanda, a son of Shiva and Parvati, going under the various names Skanda, Kumara, Karttikeya and Subrahmanya, in addition to about forty other less frequent titles that may occur further afield. Many such names come about as a result of a fusing of major deities and local gods whose identities have become absorbed for convenience and religious or political necessity. Individual deities also possess a daunting assortment of *avataras*, aspects and *shaktis*.

All of these forms must somehow be reflected in art. Deities such as Nandin, the bull, Ganesha, the elephant-headed son of Shiva, and Varaha, the boar incarnation of Vishnu, are recognizable at a glance because of their distinctive physical features, but others are more readily identifiable through their actions. A museum of Hindu sculpture will frequently possess bronzes of the god Shiva as *Shiva Mahesvara* (the Great Lord), *Shiva Nataraja* (the Lord of the Dance), *Shiva Somaskanda* (Shiva as father of a family with Parvati and Skanda) and *Shiva Candrasekhara* (Shiva moon-crested).

Each of these forms of Shiva, to name but a few, represents him enacting some role that he has undertaken in mythology. *Shiva Nataraja* is based on a propagandist myth of Shiva and Vishnu setting out to quell an uprising by ten thousand holy men. When the rebels send a tiger to attack Shiva he flays it and uses its skin as a cloak, when they send a deadly serpent he tames it and hangs it around his neck, and when they send a dwarf to kill him, Shiva defeats it by placing one foot on its back and performing a magical dance. This final act of conquest is depicted in the image of *Shiva Nataraja*, whilst the ring of flames represents the power of fire to liberate *atman* from adversity.

It is not difficult to see how, through whims of art alone, Hindu deities have succeeded in proliferating. But the sheer volume of individuals thus created also presents a challenge to the artist, particularly where they cannot be depicted carrying out some well-known mythical action. *Shiva Nataraja* is easy to spot since he is sculpted in a dancing pose surrounded typically by a ring of flames, but others may be much less obvious without deciphering an assortment of clues. The features distinguishing them one from the other must then be drawn quite distinctly and with certain agreed elements so that the image can be recognized. These elements appear in the form of vehicles, attributes and postures, particular combinations of which add up to an overall character picture.

Some attributes are straightforward and simple to understand. The Vishnu *avataras* Rama and Parasurama can be distinguished from one another in sculptures because the former carries a bow whilst the latter wields a hatchet. In the *Ramayana* epic the bow is featured as Rama's favoured weapon but the hatchet or *parasu* derives from a separate story when, at the behest of Shiva, Rama sets out against an army of demons. At the time he has left his bow behind and asks Shiva how he shall achieve victory. Shiva gives him certain instructions and, when he has conquered the demons, presents him with a magnificent axe by way of reward. This incarnation was considered distinct from Rama and became known as Parasurama (Rama with the Axe).

Deities often carry not one but an assortment of attributes reflecting their character and disposition. The goddess Kali, a terrible aspect of Shiva's *shakti* who represents a force of destruction in addition to being a cholera goddess, typically carries in her many hands such menacing attributes as a hook, knife, drum, bow, skull and noose. By contrast, Ganesha, the elephant-headed god and more amiable and approachable son of

THE GODDESS KALI, WHO REPRESENTS THE POWER OF DESTRUCTION, HOLDS A HOOK AND A SEVERED HEAD AND WEARS A NECKLACE OF SKULLS, IN THIS NINETEENTH-CENTURY PAINTING.

as sitting, bending, standing on one foot, or dancing, all of which stem from some significant aspect of the deity's mythology. Another feature may be a special pose of the arms, hands or fingers, known as a *mudra*, which is combined with the attributes. Vishnu, generally drawn with four heads and four hands, often holds a club or *gada* as an attribute which symbolizes his authority, but his right arm is typically raised with the palm open in the gesture of *abhaya mudra*, expressing fearless confidence or reassurance.

Deities are also linked with certain vehicles or mounts known as *vahanas*. These are sometimes living beings or animals, sometimes corpses, on which they ride or stand or by which they are accompanied. When the *shakti* of Shiva is in her gracious aspect as Parvati she usually stands with or rides upon *vrisan*, representing the bull, Nandin, but in her terrible aspect as Durga, she is accompanied by a more menacing beast, *sinha*, the lion.

Many of the attributes also represent mythological symbols. The wheel or *cakra* turns as the universal mind of *brahman* as well as depicting the revolving cosmos with its powers of creation and dissolution. The lotus or *padma* is the sacred emblem of creation and a symbol of the power of the sun. An object such as the club or *gada* means authority and knowledge, in addition to possessing phallic symbolism as the essence of life. The conch or *sankha*, with its spiral form, symbolizes the source of creation. These four are the principal symbols carried by Vishnu who is a positive and constructive creator force.

Shiva, holds such items as a rosary, a mango fruit and a prayer wheel.

The pose or attitude of a deity is also significant. He or she may adopt a particular position of the body or legs such

The form ultimately taken by a sculpture of a deity is based on a description which probably first appeared in a narrative text or a passage of scripture describing a ritual. The attributes and attitudes, *mudras* and *vahanas*, which embellish the basic figure all go to make up a visual character reference. They provide an esoteric name-tag and without them the tens of thousands of icons carved in stone and moulded in metal might largely remain anonymous.

PRIESTS
AND
HOLY MEN

To a westerner, the individuals involved in religious vocations amongst the Hindu population can probably be narrowed down to three familiar occupations: the priestly BRAHMANA *or 'Brahmin' member of the highest of the four social castes, the* YOGI *or contemplative ascetic, and the* GURU *or teacher. To these, in recent times, can be added the* SWAMI *or pastoral minister. India, however, is a country in which religion involves or affects virtually every aspect of day-to-day activity and where the boundaries between secular and non-secular life are blurred or overlap. The more familiar names, not surprisingly, reflect only the foreigner's popular idea of Hinduism.*

To the list should also be added the *rishis* or inspired sages who compiled the *Veda* and its commentaries, and the *sadhus* or religious mendicants who, as *samnyasis*, may undertake extremes of austerity in pursuit of their goals of understanding the scriptures and their message of *dharma*. Nor should it omit the great philosophers, such as Shankhara who lived in the eighth century CE and who delivered an important interpretation of the *Upanishads*, or other leading lights in Hindu philosophy. These include the founders of the six classical schools of thought and others such as Ramanuja who died in 1137, Nimbarka who lived in the twelfth century and Madhva in the thirteenth, all of whom founded important religious sects.

BRAHMIN

India has a current population of rather more than 900 million most of whom are Hindus governed by a strict social order known as 'caste'. The origins of the caste order trace back to the Vedic scriptures which describe how the primordial being was dismembered during the act of creation. From his head came the *brahmanas*, members of the highest of the four castes, beneath which are *kshatriyas* or warriors, *vaishyas* or farmers and merchants, and *shudras* or servant classes. The Brahmins were designated as the guardians of the sacred Vedic scriptures, the Epics and the Puranas, and of ritual procedures including *yajna* or sacrifice, the details of which were kept closely secret and handed down from generation to generation. To a non-Hindu the term Brahmin, which is a corruption of *brahmana*, may seem confusing since *brahman* also represents the spiritual totality of the universe. A member of the *brahmana* caste is, however, one who follows the way of Brahma(n), the personification of *brahman*.

The Brahmins not only uphold the old Vedic traditions but also have tended to take on missionary activities and have been selected as the natural leaders of the major sects including Vaishnavas, Shaivites and Shaktas, the devotees of the goddess Devi and other *shaktis*. Their lives are disciplined into study of the *Veda*, gathering the daily requirements of ritual such as firewood and flowers, the observation of the rituals, and earning their keep. Once Brahmins were restricted more or less to teaching but today they may be employed as lawyers, farmers, government officials and the like. Technically a Brahmin is not allowed to take formal payment for services but may request and receive 'gifts' of money.

RISHI

The *rishis* are the inspired poets, seers or sages who have achieved the perfect or blessed state of wisdom and who, in Hindu mythology, became deified as the 'sons of Brahma'. These sages of ancient times were the recipients of the divine scriptures although they are not necessarily the individuals who are accredited with writing the scriptures down. The writing of the *Mahabharata* epic is attributed to a scribe, Ganapati, but he is said to have copied down the inspired utterances of Vyasa, the *rishi* who is also believed to have compiled the liturgy of the *Veda*. Today the *rishi* is regarded as representing the ultimate ideal of Hinduism, someone who has gone beyond earthly desires, influences and moralities. He is described in the *Bhagavad Gita* as one who has attained the *supreme consummation of wisdom through leading a simple, self-reliant life based on meditation, controlling his speech, body and mind. He is free from self-will, aggressiveness, arrogance, anger and the lust to possess people or things, he is at peace with himself and others and enters into unity with brahman.* (*Bhagavad Gita*, p.210)

In simplistic terms the *guru* is the modern equivalent of the *rishi*. He is a wise teacher of the divine scriptures and the paths of loving devotion or *bhaktimarga*, which lead to liberation; he is one who shows the way and acts as a personal spiritual guide to his students (see pp.62–3).

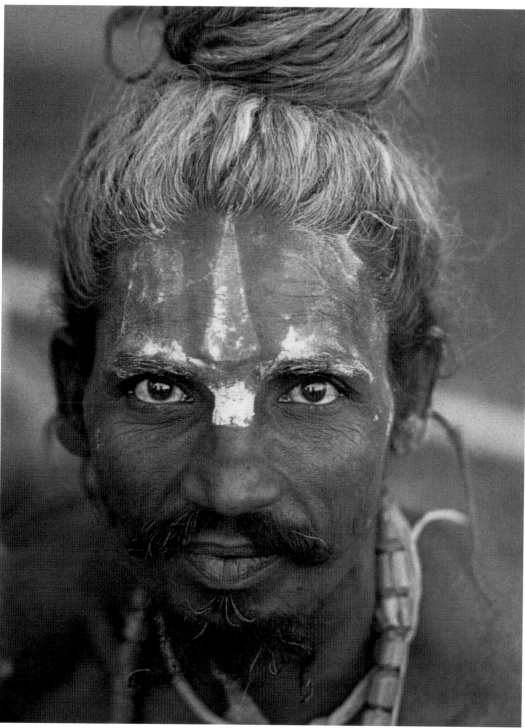

WEARING AN ASH MARK ON HIS FOREHEAD, THIS *SWAMI* IS ONE OF MANY PILGRIMS CELEBRATING KHUMBA MELA, A PILGRIMAGE FESTIVAL HELD EVERY THREE YEARS IN ROTATION AT ONE OF FOUR HOLY RIVER SITES.

PASTORAL MINISTERS AND LAYPEOPLE

Less a class of holy man than a title of respect which equates most closely with 'Reverend', *swamis* run missions and generate tracts of religious material though, in recent times, the term has achieved a degree of notoriety in the west through the cultic activities of certain well -publicized personalities. Aside from these few exceptions, however, many *swamis* in India and throughout the world continue to perform valuable and much-respected work in evangelizing the message and cause of Hinduism.

Outside of these clear-cut roles there are many thousands of men and women in India who reject the materialistic world and choose to live as ascetics with varying degrees of austerity and self-deprivation. At their most extreme, as *samnyasis*, they discard all earthly possessions other than a loin cloth, a staff and a begging bowl, occasionally even rejecting these in their pursuit of the ultimate understanding.

RITUAL

Ritual is of deep significance in Hinduism and is one of its most visible features, although the concept of ritual has changed markedly over the centuries. The earliest forms were based on the Vedic scriptures and essentially involved sacrifice of animals. In the more modern era the Vedic sacrificial rites or YAJNAS *have lost popularity and the present style of ritual tends to follow the so-called Agama tradition based largely on doctrinal writings said to have been revealed to the followers of Shiva.*

VEDIC RITUALS

Vedic sacrifice involves the vehicle of fire which not only purifies but sends the sacrificial object aloft to the heavens as smoke. It therefore requires the building of a sacred fire altar with bricks, which is then demolished after use. It also requires a number of other essential ingredients. First a recipient of sacrifice in the form of a *deva* must be named and a sacrificial object or material called the *dravya* must be made available. Then there is a ceremonial process known as *tyaga* or submitting the *dravya* to the *deva*. Finally there is the obligatory utterance of a *mantra*. Without all four of these components the ritual is considered improperly conducted and worthless.

The Vedic sacrifice can be a private family affair or it can be a high-profile and very public event. On the larger scale it is termed a *shrauta* or public ritual, designed to bring a response to a regional or national need. Such a *mahayajna* ritual will usually be performed by substantial numbers of Brahmins and the high cost of staging it will be paid for by local beneficiaries. Occasionally these large-scale events still take place, some of the most recent having been performed in response to the burgeoning nuclear threat during the 1950s.

To a Hindu worshipper Vedic sacrifice does not have the same dramatic connotations that it sometimes possesses for a westerner but rather follows the simple logic that work earns reward. Since doing a job of work in the material world earns reward in the shape of food, clothing and other necessities, it follows that a different kind of activity on behalf of a deity will

earn spiritual returns. There is a guarantee of result implicit in the understanding that every earthly requirement has a specified sacrifice and that each sacrifice has its price. This makes sacrifice and reward a kind of contractual exchange and it is understood that the gods or *devas* are dependent on sacrifice just as much as the person making the sacrifice is dependent on the *devas* for their response. It is also believed that sacrificial ritual has helped to control natural events such as floods and epidemics of disease.

MODERN PRACTICES

Sacrifice of animals is now only rarely carried out. It has been replaced by a spiritual exercise of the mind rather than a physical offering. This change has come about at the same time as the caste system has begun to lose its status. Many modern Hindus now believe that each of the four original castes is contained in every individual and therefore each person has an obligation to

THROUGHOUT THE HINDU WORLD, MILLIONS OF LIGHTS ARE SET UP IN THE STREETS TO CELEBRATE DIWALI.

ON A BOMBAY BEACH WORSHIPPERS GATHER TO CELEBRATE A FESTIVAL FOR THE POPULAR ELEPHANT-HEADED DEITY, GANESHA.

fulfil the ritual responsibilities of Brahmin, *kshatriya*, *vaishya* and *shudra*. All must learn the basics of the scriptures and rituals, undergo military service, train for a profession and also perform some kind of manual labour. These are the modern sacrificial obligations through which work earns divine reward.

Ritual still occupies a position of importance in many households when Hindus celebrate the festivals that have been a way of life in India since time immemorial. These may celebrate the changing of the seasons, an historical event or a significant family occasion, and their small rituals are passed on from one generation to the next as family traditions. Not untypical is the festival of Nirjala Ekathsi which takes place twice in every month and is intended to absolve the worshipper from sins accumulated during the previous fortnight, whilst also encouraging charity. The rites are referred to as *puja* or worship and are generally conducted in a particular room of the house which is prepared for the occasion.

In its strictest observation Nirjala Ekathsi requires fasting. The first duty is a ritual ablution followed by a cleaning of the house after which the family gathers in the *puja* room, sometimes a covered veranda. The statue of the household guardian deity,

accompanied by that of Ganesha, is placed on a raised table or altar and a lamp and joss sticks are lit. Both statues are sprinkled first with water then with a red powder known as *roli* and finally with rice, whilst the family sits around the deities. Food to be distributed to the poor and to the Brahmin is apportioned in front of each person, and water and rice are passed round whilst *mantras* are chanted. The food is distributed within two days of the festival and the object is largely philanthropic and charitable, a sacrifice from the fortunate to the less well-off.

This simple festival represents one end of the spectrum. Celebrations such as the annual Festival of Lights, Diwali, are grand affairs involving fireworks and the lighting of all the houses with lamps. Diwali marks the occasion when the exiled Rama returned in triumph to Ayodhya, having defeated the demon Ravana. It comes after what is known as the dark fortnight of the new moon in October or November. On this occasion it is Lakshmi, the goddess of fortune, riches and beauty, who is invoked alongside Ganesha since she is believed to visit everyone during Diwali. It is also a time of giving which compares in certain respects to the mood of Christmas in the Christian calendar.

TEMPLES
AND
SHRINES

ndia is a country of temples without equal but there is a certain irony in that one of the largest and most dramatic monuments to Hinduism rests not in India but thousands of miles away from the sub-continent amid the ruins of a metropolis hidden in the jungles of Cambodia. One of the largest cities of the ancient world, Angkor was built at the height of the Khmer Empire's supremacy in South-East Asia. Construction commenced in the ninth century CE, and by the turn of the millennium the city covered an area of about 40 square miles and enjoyed a population as large as half a million. In the twelfth century the vast temple of Angkor Wat, which is larger even than the Vatican, was built in the heart of the city by the god king Suryavarnam II to honour Vishnu.

Angkor Wat's distinctive terraced towers rising above the skyline are in the form of lotus buds, one of Vishnu's principal symbols. As well as being a place of devotion to Vishnu it was designed both as a monumental tomb to house the remains of King Suryavarnam, and also as an astronomical observatory.

The great holy cities of India herself, including Bhuvanesvara, Madurai, Khajuraho and Srirangam, stand as supreme monuments to a dynamic and all-pervading faith. The temple and the shrine are integral parts of the Indian landscape, and countless numbers exist in towns and villages. The simple materials with which they are often built and decorated, wood and cheap coloured paper, provide evidence of the universal interest in worship among all sections of the Indian community.

In addition to the temples, India abounds with monastic retreats such as Vimala Pitha, the *samnyasi* sanctuary founded by the sage Shankhara at Jagannatha-Puri on the east coast.

SYMBOLISM OF TEMPLE BUILDINGS

The first Hindu temples were probably no more than wooden models designed to house a statue of the god whilst the Vedic divinities were worshipped at sacrificial altars in the open air. Temple building proper in India began in about the sixth century CE and it seems that the larger temples, judging from those which have survived the passage of time, may have been copied in stone from the early wooden models. Although many Hindu places of worship were destroyed by Moorish invaders an impressive number of early historical buildings survive.

ANGKOR WAT DECAYS, BUT IN INDIA HINDUISM'S HOLY PLACES CONTINUE TO THRIVE.

Nowadays most temples and shrines belong to individual families as private properties although some of the larger buildings are administered as state-run enterprises.

By no means all the temples of India are archaic edifices: many are of modern construction; in fact, more temples have appeared since independence in 1947 than in the previous 1500 years. All are built following strict guidelines laid down in the ancient scriptures and conforming to the laws of the cosmos. Intricate calculations have to be made in order that the construction should comply with precise demands. Essential to construction are squares, symbolizing the eternal perfection of *brahman*, and circles, symbolizing the imperfect and finite principle of time. A centre square, occupied by Brahma at the core of the cosmos, is surrounded by an inner ring of the principal gods, the *devas*, and an outer ring of 32 minor gods, the *asuras*, representing the human world, at the corners of which (the 'rings' are actually arranged in a square pattern) stand the four *dikpalas* or guardians of the cardinal points of the cosmos. Each circle is interrupted by gates through which worshippers approach the ultimate object of devotion at the heart of the shrine. Outside the immediate area of the temple sanctuary are *mandapas* or cloisters where pilgrims may walk or rest in tranquillity, protected from the hustle and bustle of the outside world by high walls marking the perimeter of the temple area. The architectural principles are generally mirrored in the layout of the town in which a specified plot is detailed for temple building so the whole urban development conforms to religious as well as aesthetic requirements.

WORSHIP

The temple is an integral part of the path of devotion, or *bhaktimarga*, which most practising Hindus follow as a way of life, involving religious feasts and pilgrimages to visit holy shrines. The scriptures place strong emphasis on regular temple worship.

The embodiment of the deity in the form of a statue made in stone, wood or metal and known as the *murti* is of great importance. The imagery in the temple varies, however,

SCRIPTURES PRESCRIBE THE ESSENTIAL FEATURES OF A HINDU TEMPLE, ONE OF WHICH IS THE *DHWAJA STHAMBHA* OR FLAGPOLE. FROM HERE A SAFFRON FLAG FLIES TO ANNOUNCE THAT THIS IS A PLACE WHERE GOD RESIDES.

according to the nature of its sect. In a Vaishnava temple the image of the god Vishnu stands as an icon in more or less recognizable human form surrounded by *devas* and *asuras*. By contrast, in a Shaivite shrine, the presence of Shiva is represented by an oblong stone, the *linga*.

The temple effectively stands as a house to cater for the needs of the god, and in which to gain an audience with the god, rather than as a place of congregation. Worship is carried out according to a strict ritual by which the image is regularly bathed, sprinkled with scented water and decorated with flowers. According to some of the old texts it should also be laid down to rest at prescribed intervals and then awakened with songs and the blowing of conch shells. In addition to the main image at the centre of the temple there is often a smaller replica that is carried during processions. Some of the larger modern Hindu temples have adopted the Christian practice of offering communal worship. Unlike the decaying ruins of Angkor Wat, India's holy places are thriving testaments to the success of Hinduism in the modern world.

THE
SCHOOLS
OF
THOUGHT

*W*ithin the broad spectrum of Hindu philosophy, BHARATIYA DARSANA, there are generally considered to be six schools, the SADDARSANAS or systems of opinion. These are orthodox or ASTIKA which means that they recognize the authority of the VEDA and are Brahmanical in their discipline, contrasting with those which are heterodox or NASTIKA and which deny the Vedic authority.

A HINDU CHILD SEATED AT THE FEET OF A STATUE: ALL THE SYSTEMS OF PHILOSOPHY RECOGNIZE THE IMPORTANCE OF INTUITIVE EXPERIENCE.

The six orthodox systems are the Vedic schools of Mimamsa, Vedanta, Nyaya, Vaiseshika, Sankhya and Yoga, whilst those that are classed as heterodox include the schools of Buddha, Charvaka and Jaina. Irrespective of the particular system followed they all emphasize the need for practical realization of truth and the importance of gaining intuitive experience from religious conviction. The schools approach the matter in various ways but they are conveniently grouped in pairs which cover similar areas of discussion. Mimamsa and Vedanta go together as allied systems which try to interpret the *Veda*, whilst Nyaya and Vaiseshika tackle the problem from the viewpoint of logic, and Sankhya coupled with Yoga relies on philosophy and metaphysics. All are of classical Hindu origin, expounded by the finest of minds, yet they also have direct relevance to Indian society today and the textbooks are closely studied by modern scholars.

THE MIMAMSA SCHOOL

Mimamsa means 'enquiry' and is a theological discipline. More properly known as Purva-Mimamsa, in which the prefix *purva* means 'earlier', it is explored and analysed in the basic textbook of the school, the *Mimamsa-sutra,* compiled by the Hindu philosopher Jaimini between 200 BCE and 200 CE. It was Jaimini's intention to explain the true meaning of the *Veda* by focusing on action, *karma*, rather than thought. Purva-Mimamsa sets out to discover, through study of those parts of the *Veda* and the *Brahmanas* which deal with *karma*, the real nature of religious law or *dharma*. It reasons about the *karma-kanda* sections on sacrifice, and about the Vedic rites and the results which may be expected to come from their performance. It sets out to interpret the sense in which Vedic instructions, often terse or obscure, are to be carried out in ritual. It defends the Brahmanic view of Vedic culture on which the continuance of Vedic ritual depends and, in short, it argues that the active duty ordained by the *Veda*, including sacrifice, offerings and virtuous life, provides the surest path to the attainment of *ananda,* the ultimate bliss of paradise or *svarga*.

In some senses the Mimamsa school stands as an apology since it looks for reasons that confirm the authority of the *Veda* and argues that the liturgy of knowledge preserved in the *Veda samhita* is self-revealed rather than having been composed by human hand. On this point it compares the Vedic *shruti* (revealed) texts favourably with those of the *Ramayana* and *Mahabharata* epics and other merely 'written' literature of the *Puranas* which are *smriti* (remembered) histories. The system has attracted controversy in the past and has been attacked by other schools and sects including that of fundamentalist followers of Vaishnava who argue that it is worthless and promotes atheistic views.

THE VEDANTA SCHOOL

Coupled with Purva-Mimamsa, Vedanta is the more familiar title given to the philosophy of Uttara-Mimamsa. The prefix *uttara* means 'later' in reference to the closing chapters of the *Veda* and to a student of the school it is regarded as 'new theology' as distinct from 'old theology' contained in the Purva-Mimamsa. Uttara-Mimamsa focuses on the *jnana-kanda* sections of the *Veda* which emphasize the value of positive thought and speculation about the ultimate reality of *brahman* over that of action or *karma* involving ritual and sacrifice which it regards as passé. Much of this doctrine is set out, argued and elaborated in the *Upanishads* which are otherwise known as the *Veda Vedanta* (the close of the *Veda*) hence the 'Vedanta School'.

The basic textbook of the school, which discusses and summarizes the teachings of the *Upanishads*, is the *Vedanta-sutra* which is also sometimes referred to as the *Brahma-sutra* because it is Brahmanic in its approach. The date of the work is uncertain but its compilation is attributed to a philosopher named Badarayana and it opens with the words: 'Now, therefore, an enquiry into *brahman*'. Although the main classical work on which the philosophy relies, it is difficult to interpret since its summaries are so brief as to be largely incomprehensible to a modern researcher. It is generally assumed that a closely guarded oral tradition, explaining the *Vedanta-sutra*, was carried down from generation to generation of authorized teacher or *guru* in the school. It is also suggested that Badaryana's *sutra* was not the first on the subject but became sufficiently popular over the course of time that others, though they may have offered a clearer picture, became redundant. This argument is supported by the fact that the names of several earlier masters of philosophy or *acaryas*, whose works have not survived the passage of time, are mentioned in Badaryana's text.

The *Vedanta-sutra* consists of four chapters which deal, in order, with a detailed discussion of the nature of *brahman*, followed by an overt attack on various rival philosophies including those of the Sankhya and Vaiseshika schools and some ambiguous comments about the validity of the teachings of the Vaishnava-orientated *Bhagavata Purana*. The *sutra* goes on to discuss the nature of the living individual, and the states of waking, dream sleep, dreamless sleep and death, whilst the final section evaluates meditation and speculates on the ultimate fate of the self or *atman* of one who has come to understand the totality of *brahman*.

THE NYAYA AND VAISESHIKA SCHOOLS

In stark contrast with the theosophical systems studied by the Mimamsa and Vedanta schools, these are explorations of

A MODERN PORTRAYAL OF THE GODDESS LAKSHMI: THE VARIOUS DEITIES SYMBOLIZE DIFFERENT ASPECTS OF ONE UNIVERSAL LIFE SOURCE.

physics and logic. They tend to be linked by modern authors although they derive from different origins and demonstrate separate objectives. Nyaya is, in essence, a study in realism and singularity in the universe, whilst Vaiseshika provides a remarkable insight into an early Hindu understanding of atomic theory and the multiplicity of existence.

From about the tenth century onwards there were moves to combine the historically separate Nyaya and Vaiseshika Schools. They developed as sister academies and although their systems follow wholly different aims they have never stood as rivals. Many authors point to the fact that, in certain respects, they supplement one another and refer to them as the amalgamated Nyaya-Vaiseshika School.

The Nyaya School

This system is of ancient origin and is based on the *Nyaya-sutra,* allegedly compiled by the Vedic authority Gautama-Aksapada (distinct from Gautama Buddha) in about 300 BCE. In the sixteenth century the original treatise of the *Nyaya-sutra* was streamlined and modernized by an emergent school of Navya-Nyaya or 'new logic' whose founder, Gangesa, produced a textbook called the *Tattva-cintamani.*

The Nyaya system argues a mixture of philosophy, metaphysics (the first principles of nature and thought) and logic in the form of deductive reasoning, properly known as syllogism, which requires that a logical conclusion is drawn from two theoretical proposals, a major and a minor premise. The *Nyaya-sutra* comprises two sections: the first or *adhyatma-vidya* (the knowledge of the supreme being) deals with metaphysical questions and the second or *tarka-sastra* (doctrine of logic) with the rules of reasoned debate.

The system does not claim to devote itself to pure logic but concentrates on the theory of knowledge. It stresses that the best means of achieving ultimate knowledge is through reasoning or logic and argues that the pursuit of logic is a sure path to truth, and therefore to salvation. In support of this theory the older system offers sixteen categories by which the path may be achieved. They cover all aspects of comprehension and knowledge, from the means and objects of correct comprehension, through theory, discussion and contention, to its final section, the conclusive argument.

The newer Navya-Nyaya system, expounded in the *Tattva-cintamani,* downgrades the metaphysical arguments and places emphasis on working through four legitimate means of discovering reality by concentrating on objects of knowledge. These objects may be *atman* or self, the body and the physical senses, the mind and understanding, endeavour, pain and pleasure, suffering and liberation, rebirth. The various means of discovery include perception or *pratyaksa* (the result of contact between sense and desired object), inference or *anumana* (cause leading to effect or vice versa), analogy or *upamana* (recognizing anything on account of its similarity to some well-known thing), and the spoken testimony or *sabda* of some well-established authority.

Pursuing either the old or the new metaphysical thesis will, the school claims, lead to attainment of the goal. Respect for both developments of the system has been kept and they are probably followed equally today although some, including Buddhist logicians, regard them scathingly.

The Vaiseshika School

This system, which is in fact older than Nyaya, does not pursue some all-embracing Brahmanic concept of the universe, but expounds the theory that the soul of the cosmos, *brahman,* is hugely diverse and pluralistic. It draws on physics and metaphysics to argue its case into which, in common with the Nyaya School, it also weaves logic and the theory of knowledge.

The founder of the school is the ascetic Kanada who also compiled its standard textbook, the *Vaiseshika-sutra.* Subsequent commentaries and revised versions of the system were developed by classical scholars, amongst whom the philosopher Prasastapada wrote a work on the subject known as the *Padartha-dharma-sangraha,* now regarded as a standard by students of Vaiseshika. Prasastapada elaborated seven categories of substance, the full understanding of which provides a route to salvation. They include earth, air, fire, water, ether, time, space and *atman* which must be evaluated on the basis of a number of qualities — touch, taste, smell, colour, quantity, volume, proximity, understanding, pleasure, pain, desire or otherwise, and self-will. All of these things are viewed in a multiple sense, including the *atman* or self, since there are, according to the Vaiseshika system, many *atmans* distinguished by their specific properties and relationships. They inhabit physical beings temporarily but their great diversity is perceptible only to a *yogi* who has achieved true insight into the meaning of *atman.*

Perhaps the most remarkable aspect of Prasastapada's work is his explanation of atomic theory. He describes the physical elements of earth, air, fire and water as possessing mass, number, weight and other features. They are made up of atoms which, prior to creation and after apocalypse, exist as single particles. Whilst ether is wholly inert and eternal, these physical elements are partly temporal and partly eternal and only through the act of creation do they become combined into molecules under the control of the creator being who melds and arranges them into an orderly cosmos. Prasastapada also examines heat and light with remarkable insight, explaining them as tiny particles which move through space at tremendous speeds. Those of heat either pass through spaces in matter or collide with its atoms and rebound, which explains how materials either conduct or reflect.

SANKHYA
AND
YOGA

In the BHAGAVAD GITA, Krishna explains to Arjuna the various routes by which to achieve full consciousness of ATMAN and therefore perfect unity with BRAHMAN. One of these is the passive discipline of SANKHYA but Krishna goes on to place greater importance on its more active counterpart, YOGA, which he describes as being neither inaction nor unqualified action but rather action with authority and understanding. The two disciplines are intimately connected and together represent perhaps the oldest of the Indian philosophical systems.

SANKHYA

Founded according to mythology by the *rishi* or sage Kapila who, it is believed, lived in the sixth century BCE, *sankhya* offers freedom from the pain and misery of *samsara*. The oldest textbook on the subject, probably written by Isvara Krishna in the third century CE, is the *Sankhya-karika*, although this evolved into a much lengthier later work, the *Sankhya-sutra*. The philosophy argues the existence of two realities, *prakriti* and *purusha*, the male and female principles of matter and spirit which, although possessing a certain polarity, combine and interact. It claims a multiplicity of *purushas* which, at the very beginning, disturbed the equilibrium of matter and caused evolution to start. The aim of *sankhya* is to free *purusha* from *prakriti* by abandoning perception through the objective senses and coming to understand that the true nature of matter is contrary to the true nature of spirit. Only then, and at death, can the *purusha* be alone and wholly liberated into bliss.

YOGA

The word *yoga* derives from a Sanskrit root meaning 'to join', suggesting the fusion of the two principles *atman* and *brahman*, self and totality (see p.42). It is suggested that it may have been practised since very early times in India and the argument is supported by engraved seals discovered at Mohenjo-Daro, one of the two main centres of the Indus valley civilization. Some of these seals depict postures which compare closely with at least one of the meditative positions or *asanas* described for classical *yoga*.

The aim of the practitioner, the *yogi*, is to achieve spiritual fulfilment and discovery of the ultimate reality through austerity and the rejection of earthly desires. The insight said to be gained through this process represents the highest and most virtuous way of life and even within the six orthodox schools of Hindu thought, which often promote rivalry, the *yoga* system is fully incorporated into the principles of *Advaita Vedanta*, the Vedanta treatise of the great philosopher Shankhara, who believed it to come closest to the 'true way'.

As a discipline *yoga* is most closely followed by Shaivites, members of the sect which devotes itself to the worship of

THROUGH THE MENTAL AND PHYSICAL DISCIPLINES OF *YOGA*, THE PRACTITIONER ASPIRES TO ACHIEVE SPIRITUAL FULFILMENT.

A *YOGA* POSTURE, INCLUDING FOUR DIFFERENT HAND GESTURES, IS DEMONSTRATED BY A STATUE INCORPORATED IN THE EXTERIOR OF THE LAKSHMANA TEMPLE AT KHAJURAHO, INDIA, DATING FROM C.950 CE.

In the modern western sense, *yoga* has been used to describe various meditative forms of popular spiritual practice which may, in reality, have little in common with the classical Indian concept of the word and which are generally termed *hatha yoga*. The true *sankhya yoga* or *raja yoga* discipline was first detailed in a religious text, the *Yoga-sutra* compiled by Patanjali, a philosopher who lived some time between 200 BCE and 500 CE and whose knowledge stemmed, it is said, from the teachings of Shiva. The *Yoga-sutra* does not actually refer to Shiva by name but uses the title Ishvara or *purusha*, the Supreme Lord, which is nowadays regarded as an epithet of the god. In theory classical *yoga* is believed to replicate the trances engineered by the ancient seers and sages in order to receive divine revelation and wisdom, whilst in practice Patanjali described it as being the cessation of all changes in consciousness through physical training and will-power.

The path of the true *yogi* towards spiritual fulfilment lies somewhere between, on the one hand, self-destruction and, on the other, even the most fundamental self-indulgence such as cure of bodily ills. At its core lies the discipline of *pranayamana*, the control of life-breath or *prana*. It is claimed that after extensive training a *yogi* can reduce his body metabolism so that the heartbeat falls to a more or less imperceptible level and the person appears not to be breathing at all. In this state he has overcome all fear about keeping his vital processes going, has entered a state of purification and is capable of achieving full mental realization. This involves three stages known as *samyama*. Initially the disciple concentrates his intellect towards a single topic in a process known as *dharana*; next comes *dhyana* when the mind has achieved its focus and must remain concentrated upon it; finally *samadhi* requires the object in focus to be divested of form and to become merely an abstract understanding.

Shiva, whom they regard as the *Mahayogi*. Fettering of the spirit, which prevents absolute knowledge of self, is one of the fundamental principles of *Shaiva-siddhanta* (the worship of Shiva which reveals the final truth) and by means of its ritual acts *yoga* is regarded as the most effective way to obtain freedom from this bondage.

In practice *yoga* requires training in a number of routines, partly physical and partly mental. These include breath control, directing the vital breaths through six body centres or *chakras*, withdrawing the senses from material stimuli, suspending mental activity, and recitation of *mantras* including repetition of sacred words such as OM.

Physically the *Yoga-sutra* recommends adoption of certain positions or *asanas* during meditation which enables the disciple to remain motionless in comparative comfort for long periods of time without falling asleep. Most people never pass beyond the basic meditational exercises but the most advanced *yogis* are claimed to have reached a state of control that allows them to perform miraculous acts including expanding to giant dimensions, reducing to the size of a grain of sand or even becoming wholly invisible, as well as leaving the body for temporary periods.

The ultimate aim of the quest, gained through complete achievement of *samadhi*, is to reach the spiritual height of *kaivalya* or 'oneness', the joining of *atman* and *brahman*. *Yoga* represents one amongst a number of ways by which the philosophers of Hinduism believe it is possible to achieve perfect understanding and liberation from *karma*. In spite of the close connection with Shiva the popularity of *sankhya yoga* has spread and it is now practised by Shaivites, Vaishnavas and Shakti worshippers alike. As a general spiritual path *yoga* remains the most popular and the most widely followed and it has also gripped the imaginations of devotees in many parts of the world beyond the borders of India.

SHANKARA

Shankara was a great philosopher and writer of the Indian medieval period who compiled one of the finest discussions of the VEDANTA. His work, the ADVAITA VEDANTA, is regarded as a classic commentary on the Vedic liturgy and the texts of the UPANISHADS. He was born at Kaladi in Tamilnadu, Tamil country, in about 788 CE and grew up in the south of India deep within the Dravidian heartland which, in his time, was the focus of Hindu civilization. Here the Dravidian language was the common tongue and the old traditions of pre-Sanskrit Tamil culture were fiercely guarded.

Shankara was a *samnyasi* (see p.48) by the age of 18 and he became deeply concerned with what he saw as the heresies of Buddhism and Jainism. His own *guru* is thought to have been Gaudapada who compiled a set of principles in a work known as the *Karika*, based on the *Mandukya Upanishad*. He set out to restore, through the writing of numerous books, teaching, and the establishment of missionary schools, the principles of the eternal religion of Hinduism, *sanatana dharma*. He saw this as having become adulterated and felt a deep necessity to return to a purer form of doctrinal belief drawn from the *Veda* and the *Upanishads*. Shankara died at the age of 32.

Although loyal to his Tamil roots Shankara, nevertheless, spoke to the whole of India. He wrote in Sanskrit and thus gained a vast following outside the Dravidian-speaking areas of the south. Shankara was a passionate believer in the validity of the *Veda* and in order to convey his message he founded a missionary order, the Dasanami, the so-called 'ten named'. This was based on his doctrine of *dasanami samnyasi* which draws on the work of ten illustrious *samnyasis*, including Gaudapada and others, whose thinking Shankara respected and followed. He demanded strict discipline and study and an indication of his devotion to the Vedic scriptures lies in the fact that his disciples were given a *sloka* or double verse from the *Upanishads* as their personal *mantra*. From its monasteries or *mathas* the true message of the Dasanami was taken to the whole of India. The four principal Shankara religious centres,

each headed by a *guru* known as a *shankaracarya* who is the living successor to the founder, include Jyoti Matha in the foothills of the Himalayas in the north, Vimala Pitha at Jagannatha on the east coast, Sarada Pitha in the south, and Kalika Pitha on the west coast.

Shankara was not universally popular amongst Hindus, however, and many Vaishnavites saw his arguments as being heretical. His alleged misdeeds included compiling the *Advaita Vedanta* as a cover for spreading the alien message of Buddhism, encouraging the murder of women and children and irresponsibly employing the magic arts. Ironically, from the opposing ideological camp Buddhists also saw Shankara and his followers as the 'enemy'. At one time matters became sufficiently heated that the Dasanami order had to resort to the employment of armed guards, the *dasanami nagas*, who lived in military-style camps or *akhadas* and carried heavy metal tridents. It was their responsibility to protect the *samnyasis* against attack from Vaishnavites and Buddhists and their discipline included yoga and physical training, the combination of which was believed to provide them with supernatural powers. The violent skirmishes between religious factions are on record as having continued, sustaining large numbers of casualties, until the nineteenth century.

Shankara succeeded in outclassing his rivals and quelling the voices of opposition not least because of his superior powers of oratory and his command of public debate. Far from being a supporter of Buddhism he saw his monastic order as providing a bulwark against unorthodox beliefs. He believed that knowledge of *brahman* was the essential goal, that the only authoritative *guru* was a member of the Brahmin caste who fully understood the arguments and could discuss them in a calm and reasoned manner, and that the most effective route was through the discipline of *yoga*.

Shankara was a supporter of the philosophy of *advaita* or non-dualism, in which there is no separation between *brahman* and *atman* and liberation can be achieved only through knowledge rather than action. He believed that the tangible and visible world has its origins in *brahman* but that this same material world is only an illusion and is not a part of *brahman*. Shankara was one of a number of philosophers who considered that the individual self or *atman* is shackled permanently by ignorance and that knowledge is distorted in such a way that the subject is prevented from discovering objective reality. He explains that the ordinary person is tied in ignorance because he cannot distinguish what is *atman* and what is purely

WOMEN CARRY PITCHERS OF HOLY WATER FROM THE RIVER GANGES FOR A RELIGIOUS RITUAL KNOWN AS ASHWAMEDH YAJNA. THE IMPORTANCE OF UNITED WORSHIP OR *YAJNA* IS EMPHASIZED IN THE HINDU SCRIPTURES AND ADVOCATED BY MOST SCHOOLS OF THOUGHT.

material, in other words between 'things' and 'being' or between relative and absolute. Shankara gives an example of the person walking along a road who mistakenly identifies a piece of rope as a snake or, conversely, a snake as a piece of rope. He extends this simple illustration infinitely by calling into question the reliability of all human perceptions gained through the physical senses. The *Advaita Vedanta* doctrine is described as *maya* or 'illusion' and it is because of this that rivals have claimed Shankara's philosophy to be 'Buddhism in disguise', but its true wisdom remains that the only reality is *brahman* and that we are all part of this undivided consciousness.

MODERN GURUS

M odern Hinduism and the understanding of its complexities owes much to the GURU or teacher. In ancient times the term referred specifically to a Brahmin priest who instructed his young scholars in the religious lore of the VEDA and the UPANISHADS. The definition is now broader and encompasses the role of any teacher who offers personal instruction to a disciple or CHELA. Many such GURUS go unnoticed beyond the immediate confines of their village or religious retreat, the ASHRAM. Others achieve worldwide recognition and exert considerable influence far beyond the borders of India.

REFORM MOVEMENTS

The modern *guru* phenomenon probably began with nineteenth-century social reformers including Ramadasa and Ramakrishna. Ramadasa was born in 1865 in Bengal and founded an order of Ramadasis which became popular amongst people of lower caste. Ramakrishna was a contemporary and fellow Bengali who lived from 1836 until 1886 and was a staunch devotee of the goddess Kali. He lived as a reclusive temple priest who apparently displayed no interest in social reforms but, nonetheless, his personality exercised a strong influence on many of those who met him. One of his disciples, Vivekananda, went on to found the best known of the Hindu reform movements, the Ramakrishna Mission, which he represented at the World Parliament of Religions in Chicago in 1893. The avowed intention of the mission was to improve living conditions for large numbers of Hindus and to provide better schools and hospital facilities.

Hindu *gurus* and *swamis* have been unusually successful in adapting their religious beliefs to suit the western mentality. Undoubtedly the best known of the *guru*-inspired movements in the western world is that of Hare Krishna, properly known as the International Society for Krishna Consciousness, which was founded in the United States in 1965 by Swami Prabhupada, otherwise known as Swami Bhaktivedanta. Its disciples became instantly recognizable, with their shaven heads and saffron robes, dancing, chanting and selling trinkets and religious tracts in city streets in America and Europe. Prabhupada gained inspiration from the teachings of a medieval Vaishnavite *guru*, Caitanya, whose school is most influential in Bengal and other parts of northern India. He took one of the most compelling Vaishnavite texts, the *Bhagavad Gita,* to the hippy movement at the height of the Cold War and popularized its message as propounded by Krishna. An element of Armageddon mentality was also introduced in as much as the movement's disciples were ordered to wear a topknot of hair by which Krishna would pluck them to safety at the moment of nuclear holocaust. Hare Krishna has done much to bring to the west, through translations, the classical texts of Hinduism which focus on *bhakti*, the path of love and devotion. At its higher levels of commitment its disciples live in a religious commune and practise strict austerity, including total celibacy outside of marital procreation, vegetarianism, and abstinence from alcohol and tobacco. The international acclaim of Hare Krishna was raised further by former Beatle George Harrison, who wrote a much publicized song based on their *mantra* 'Hare Krishna, Hare Krishna, Krishna Krishna, Hare Hare, Hare Rama, Hare Rama, Rama Rama, Hare Hare'.

Some of the minor movements have started with good intentions and descended into infamy. One of the more notorious is the Rajneeshis founded in the late 1960s by the self-styled Bhagwan Shree Rajneesh who based his spiritual headquarters in Bombay and made the dubious claim that only the rich could find spiritual fulfilment. Others with proven credentials, including the Transcendental Meditation Society of Mahesh Yogi Maharishi, introduced to the west in the 1960s, have achieved phenomenal success and have succeeded in recruiting large numbers, particularly of young people, to

THE MUSICIAN RAVI SHANKAR WITH FORMER BEATLE GEORGE HARRISON,
ONE OF HARE KRISHNA MOVEMENT'S MORE CELEBRATED FOLLOWERS.

MAHATMA GANDHI

Of all the great modern *gurus* in India, none achieved more international repute than Mohandas Karamchand Gandhi who was born in 1869 and assassinated by extremists in 1948. He managed to combine politics and religion in a way that was unique even by Indian standards, bringing India out of British colonial rule and at the same time introducing a wide-ranging package of social reforms. He expressed a solid aversion to modern technology which he rightly believed had the potential to leave jobless vast numbers of the lowest workers, including the untouchables for whom he had special concern. He also supported the rights of women in a climate of sex discrimination and attempted to integrate elements of the Christian faith of the British raj with Hinduism. Amongst Gandhi's favourite scriptures was the *Bhagavad Gita* which he referred to as his 'mother' and in which he found the quintessence of the age-old battle between spiritual duty and personal interest. He took the *Bhagavad Gita* as the basis for his philosophy on modern living.

WOMEN GURUS

India has enjoyed her share of women *gurus*, known as *mas* or mothers, during the twentieth century, though these have been in a minority. Amongst the celebrated is Anandamayi Ma who lived in Bengal from 1896 to 1982.

Hinduism in Europe and North America. Much of their attraction has lain in the use of *mantras* and meditative techniques that relieve stress and induce feelings of calm and well-being.

Although at first she was labelled as 'deranged' she gained a substantial following both in India and abroad and developed a number of influential and successful *ashrams*. She became recognized as a Hindu *sant* or saint and was a living *deva* to many of her followers, who described her as an *avatara* of the goddess Mahadevi or Parvati.

MODERN HINDUISM

*H*induism is not a missionary religion and it has remained largely a belief shared amongst people of Indian culture and background. Nor is it a strictly uniform faith: its 400 million or more devotees in India form clearly defined sects, whose forms of worship and objects of devotion are sometimes accountably different. These divisions have come and gone throughout its long history, some being ephemeral, others surviving for centuries.

Beyond the borders of India, Hinduism was once very strong in a number of South-East Asian countries but many of these have since become predominantly Buddhist, and it now continues to attract the majority of the population only in the Indonesian island of Bali. Indians have, however, migrated extensively to Europe, the United States, South and East Africa and the East Indies, as well as to neighbouring countries such as Nepal, and have carried their faith with them. Hinduism is particularly strong in the United States, but in England, north London claims the biggest Hindu temple in Europe with a congregation of many thousands of devotees.

THE INFLUENCE OF LANGUAGE

Within the Indian sub-continent Hinduism remains divided to no small extent on the basis of language. Most of its religious texts were composed in Sanskrit, which was spoken in north-western India from about 1500 BCE and was the archaic language of the first works of Hinduism to emerge in written form, the Knowledge or *Veda*. Sanskrit was then 'modernized' as the classical written language of culture and, in spite of its antiquity, has remained the literary and sacred language of India.

In southern India and Sri Lanka, however, Dravidian is the religious lingua franca. Its dialects represent the ancient tongues of India before the invasions from the north-west and have been spoken from at least 2000 BCE. They include Tamil, with Kanarese, Telugu, Malayalam and Tulu, although one Dravidian language is also spoken in parts of Pakistan. Hence the religious tradition of the south shows clear differences from that of the north.

Notwithstanding the distinct tongues and separate cultures, Hinduism has been adopted as the religion of the majority in both north and south India. One of the more unusual aspects of Hindu faith – perhaps a significant key to its tenacity – is that it is based on no formal creed and permits a great number of diverse traditions and practices. Its classical liturgy, the *Veda*, has been constantly reinterpreted to suit changing social and economic conditions, politics, personal needs, aspirations and horizons. There are also substantial differences between the theory of Hinduism and its practice. The actual way of devotion varies considerably from one locality to another and this underlines the great flexibility of the religion. The constant figure within this great diversity is the *guru* or teacher who conveys his own idiosyncratic understanding of the enormous scope of Hindu scripture and doctrine.

BLENDING THE RELIGIOUS AND THE SECULAR

One of the most significant aspects of life in modern India is the extent to which Hindu religion remains a part of everyday experience. The Bombay film industry turns out celluloid interpretations of ancient religious stories in a way that the west has never equalled; the great epics are best-sellers and vivid posters romanticizing Hindu religious scenes grace hoardings in most cities. Devotion to festivals and holy days attracts tens of thousands of worshippers, as does adherence to fasts and penitential rites.

One of the most popular and grandest festivals is Diwali or Dipavali, the Festival of Lights, which takes place at the onset of winter and commemorates the return of the heroic *avatara* of Vishnu, Rama, to Ayodhya, the capital of his kingdom, after

HARE KRISHNA FOLLOWERS ARE NOW A FAMILIAR SIGHT ON THE STREETS OF MOSCOW.

fourteen years of exile. In addition to the emphasis on *puja* or worship, every household is cleansed, lit with lamps and candles, special foods are prepared and fire crackers are set off.

Preceding Diwali by twenty days is the festival of Dussehra or Dasara which marks the triumph of Rama over Ravana, the demon king of Sri Lanka, and the heroic rescue of Rama's wife, Sita. Effigies of the central characters are paraded and the *Ramayana* epic is re-enacted in dramas and tableaux known as Ram Leelas. There are parallels with the English Guy Fawkes day in that a dummy of Ravana, filled with fireworks, is shot through the navel with an arrow and set alight, but the festival is essentially one which celebrates the triumph of good over evil. In this vein the festival is also a celebration of the slaying by Durga, the vengeful aspect of the goddess Parvati, of the demons, and in particular the buffalo demon Mahisa.

In the spring, in February or March, the festival of Holi is celebrated, marking the end of winter and, in some traditions, the Hindu New Year. This is a joyous occasion of thanksgiving for the change of seasons from cold to warm and for the renewal of life. Holi is largely devoted to the other great human *avatara* of Vishnu, Krishna, who is said to have celebrated Holi with great enthusiasm as a child, armed with a kind of water pistol known as a *pichkari*. Today these are popular toys and are used by both adults and children to squirt coloured water at one another. There is also a tradition of throwing brightly coloured powders, known as *gulal*, mixed with small crystals, *abeer*, which give the powder a sparkle.

These festivals, coupled with a host of minor festivities throughout the year as well as longer fairs termed *melas* that are held at places of pilgrimage, are designed to involve all levels of Hindu society and to shade any distinction between the religious and the secular in the life of India.

SIKHISM

SIKHS REVERE GURU NANAK AS THE FOUNDER AND FIRST *GURU* OF THEIR FAITH.

The Hindu teacher and philosopher, Guru Nanak, was born near Lahore and lived from 1469 until about 1539. Nanak saw benefits in blending certain elements of Hinduism and Islamic tradition and he went on to found Sikhism as a new and more universal religion. Sikhism sets out to forge a link between the two religions and combines their ideologies where these are seen to converge or overlap.

Islam promotes the concept of a universal divinity as the only true reality, a singular God before whom all worshippers stand as equals and in whose sight human virtues take a higher place than status and material wealth. Most of these principles also constitute a fundamental part of the *bhakti* or devotional path followed by Hindus in north India.

Nanak travelled extensively in his occupation as a merchant and in doing so became influenced by Islamic teachings. He eventually settled in Kartapur where he began teaching and gaining a following of converts. The tenets of the faith he created, including a large number of his hymns, are contained in the holy book of the Sikhs. Originally titled the *Granth Sahib* or 'Revered Book', this was compiled, some time after his death, in about 1603 by Arjan, the fifth of ten celebrated *gurus,* who followed in Nanak's footsteps. The cult of the *guru* is much more prominent than in Hinduism. Sikhs believe there is only one *guru* and that these teachers have carried the spirit of Nanak onwards through successive reincarnations. Arjan incorporated the teachings of his predecessors with his own to reflect this spiritual continuation.

MEMBERS OF THE *KHALSA* WEARING THE FIVE KS, SYMBOLS OF THEIR RELIGION.

DOCTRINE AND DEVELOPMENT

The essence of the Sikh doctrine laid down by Nanak is contained in the opening section of the *Granth Sahib* and is known as the *Mul Mantra.* It describes God as being without form but immanent throughout the whole of creation as *nam,* the essential name of the divine. This equates, more or less, with the Hindu idea of *brahman. Nam* is the Eternal One, *Akal Purakh,* and the enlightened believer who truly knows *nam* has found the path to ultimate release. The spiritual road of Sikhism, towards this state of bliss, is travelled in much the same way as it is by Hindus, through the recitation of *mantras,* meditation and active service in pursuance of the faith. There are, however, distinctions between the faiths. Sikhs believe that ultimate knowledge and revelation is possible only through the grace or *nadar* of God and, whilst the Hindu principles of *karma* and reincarnation are accepted, the caste system, integral to Hinduism but anathema to followers of Islam, is denied.

The word Sikh, in its original use, means 'disciple' and Nanak envisaged the religion of Sikhism purely as a peaceful search for spiritual truths. Over centuries, however, the meaning of the term has altered and now reflects a religious fraternity which has taken on a more militaristic character. Sikhs believe that they are representatives of a chosen race of warrior saints known as the *Khalsa,* the Company of the Faithful, and they follow a strict personal code in which five articles of dress have become an obligatory part of their religious tradition – uncut hair on the head and face called *kesh,* the wearing of the comb or *kangha,* short trousers or *kach,* the sword or *kirpan,* and a steel bracelet known as the *kara.*

The concept of the *Khalsa* and the traditions which accompany it were introduced by Guru Gobind Singh who lived from 1666 until he was slain by a Muslim assassin in 1708. Gobind Singh was the last in the succession of ten *gurus* who not only carried the message of Nanak but gradually transformed the movement into a political and military force. Since the death of Gobind Singh the holy book, the *Granth Sahib,* has been recognized as the embodiment of the driving force of Sikhism in place of a living leader and its title has become expanded to the *Guru Granth Sahib.* It is also known as the *Adi Granth* or 'First Book' which distinguishes it from a subsequent work, the *Dasam Granth,* the 'Book of the Tenth Guru'. This collection of works was not necessarily compiled by Gobind Singh as its title implies; whilst it is generally believed that he wrote parts, the bulk was probably amassed by his students. *Dasam Granth* closely reflects Gobind's message but also includes substantial retellings of the Hindu mythology of Krishna.

PUNJAB

The state of Punjab is the religious home of Sikhism, where about 9 million of the 14 million devotees live, and contains the Sikhs' holiest city, Amritsar. It was here in 1984 that Indian troops laid siege to the Golden Temple and occupied it after killing 325 armed demonstrators, an act of desecration which resulted in the assassination, by her Sikh bodyguards, of the prime minister, Indira Gandhi. In subsequent riots and reprisals more than 1000 Sikhs were killed.

It was not the first time in Indian history that there had been trouble between Sikhs and Hindus. In 1845, Sikh forces invaded British India and were defeated with the loss of territory, including Kashmir. In 1848 there was a second Sikh uprising that resulted in the British annexation of the Punjab and, ever since, this has been the focus of rumbling dissent.

In 1915 there took place the infamous Amritsar Massacre in which 379 were killed and many more wounded. The attack was ordered by the British commander in the area, General Dyer, the target being a crowd of some 10,000 demonstrators who were protesting against the arrest of two National Congress leaders. In 1966 a Sikh state was created by annexation of part of the Punjab but political and religious fundamentalists continue to air demands for a wholly independent state of Khalistan.

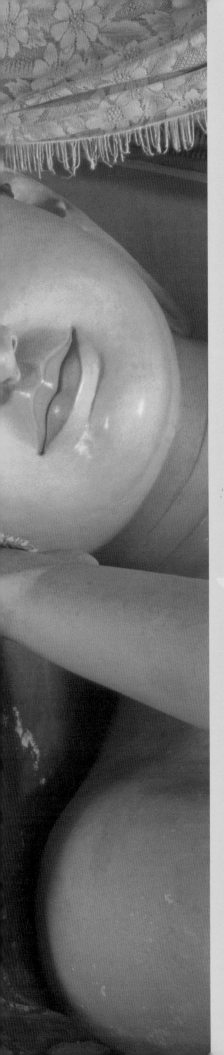

BUDDHISM

*B*uddhism is an essentially monastic but also non-theistic religion. It rejects the idea of the existence of a God or gods who stand distinct and separate from humankind and instead argues in favour of a transformation of consciousness resulting in enlightenment which breaks the painful cycle or 'Wheel' of death and rebirth. In certain respects Buddhism evolved as a reaction against aspects of Hinduism and the two, though often existing side by side, have never rested as particularly easy bedfellows. The teachings of the *buddha* are considered heretical by Hindus, who regard all Buddhists as atheists.

The founder of Buddhism, Siddharta, who later became recognized as the historical *buddha*, Gautama Buddha or Shakyamuni, experimented with the self-mortifying practices of Hindu *samnyasis* or wandering mendicants and rejected them in favour of a Middle Way which sought to compromise between material indulgence and extreme asceticism. He urged people from all walks of life to follow his teaching of *dharma* or truth, with the promise that the Way could lead them to enlightenment and the cessation of suffering represented in repeated cycles of reincarnation. In his teachings he claimed that all things in the material world are illusory, including the self, and that the secular world is one of impermanence and, ultimately, disappointment. We are prevented from understanding the true reality because we are controlled by material values. The object of the Way is to reach perfect enlightenment and thereby vanquish self and, with it, the need for death followed by rebirth. One fundamental disparity with the 'self' of Hinduism is that in Buddhism the 'self' is not a permanent entity like *atman*, but something that is subject to change through attachment to objects that are, in themselves, impermanent and illusory.

Through Buddhism we may reach the ultimate state of bliss or *nirvana*. Our success or failure is dependent on our actions or *karma* in each earthly existence, when good or evil deeds are placed 'on account' and their sum determines our luck when we are next reincarnated. The object is to achieve an upward spiral of life until we reach the summit.

BUDDHA MYTHOLOGY

*B*UDDHA *is a state of perfect being which, it is accepted, did not begin with Gautama Buddha in the fifth century* BCE *but has existed since the very beginning of creation. Gautama Buddha was merely the last in a line of succession and, distinct from spiritual beings, was a* MANUSIBUDDHA *or human* BUDDHA. *Gautama will, at some time in the future it is believed, be succeeded by another, the* MAITREYA *or Benevolent One who is yet to be born.*

Mythology of the Mahayana school of Buddhism accounts for a series of five spiritual meditation *buddhas* or *dhyanibuddhas* all of whom emanate from the original or primeval divinity, Adibuddha, who is also sometimes referred to as Vajradhara, particularly in Nepal and Tibet. This being is largely symbolic and is envisaged as *sunya*, the void. The term *sunyata* means zero or emptiness and signifies a state of mind that equates with neither existence nor non-existence but lies somewhere between the two extremes, a state of mind that the advanced disciple seeks to achieve as a penultimate stage before total enlightenment.

The name *dhyanibuddha* is a comparatively late term which does not appear in the original Buddhist scriptures. These tend to refer to *tathagata* which translates roughly as 'he who has arrived at the truth', meaning one who has reached the ultimate state of perfection. He is the mystical and spiritual counterpart of the *manusibuddha*. The traditions of the school of Vajrayana Buddhism also recognize the five *dhyanibuddhas* and describe each of them as personifying one of the five cosmic

elements, the *pancaskandhas*. These include bodily form, sensation, perception, consciousness and conformity.

The first of the *skandhas*, bodily form or *rupa*, is represented by Vairocana, which means 'coming from the sun'. He is the oldest of the *dhyanibuddhas* and is the personification of the nature of the sun as a creative force in the cosmos but he is also envisaged as the abstract body of Adibuddha. His colour is white and he lives in the zenith of the cosmos. Sensation or *vedana* is represented by Ratnasambhava, meaning 'born of a jewel'. He is described as the head of a group of deities, the *ratnakula*, all of whom wear a jewel as a family symbol. His *shakti*, or female aspect, is Mamaki and his colour is yellow. Ratnasambhava lives in the southern quarter of the cosmos, the direction of sun.

The third of the *dhyanibuddhas* is Amitabha, who represents perception or *sanjna*. Amitabha means 'of unlimited splendour' and this being lives in a paradise known as Sakhavati. His colour is red and his place in the west and there is some argument that the concept of this *skandha* was influenced by the Iranian (Persian) light religion of Ahura Mazda. He is also strongly involved in the process of creation. The fourth, Aksobhya or 'imperturbable', representing consciousness or *vijnana,* lives in the eastern heaven of Abhirati and his colour is blue. The fifth and last of the so-called 'meditation *buddhas*' is Amoghasiddhi, whose name means 'unquenchable power'. He embodies conformity or *sanskara*, his colour is green and his cosmic direction is north. To these five is sometimes added a sixth *dhyanibuddha*, Vajrasattva, although he is more generally accepted to be Adibuddha by another name since Vajrasattva translates as 'the supreme being of the Vajra sect'.

A SIXTEENTH-CENTURY TIBETAN STATUE OF THE *BODHISATTVA* AVALOKITESVARA.

In the theosophy of the Mahayana sect each of the *dhyanibuddhas* may also appear as an emanation or distinct aspect which is known as a *dhyanibodhisattva*. The five *dhyanibodhisattvas* include Samantabhadra, Ratnapani, Avalokitesvara or Padmapani, Vajrapani and Visvapani. Of these, Avalokitesvara, the 'merciful Lord', is probably the best known since he is the guardian deity of Tibet and a highly popular figure of devotion amongst the Mahayana Buddhists. His *shakti* is Pandara and he is envisaged to be the Buddhist counterpart of the Hindu god Vishnu, placed as the most auspicious of the creator deities. In the *rNin-ma-pa*, one of the smaller Tibetan schools, the *dhyanibodhisattva* Samantabhadra is generally recognized as the emanation of Vairocana, but is also regarded as being identical with Adibuddha.

As Buddhist mythology has developed so the number of *buddhas* has also expanded from the essential one plus five recognized in the Mahayana school. As many as 25 are recognized at one extreme whilst, at the other, the Hinayana school dispenses with all the mythical *buddhas* and their various emanations and recognizes only one category, the 'historic' or *manusibuddhas*. The latter include Gautama Buddha along with a list of other names among which are Dipankara the 'light bringer', Bhaisajyaguru the 'supreme physician' who, in Lamaism, is the first of a series of medicine *buddhas* or *sMan-bla*, Kasyapa the predecessor of Gautama, and Maitreya the *buddha* yet to come. The existence of these five *manusibuddhas* is also recognized in Lamaism.

Maitreya, the *buddha* who is not yet born on earth – in other words, the next *manusibuddha* – is to be regarded, technically, as a *bodhisattva* or 'Buddha-designate'. As a group these mythical

THE ORIGINAL DIVINITY, ADIBUDDHA OR VAJRADHARA, DEPICTED WITH THE FIVE SPIRITUAL MEDITATION *BUDDHAS*, IN A VIVID TIBETAN PAINTING.

bodhisattvas live, temporarily, in a heavenly realm known as Tusita or 'satisfaction' and lists of them, including some of the named *dhyanibodhisattvas* such as Avalokitesvara, are described in various religious texts. Another *bodhisattva* who has gained considerable popularity in most Buddhist countries, though especially in Tibet, China and Japan, is Manjusri, who is the Buddhist personification of wisdom and therefore the counterpart of Brahma, one of the trio of creator gods in Hinduism.

GAUTAMA BUDDHA AND SOME NOTABLE DISCIPLES

*T*radition has it that there has been a succession of BUDDHAS since the beginning of time, each of whom, in their mortal life, has reached the state of enlightenment known as BUDDHA. Thus BUDDHA is a term for a state of being rather than strictly the name of a person.

The *buddha* of the present age is the only one known to have existed other than in myth. According to records Gautama Buddha lived in northern India during the late sixth and early fifth centuries BCE and he is therefore the 'historical *buddha*'. His personal name is Siddharta and Gautama (in Sanskrit) or Gotama (in Pali) refers to his family name, although he is also described in texts as Shakyamuni or, more commonly, Bhagavat. *Muni* is a Sanskrit term for a religious ascetic or monk and therefore Shakyamuni means the 'ascetic of the Shakya people' since Gautama was a member of the royal clan in the small country in north-eastern India that belonged to the Shakya clan (modern southern Nepal), whose capital was Kapilavastu. *Bhagavat* simply means 'master'.

A WALL PAINTING DEPICTING THE *BUDDHA* AND SOME OF HIS FOLLOWERS.

Little more than the most fragmentary glimpses of Gautama's biography are contained in Buddhist scriptures, the *Theravada* or 'doctrine of the elders', and the only part of his life which is described in any detail includes the final days prior to his death. Mythology tells that in about 563 BCE Siddharta was born into a royal lineage. His mother was Queen Maya, the consort of King Suddhodhana, but she experienced a virgin birth after an elephant placed a white lotus in her womb. On the night she conceived, she dreamed that the Buddha-designate or *bodhisattva* would enter her body, and on the following day 64 *brahmins* presented themselves before her and confirmed that she was to be the mother of the future *buddha*.

As a youthful prince, aged about 16, Siddharta became wedded to his cousin, Princess Yasodhara, and he seems to have lived a more or less uneventful life of regal luxury until some 13 years later when he was 29. Shortly after Yasodhara had borne him a son, Rahula, he abandoned his worldly existence, including his wife and child, to assume the name Gautama (Gotama) and to become a wandering ascetic. The story goes that, in spite of his father's objections, Siddharta began wandering abroad from the royal palace accompanied only by his charioteer and mentor, Chandaka (charming). On

MAHABODHI TEMPLE AT BODH GAYA, THE SPOT WHERE THE *BUDDHA* ACHIEVED ENLIGHTENMENT.

four separate excursions Siddharta was to discover 'Four Sights', experiences which prompted the course that was to command the remainder of his life. These experiences involved four encounters: with old age, from which Chandaka reminded him that no one escapes; with disease, which Chandaka pointed out may strike at anyone regardless of their station; with death, about which Chandaka also advised him; and with a begging ascetic who was searching for the path which would enable him to transcend the first three obstacles.

These meetings provided the catalyst. Siddharta shed his royal trappings and donned a pilgrim's garb before setting out into the Ganges plain to seek wisdom from the holy men and philosophers of his day. He joined the *sangha* or religious community of an ascetic named Alara, the first of a number of teachers, and learned his system of meditation. The path he took was aimed at preparing himself, initially by extreme self-denial and meditation, almost starving himself to death, for the moment of perfect enlightenment and liberation as the *bodhisattva*. Later, however, he became disillusioned with this form of self-mortifying asceticism and it was not until he steered a more moderate path between asceticism and indulgence that he achieved his goal.

True understanding eventually descended on Gautama after about six years of pilgrimage, at a place called Gaya. By tradition, enlightenment came whilst he was seated in a contemplative mood beneath a bodhi-tree on the west bank of the river Nairanjana in the kingdom of Magadha (modern Bihar), in circumstances which are fully described in a sacred text known as the *Sutta-pitaka*. The place became known as Bodhgaya and it has become revered by Buddhists as the 'Navel of the Earth'. Their holiest shrine, the Mahabodhi temple, stands upon the spot.

When he achieved the state known as *buddha*, the 'enlightened one', Gautama began a path of teaching which lasted some 40 years. He spent much of this time travelling through northern India, still in the manner of an ascetic, and teaching the 'Way of the Buddha' which included the so-called 'Eightfold Path' involving an amalgam of wisdom, meditation and morality. This Path was based on the Four Noble Truths which, if followed resolutely, will lead to release from the eternal cycle of death and rebirth and allow discovery of the final bliss or *parinirvana*.

Gautama became known by a variety of epithets, the most familiar of which is Shakyamuni, but he is also referred to as the *tathagata* which is difficult to translate but means approximately 'Some-come, some-gone' or 'He who has entered into the Suchness'. He collected a body of disciples into his own *sangha* which formed a migrant community and followed him in his wanderings. The *sangha* was initiated with five ascetic mendicants – Kaundinya, Vaspa, Bhadrajit, Mahanaman and Asvajit – and its numbers were swelled by the missionary activities of this group of begging disciples who had achieved enlightenment and become known as *arhats*. The disciples were required to observe his strict form of discipline based on self-denial, known as *vinaya*. This, however, was not a discipline of extreme austerity such as the one Gautama had experimented with previously. Rather it was a Middle Way which recognized that the body must remain fit and healthy in order to sustain the mental rigours of progressing towards enlightenment. The teaching of this discipline is contained in the *Vinaya-pitaka,* the first of three divisions of Buddhist scripture.

As an old man Shakyamuni suffered repeated bouts of debilitating illness and became progressively more frail. His final journey was made on foot, as was his custom, when he travelled from Rajagrha (modern Rangir) in north-east India to a small village called Kusinagara near the Nepalese border. There he is believed to have achieved the final *parinirvana*. Many myths have arisen regarding the circumstances of his dying. It is said that, for his last meal, he commanded his disciples to bring him the 'food of pigs' which he alone ate. He suffered a severe

THIS RELIEF SCULPTURE OF GAUTAMA BATHING STANDS AT BOROBUDUR TEMPLE IN JAVA AND DATES FROM THE NINTH CENTURY.

haemorrhage shortly afterwards and, in great pain, asked to rest beside a small muddy stream. As a final miraculous act he cleansed the flowing water before being taken on to Kusinagara. There he was laid upon a couch on his right side and with his head facing to the north. A monk stood fanning him until commanded to move away since the entire countryside was filled with watching deities whose view was being obscured by the attendant. The scriptures tell of a last conversion made by the dying *buddha* upon a man named Subhadra and his final recorded words of instruction to his assembled *arhats* were: 'Impermanent are all composites, strive earnestly.'

The earthly life of Gautama Buddha was extinguished that night and he was cremated by his closest disciples, his ashes being distributed and interred in reliquary mounds or *stupas*. His death is believed to have occurred in about 483 BCE. When he died Gautama had omitted to name a successor. There was no *maitreya* or future *buddha* incarnation waiting in the wings, no *bodhisattva* preparing for ultimate enlightenment and so, for some 25 centuries, Buddhism has been without a central authority. In their first council or *sangiti* after his death, his disciples within the *sangha* community elected to rely on the teachings of Gautama, the discourses contained in the *Sutta-pitaka* and the discipline of the *Vinaya-pitaka* in place of any living authority.

SARIPUTRA

Before meeting Shakyamuni, Sariputra was an ascetic wandering the pathways of northern India with a companion named Maudgalyayana. A chance meeting with one of the original members of Shakyamuni's *sangha*, Asvajit, at Rajagrha made a profound impression on Sariputra. Asvajit related to Sariputra a now famous utterance of the *buddha* and it persuaded Sariputra to seek out Shakyamuni and learn from him. The verse which Asvajit recited with such effect begins:

Dharmas which are created from a cause
The Tathagata has proclaimed
The cause as well as their stopping
So teaches the great ascetic.

Although Sariputra was never the personal attendant of the *buddha* – a duty that was allocated to Ananda, another of the close *arhats* who joined the original group of five – he remained the most devoted disciple and was one of the foremost amongst the trusted teachers. He is said to have been at the head of the crowd who greeted the *buddha* when he descended in triumph from the triple stairway at Samkasya (see p.79).

Sariputra's death came shortly before that of Shakyamuni and the scriptures indicate that, when he knew he was dying, he left the *sangha* community and returned to his birthplace, a village near Rajagrha. Not least among his intentions was to convert his mother to the path of Buddhism and it is said that as dawn broke following his mother's attainment of the True Path, he died and attained final *nirvana*. The monks who had accompanied him on this last journey supervised his funeral rites and then returned to the side of Shakyamuni.

ANANDA

Shortly after the incident which became known as the Miracle of Fire and Water (see p.79), the *buddha*'s father, Suddhodhana, felt obliged to provide his errant son's entourage with some members of family. Accordingly he passed a decree that one male heir from each branch of the Shakya nobility should enter Shakyamuni's *sangha* community. One of these was named Ananda. In subsequent years he was largely responsible for persuading the *buddha* to allow women to enter the *sangha*, albeit enjoying a lower social and religious position than the monks. Shakyamuni is said to have been highly reluctant to allow this to happen and when he finally acquiesced it was with the complaint that the potential of *dharma* would henceforth be diminished. One of the women who entered the Order was Mahaprajapati, the surviving widow of Suddhodhana.

Ananda came to notice as the personal assistant of the *buddha*. At an age thought to have been between fifty and sixty Shakyamuni was found to need assistance. Though he was not of particularly advanced years, the incessant journeying on foot and the general deprivations of the itinerant monkish life had taken their toll physically. Shakyamuni was no longer a fit man. It is said that Sariputra was keen to take on the responsibility of caring for his Teacher but Shakyamuni considered that his work in the wider ministry of north India was too important to allow him to stay closeted 'at home'. So Ananda was selected for the role which he maintained for about 25 years until the death of the *buddha*.

Ananda was the disciple, therefore, who was perhaps closest physically to the Teacher on a day-to-day basis. There exists a tradition that the *buddha* delivered nearly 50,000 sermons, of varying length, over the 40 or so years between his enlightenment and death, and that, subsequently, in the first Buddhist Council, Ananda proved an ability to recite all these teachings from memory. Tradition also has it that Ananda received advice from the dying *buddha* confirming that he had not appointed a successor and that the combination of the teaching, *dharma,* found in the *sutras,* and the discipline, *vinaya,* would serve henceforth as the driving force of Buddhism.

As the last days of the *buddha*'s life approached, Ananda was required to gather together the members of the *sangha* to hear the Teacher's final address at Vaisali. It was only after the death of the *buddha* that Ananda is said to have achieved enlightenment and the level of *arhat*. He was asked to recite the entirety of the *buddha*'s teaching in the first major Council at Rajagrha and, according to some disputed sources, impressed his fellow monks by doing so. It is, however, suggested that his recollection was incomplete and that he was not the only individual who was able to recite large parts of the *dharma* since another monk named Gavampati had been the first choice to deliver the teachings but had declined the task. There was also perhaps some continuing debate about whether or not he had achieved the level of *arhat*.

MAUDGALYAYANA

As a wandering mendicant and the companion of Sariputra, Maudgalyayana first came into contact with the *buddha* at Rajagrha. After conversion he became recognized, with Sariputra, as one of the two senior disciples of the early Order. Little detail is given of his lifetime of devotion, but there is a description of his death which occurred at about the same time as that of Sariputra. It was claimed that, on achieving the level of *arhat*, Maudgalyayana had developed superhuman powers, known as *rddhi*, which included an ability to travel between the temporal and spiritual realms and to report on the fate of deceased individuals. This was used to political advantage on occasions by the *buddha* to press home the benefits of pursuing his Middle Way to enlightenment against those of other teachers. Eventually some of his rivals hatched an assassination plot against Maudgalyayana, whom they saw as the source of damage to their reputations.

Maudgalyayana was said to have used his magical powers to elude his enemies, but when these weakened he was set upon and beaten almost senseless. He retained enough of his abilities to travel in spirit to the *buddha* for a final farewell before he died and achieved *nirvana*.

DEVADATTA

During the later part of Shakyamuni's life as the *buddha*, a schism was threatened amongst the ranks of disciples in the *sangha* community. This rival movement was spearheaded by a cousin named Devadatta. At first he was a staunch adherent to the doctrine of the *buddha* but then showed himself to be a turncoat. Tradition has it that Devadatta joined the *sangha* community when Shakyamuni first visited his family in Kapilavastu. As the years passed, however, Devadatta developed a jealousy over his illustrious cousin's authority and a burning ambition to take his place. He had practised asceticism to the extent that it was claimed he was also in possession of magical powers enabling him to transform into any shape at will and to make himself invisible. He also cultivated the patronage of the then ruler of the country, King Ajatasatru, persuading him to support a move whereby the *buddha* would be overthrown and Devadatta would assume control of the *sangha* community. In this way the spiritual and temporal leadership of the country would be safely in the hands of like-minded members of the Shakya nobility.

When Shakyamuni was about 70 years of age he was first approached by Devadatta with the suggestion of relinquishing authority and handing over the reins of leadership. It was when the *buddha* refused that Devadatta became violently antagonistic and resorted to several attempts at murder. The first of these involved an ambush along one of the paths which Shakyamuni regularly walked, but at the last minute the bowmen who had been employed as assassins refused to carry out their task. When Devadatta saw that the original plan had misfired he levered a large boulder off the top of a cliff which narrowly missed its target. It did, however, create splinters when it dashed against the ground and one of these pierced the foot of the *buddha*. Another tradition relates that Devadatta sent an enraged elephant stampeding in Shakyamuni's path but that this attempt also failed when the *buddha* used his telepathic powers to calm the animal.

A schism within the ranks of the *sangha* was opened when Devadatta turned his attention to the monks and started a political campaign in support of a rival Order. He advocated the voluntary adoption of a somewhat more austere discipline amongst the disciples which included five rules in addition to those laid down by Shakyamuni. Aware of the potential disaster facing the Order, the *buddha* instructed one of his most senior devotees, Sariputra, to persuade the breakaway group, amounting to several hundred monks, to return to the main Order and eventually the rebellion was ended.

Disillusioned, Devadatta spent his remaining years as an outcast. One further myth surrounds his demise. Terminally ill, he asked to be allowed to visit Shakyamuni and, when his request was refused, he had himself placed in a litter and carried to where the *buddha* was residing. Before he reached the place, however, the earth opened and he fell into a chasm leading to the underworld kingdom of Avici, the lowest of all the hells.

AN EIGHTEENTH-CENTURY TIBETAN INTERPRETATION OF THE DEATH AND CREMATION OF THE *BUDDHA*.

MYTHS
OF
GAUTAMA
BUDDHA

*A*lthough little can be confirmed historically through the THERAVADA, the Buddhist 'doctrine of the elders', a rich apocryphal tapestry of tradition has grown up around the life of Gautama Buddha. Much of it is found in a limited number of ancient religious texts composed in Sanskrit — the AGAMASUTRAS, the second-century-CE BUDDHACHARITA and, to a lesser extent, the LOTUS SUTRA.

THE BIRTH AND EARLY LIFE OF SIDDHARTA

The myths begin with the birth of Siddharta and a tradition that the virgin Queen Maya went into labour whilst strolling in the gardens of Lumbini, a park filled with trees, lakes and beautiful flowers. The child was born from her right side as she reached out to touch the blossoms on a *plaksa* tree, whereupon the Hindu gods Indra and Brahma descended from above and cradled the infant. Almost immediately after his birth Siddharta took seven steps in each quarter with his right hand raised in the gesture of *abhayamudra* (fearlessness) and his left turned downwards in *varadamudra* (granting wishes). The symbolic implication is that he was to be honoured in both heaven and earth.

This notion of an individual with a special destiny was reinforced by myths that grew up surrounding the childhood of Siddharta. When still at an early age he was taken to a local Hindu temple by his aunt and foster mother (Queen Maya died

IMMEDIATELY AFTER HIS BIRTH, SIDDHARTA TOOK SEVEN STEPS IN EACH QUARTER, A MYTHICAL EVENT DEPICTED IN THIS EIGHTEENTH-CENTURY TIBETAN PAINTING.

prematurely) in order to pay devotion to the gods. It is said that Siddharta told his relatives that he was already acknowledged by the great deities to be their superior and that when he entered the temple the icons of the gods took life, descended from their shrines and gave him their respect.

Tradition has it that as Gautama, the ascetic preparing for *buddha*-hood, he was subjected to a series of temptations paralleling those of Jesus Christ in the wilderness. The evil influence on Gautama was a demon named Mara whom he did not attempt to vanquish in the Christian style but viewed rather with compassion and a desire to enlighten. The *bodhisattva* was first approached by beautiful women whose seductions, on behalf of Mara, proved unsuccessful; then demonic forces were sent to intimidate him but their aggression was quelled by his fearlessness and air of benevolence. After these tactics were seen to fail, Mara tried the more subtle intellectual stratagem of taking on Gautama in debate and when this ploy turned out to be equally futile, he gave up.

ENLIGHTENMENT

The story of the enlightenment has been elaborated in several versions. It is suggested that, prior to the event beneath the bodhi-tree on the banks of the river Nairanjana, Gautama had undergone a long period of intense fasting, eating no more than a single grain of rice a day, and was near to death from starvation. He became profoundly disillusioned that these extremes of physical deprivation and mental discipline had not resulted in enlightenment and was tempted again by the demonic Mara. Gautama went to the river to bathe himself and when he returned to his seat of contemplation beneath the tree was persuaded to accept food from a peasant girl. Regaining a little strength, he determined to remain seated on the spot until supreme wisdom was achieved. Again Mara came with further attempts at temptation and challenged Gautama to prove that he was the *bodhisattva* whereupon Gautama touched the ground with his right hand and a great earthquake followed, causing Mara and his demonic attendants to flee in terror.

During the night that followed Gautama experienced a revelation of all his past incarnations and of the reality of *samsara*, the wheel of life and the material world. Beneath the bodhi-tree perfect enlightenment had reached him and he had become the *manusibuddha*, the living *buddha*, Shakyamuni.

MIRACULOUS EVENTS

A series of miraculous happenings are recorded during the *buddha*'s subsequent time on earth. One of the symbolic icons of the *buddha* is a pair of footprints on to which are superimposed spoked wheels. The origin of this device lies in a tradition that, on a journey from Benares to Rajagrha, Shakyamuni was met by a *brahmin* named Dona who walked respectfully just behind the *buddha*. As he followed the Teacher's footsteps he noticed that the imprint in the soft earth included the outline of a wheel with 1000 spokes representing the combined following of the initial Buddhist community in northern India. It is suggested that such revelations, including special marks on the body of the *buddha,* could be detected only by the enlightened few to whom he chose to show them.

Amongst the more dramatic episodes revealing the larger-than-life powers of the *buddha* was that of the Miracle of Fire and Water. Shakyamuni had elected to return to Kapilavastu from Rajagrha where he and his entourage, the *sangha* of

THE *BUDDHA*'S FOOTPRINT, SUPERIMPOSED WITH A SPOKED WHEEL, IN MAHABODHI TEMPLE.

disciples, had been staying. Travelling north-west towards the foothills of the Himalayas they entered the Shakya country but the clansmen of the former Siddharta did not recognize or acknowledge him as the *buddha*. In order to persuade them of his credentials he suddenly levitated into the air before a crowd of onlookers and, suspended high above them, caused flames to erupt from his head and torso whilst streams of water cascaded from the lower part of his body. He then made a pavement of gems appear in the sky, along which he walked. Despite the new-found respect from family and clansmen which this awakened, Shakyamuni elected to continue with his austere life as before, going around in simple garments and holding out his begging bowl for food. This act of defiance caused his father, Suddhodhana, considerable grief since, to him, it amounted to a public disgracing of the royal family. Shakyamuni, however, eventually persuaded his father that he was truly the next living incarnation of the *buddha*, following in the footsteps of his venerated predecessor, Kasyapa.

Another sensational event in the life of the *manusibuddha* occurred after the premature death of his mother, Maya. Tradition has it that she was transported in spirit to the Heaven of the Thirty-three, the *trayastrimsa*, so-called because it is believed to be the residence of the thirty-three gods known to Indian religion. Shakyamuni went there for three months, wishing to convert her to the True Path of enlightenment and he tutored her from the philosophical scripture of the *Theravada*, known as the *Abhidharma-pitaka*.

Having persuaded his mother to adopt the True Path, the *buddha* chose to return to earth at a place called Samkasya on one of the westernmost tributaries of the Ganges. On the night of the full moon he constructed a triple staircase from gold, silver and precious stones and could be seen by the townspeople descending to the ground in splendour, surrounded by a retinue of divinities, Brahma to his right and Indra to his left. This moment was, arguably, the climax of the miraculous occurrences attributed to Gautama Buddha during his lifetime.

MYTHS
OF THE
BUDDHA'S
PREVIOUS
LIVES

*O*ne of the most significant texts which details
the past lives of Gautama Buddha is the
scripture compiled in about the fifth century CE and
known as the JATAKANIDANA. This includes some 550
stories constituting part of the canon of Buddhism
known collectively as the TRIPITAKA, the 'Three Baskets
of sacred writings'. As with those of the Hindu VEDA,
these written texts are the culmination of a long period
of oral tradition during which stories were handed down
from generation to generation by word of mouth.

The *Jatakanidana* myths are composed in a style which
makes them difficult to follow without an understanding of the
'format' since the beginning of each chapter seems to have
little or nothing to do with the *buddha* or *bodhisattva*. Each
begins with an anecdote given by the Teacher, Shakyamuni,
the historical *buddha*, and called the 'story of the present'. It
describes an event involving the *sangha* or disciple community
in the recent past which needs further discussion. This comes
in the 'story of the past' which then follows. The Teacher
relates an event from one of his previous incarnations, the
memory of which has been triggered by the 'story of the
present' and which amplifies the topic of discussion in the
form of a parable.

The *Deva-dharma jataka* (the Divine Nature Jataka) begins
by explaining where the Blessed One, Shakyamuni, was when
he related the 'story of the present', in this instance at a
retreat called the Jetavana Park which had been donated to his
sangha community by a benefactor. The 'story of the present'
concerns a wealthy landowner who became a monk on the
death of his wife, confining himself to a hermitage he had
built, but adopting a lifestyle of considerable opulence with
plenty of food, good clothing and a team of servants. Other
monks soon admonished him for this and took him to the
Teacher.

Shakyamuni asked the monk: 'Why are you a man of many
goods? Am I not one who praises few wants and possessions,
seclusion and the stirring up of spiritual energy?' Distressed,
the monk stripped off his clothes and threw them away, apart
from one sparse garment. Shakyamuni, however, cautioned him
again, saying: 'Were you not once a seeker after modesty and
discretion? If so, why do you now stand before me lost to
modesty and discretion?' On hearing this the man collected up
his cloak and put it on again, whilst the disciples, confused by
what had taken place, asked the Teacher to explain more fully.

Shakyamuni then took his disciples back, for the 'story of
the past', to one of his previous lives. He explained that the

bodhisattva had been born as a prince named Mahingsasa, the son of King Brahmadatta and his chief consort, at Benares in the kingdom of Kasi. Soon after his brother Chanda (moon) was born his mother died and the king replaced her as his senior queen. When the new queen bore a son he was named Surya (sun) and when the boy came of age she reminded Brahmadatta of a pledge he had once made that Surya could, if he wished, inherit the kingdom. The king refused, pointing out that he had two fine sons who were senior in line of succession.

Fearful that the queen might be plotting against his rightful heir, the king sent Mahingsasa and Chanda into the forest for their own safety. When they departed, however, Surya elected to go with them. The three journeyed to the Himalayas where they rested beside a lake controlled by a water demon, reputed to consume those who were ignorant of the nature of the divine. Surya was sent by Mahingsasa to fetch water, but when he could not provide the water demon with the correct answer about the nature of the divine, the youngest son was incarcerated in the demon's abode. Chanda was sent but suffered the same fate and eventually Mahingsasa investigated, prudently keeping back from the shore with his weapons ready.

The water demon approached him with the familiar challenge but Mahingsasa complained that he was tired and so the demon bathed him and provided food and drink before receiving an answer.

> *Those who are modest and discreet,*
> *On things that are pure intent,*
> *The holy men, the lovely men,*
> *These the world calls divine.*

The demon agreed that this was a fair response and offered to return one of the brothers. When Mahingsasa asked for the youngest son the demon queried his choice. Mahingsasa explained that Surya had come with them in good faith and if they returned without him people would naturally assume his siblings had killed him. This pleased the demon who now considered that Mahingsasa knew divine things and acted accordingly and so he returned both brothers safely.

Mahingsasa, however, admonished the water demon, saying that, through evil, he had been reborn as this malevolent creature who was still doing evil by eating people. Through his patient teachings he converted the demon and remained by the lake until word came that his father had died, whereupon he went home, took his rightful crown and ruled wisely.

The Teacher explained that the water demon was the monk with his many goods, Surya was Ananda, the half-brother of the *buddha*, and Chanda was Sariputra, one of the *buddha*'s first disciples. Mahingsasa was, of course, the *buddha* Shakyamuni himself.

BUDDHA ICONOGRAPHY

*B*uddhism has generated some of the most stupendous religious sculptures of any in the world. Amongst the most awesome is a colossal bust of Gautama Buddha set in a wooded ravine at Leshan in the Szechuan province of western China. Hardly less impressive are the portraits in stone of the serenely smiling face of the BUDDHA at the temple city of Angkor in the jungles of Cambodia. There are some 200 of these images, each about 8 feet high, in its Bayon temple. The features are said to be modelled on those of King Jayavarman VII who was crowned in 1181 and promptly declared himself the MANUSIBUDDHA.

At first there was a strong reluctance to depict the *buddha* in iconography since it represents a transcendental state of being rather than a named individual, so the divine presence was often indicated by a symbol such as an empty throne, the bodhi-tree with an empty seat at its foot, or the thousand-spoke wheels of *dharma* impressed into the footprints of the

A ROADSIDE STATUE OF THE *BUDDHA* TOWERS OVER TRAFFIC IN SRI LANKA.

buddha. The vogue of creating *buddha* images is believed to have begun in Indian colonial provinces under the domination of the Kusana Empire in central Asia during the second century CE. Subsequently, similar early schools of iconographic Buddhist art arose in Mathura and Gandhara in northern India.

SIGNIFICANT STYLES AND ATTRIBUTES

The style in which the various emanations and forms of *buddha* are portrayed in art is important when it comes to identifying who is who in the confusing lists of *dhyanibuddhas, manusibuddhas, dhyanibodhisattvas* and their respective *shaktis*, since each is provided with a distinctive colour, direction, vehicle or *vahana* and attributes or *mudras*.

Major deities are generally right-handed, a convention which derives from the idea, common to all Indian religions, that the right side is the honoured side and therefore turning to the right is considered auspicious. It is also conventionally the male side since women are always positioned to the left in iconographic groups. The *buddha*, in company with such major divinities as Vishnu in Hindu iconography, performs a significant right-handed gesture known as *abhayamudra*. This is a motion of reassurance or safety and it conveys tranquillity and protection from the deity to the worshipper. The right hand is raised, palm outward and fingers pointing upwards, towards the devotee, a gesture which also became popular amongst artists and sculptors in the Christian tradition who modified it as a sign of benediction.

The sacred texts identify 32 features or characteristics by which a *bodhisattva* or Buddha-in-waiting may be distinguished. These include a curl of hair or *cuda* between the eyebrows which evolved into a round mark or lump on the forehead known as the *urna*.

The *buddha* is typically shown with his head shaven or covered with tight short-cut curls, and the curls also usually turn to the right following the right-hand principle. The closely cropped hairstyle, known as a *cudakarana*, may be reduced to a tonsure along the top of the scalp which, according to tradition, was the style adopted by Gautama, achieved with a single cut immediately before he departed from his family home to begin life as an ascetic.

Dhyanibuddha and *bodhisattva* images are frequently drawn in terrific aspect. The *bodhisattva* Avalokitesvara, for example, is drawn with up to eleven heads, whilst icons generally have pairs of arms and legs in excess of the normal two. The hands of deities may also hold objects of significance. These often include a *sutra* or religious text and sometimes a sword which is used symbolically to cut through the bonds of ignorance, but objects may be more specifically related to a particular image. The attributes of Amitabha, for example, include a water jar and a lotus.

The icon of a *dhyanibuddha* may also bear a small model or image known as a *bimba* which represents an emanation of the *dhyanibuddha*. He either holds it in his hand or balances it on his head. Amitabha may, therefore, have on the crown of his head an *amitabhabimba*, whilst his hands are in the gesture of meditation or *dhyanamudra*.

Attributes may be selected to emphasize the character or quality of the divinity. Kwannon, the popular Japanese Buddhist form of Avalokitesvara, whose sex, incidentally, has been changed to female, is recognized as a goddess of mercy, so she carries objects which express the idea that the *bodhisattva* is always ready to ameliorate disease and suffering. She typically holds a vase filled with the tears of compassion and a willow branch.

An image may also adopt a distinctive attitude of sitting or standing and this may be equally significant for identification, particularly in association with the vehicle or *vahana* of the divinity. Amitabha is usually depicted seated in the *padmasana* or lotus position with a *vahana* in the form of two peacocks or, less frequently, a pair of geese.

The *buddha* is not always reborn in human form: in a number of the *Jataka* stories he is incarnated as an animal, including Mahakapi, the Great Ape, and other creatures like the deer. He may be represented thus in iconography.

HOLY PLACES

Specific iconography is associated not only with figures but also with holy places or *ananda*, including those which the historical *buddha* is said, by tradition, to have visited during his pilgrimages prior to *parinirvana*. Originally there were four sites – Lumbini, his place of birth, Bodh Gaya, where he achieved enlightenment, Sarnath, where he first taught and Kusingara where *parinirvana* was entered – but the number was later increased to eight, the new sites including Rajaghra, Sravasti, Vaisali and Samkasya. These holy places were popular subjects for artists to represent in bas relief carvings on *stupas* and temples (see p.98). Their art symbolized the way to enlightenment, the process of transformation associated with the acts of the *buddha* and with the corresponding stages on the pilgrim's journey, and this style of art became standardized in *stupas* throughout Buddhist lands.

THE FACE OF THE *BODHISATTVA* AVALOKITESVARA AT ANGKOR, CAMBODIA.

THE FOUR NOBLE TRUTHS

*G*autama Buddha emphasized that his teachings or DHARMA were not to be regarded as some kind of inflexible creed engraved in letters of fire but a working manual to be adapted and to evolve as necessary. Much of the teaching of the BUDDHA is founded on a number of simple premises regarding the nature and limitations of mortal existence. It can be summarized in ARYASATYA, the Four Noble Truths, which reflect the sum of his experience as the BODHISATTVA resulting in his enlightenment beneath the bodhi-tree.

A WALL PAINTING AT THE THIKSE MONASTERY IN LADAKH SHOWS THE DEMON MARA GRIPPING THE WHEEL OF LIFE.

Apart from the pronouncement of the Middle Way, in which he turned away from destructive self-mortification and moved towards a path that was neither extreme asceticism nor indulgence, the Four Noble Truths represent the first public teaching of the *buddha* after he left the Seat of Enlightenment. Tradition has it that he travelled to the town of Benares where he gathered his fledgling *sangha* in the deer park of a benefactor and delivered what has become known as the First Turning of the Wheel of the Law. The tutorial was given to the original five *arhats* or disciples and effectively represents the moment of transition from Gautama the *bodhisattva,* to Shakyamuni the *buddha,* the fully enlightened Teacher or *tathagata*. It was this initial and deceptively concise teaching, and the explanation of the Eightfold Path which stems from it, that the ranks of disciples, swelled to some sixty in number, were instructed to take out and promote along the highways and byways of northern India.

Behind the Four Noble Truths lies a more fundamental concept. In the *Theravada* scriptures of mainstream Buddhism it is explained that there are three general characteristics of existence, the so-called *ti-lak-karma*. The first of these, and the basis for the other two, is *anicca* or 'non-permanence' which implies that nothing exists in the same state for more than a moment in time and that to believe otherwise is illusory. The second is *dukkha* which reflects sorrow and suffering stemming, not so much from the non-permanence, but the blindness to its illusion and the lack of true understanding of its reality. The third, *anatta*, argues that, because of the impermanence of any phenomena there is no lasting sense of personality and therefore 'self', the Hindu *atman*, is something that is in a constant state of flux.

It is from the *ti-lak-karma* that the Four Noble Truths evolved. It is claimed that when he delivered them, the *buddha* relied on a great economy of words — just twelve sentences by which he explained these truths in three different ways — and that when he had given the explanation, the five disciples became fully-fledged *arhats* and the pantheon of gods, who had also been listening to his words, became *bodhisattvas*.

The first Noble Truth, the Truth of suffering, focuses on *dukkha* and reveals that the pain experienced by humanity, both mental and physical, is universal and comes as a consequence of our *karma* or actions in past lives, both negative and positive. All of existence is *dukkha* and it is experienced in six of the realms of existence from the lowest hell to the high heaven of the gods. Only beyond this, in the highest realm of *nirvana,* is *dukkha* eliminated, since even gods may die and, when they do so, they experience pain and suffering.

The second is the Truth of origin in which the *buddha* advises that our suffering is caused primarily by reaching out either for the wrong things in life, or for the right things but in the wrong way. In other words, we have a misplaced sense of values and we tend to put a price on material things which can be sustained to only a limited extent. All of these strivings represent the mainly negative aspects of *karma*, described as the chain of Dependent Origination or the Chain of Causation, *pratityasamutpada*, whose twelve links, beginning with ignorance, encircle a wheel controlled by the demonic anti-*buddha*, Mara. We must understand the true origination or *samudaya* of our pain.

The third of the Noble Truths, the Truth of cessation or *nirodha*, is that we can escape from *dukkha* and the pain of suffering, or *klesa*, if we wish to do so by applying the proper disciplines which will free us from the adverse effects of the laws of *karma*. We are required to shed those negative desires which tie us to the material world, *samsara*, with its endless cycles of birth and death. They are encapsulated as the cravings for sensual pleasure – such things as dependence on material possessions, greed, jealousy, anger, covetousness and sexual lust. In their place, the vacuum left when they are disposed of, come the positive qualities of wisdom, understanding, spiritual love and compassion. If we possess compassion and love for others these plus factors will, in themselves, negate anger and jealousy. If we require nothing for ourselves of material worth, we cancel out greed and covetousness.

A DISTINCTIVELY CHINESE INTERPRETATION OF THE *BUDDHA* PREACHING, FROM AN EIGHTH-CENTURY BANNER FOUND IN DUNUANG CAVES.

The fourth and final Truth, the Truth of the Path, offers the means of escape from *dukkha* – the Eightfold Path to enlightenment, known as *marga*.

The *buddha* elaborated on these themes by stressing that we have to learn to understand the nature of suffering before we can control it by eliminating its source. In order to abandon the origin of suffering it is necessary to follow the Path. Having done so we will know the end of suffering, part of the ultimate experience, because to understand fully the reality of suffering means there is nothing more to understand.

THE
EIGHTFOLD
WAY

*I*n many respects the entire Buddhist teaching or DHARMA can be defined as an elaboration of the Four Noble Truths. The way of putting into practice the final objective contained in the Four Truths, the means of escape, was described by the BUDDHA as being the Noble Path. This he offered to his disciples in the form of eight parts – Right Understanding, Right Purpose, Right Speech, Right Action, Right Livelihood, Right Endeavour, Right Mindfulness, Right Concentration. These eight aspects tend to be collected under three headings.

Understanding and Purpose, grouped as *prajna* or wisdom, require a clear view of the human condition and the necessary resolve to overcome it. The proper application of Speech, Action and Livelihood, under the heading of *sila* or morality, requires avoidance of defamatory words or lies, coupled with rejection of dishonest, sensual or injurious behaviour and the active pursuit of an occupation which does not involve hurt to others. Correct Endeavour, Mindfulness and Concentration are classified as *samadhi* and demand the cultivation of a morally pure state of mind, awareness of one's actions, and the ability to focus consciousness through meditation.

The Path later became partly redefined by the disciples into five stages, described as accumulation or *sambharamarga*, preparatory conduct or *prayogamarga*, vision or *darsanamarga*, meditation or *bhavanamarga* and no further training or *asaiksamarga*. The object of these exercises is progressively to eliminate the impurities which occur throughout the spheres in which *samsara*, the material world, exists. These are recognized as those bounded by earthly constraints from the lowest hell to the tips of the highest mountains and the two lowest heavens which lie immediately above the earth. They are, respectively, the realms of *kamadhatu* or desire, *rupadhatu* or form, and *arupyadhatu* or no-form.

The first two stages are preparatory levels from which the initiate launches on to the Path proper. The stage of Accumulation, also known as the Path of Acquiring Equipment, may take place in a present life as a groundwork process of preparation or it may have taken place gradually over several previous lives. It includes the first contact with *dharma* and entering upon the discipline which provides the morality factor – the right view and intent – and begins to eliminate *dukkha*. This preparation stage may also be defined as laying down 'good foundations' for the progressive phases of the Path that follow.

By the end of this first stage the initiate is probably a committed monk or nun living in a *sangha* community and following an ascetic lifestyle, ready to enter fully upon the stage of preparatory conduct. He or she acquires, at the same time, a degree of expertise in meditation techniques and controlled breathing known as *dhyana*, detaching still further from the negative aspects of *karma*. *Dhyana*, according to the explanations of the *buddha*, proceeds in four stages, beginning with the acquisition of joy and peace in exchange for anger and angst. It goes on to achieve serene concentration devoid of reasoning or investigation. From there the sensation of joy subsides, though the tranquillity remains and this leads to the final stage of *dhyana* which results in an evenness of mind and temper, verging towards neither ease nor unease, and with a concentration that is firm and yet flexible.

From the point of acquiring *prayogamarga* the monk effectively leaves the material world and steps out upon the True Path, *aryamarga*, towards enlightenment. *Darsanamarga*, the Path of Vision, includes sixteen key points described as moments of comprehension, and with the last of these the disciple enters upon the next stage, known as *bhavanamarga*. Through the revelations, which are achieved by intensely disciplined mind control, the practitioner comes to understand the true meaning and reality of the Four Noble Truths and, in particular, the source and means of preventing *dukkha* or suffering. *Samsara* is open to spiritual conquest only when he or she who follows the Path has risen above and beyond materialism, desire, pain and grief. Separate traditions maintain that the disciple or *arhat* who has achieved this series of visionary experiences has entered into the 'Stream' and is either destined for no more than seven future incarnations on the Wheel of Life before achieving perfection and *nirvana*, or will achieve the same state of bliss in a shorter time period, within seven years. The former school of thought is that followed mainly in Hinayana Buddhism, whilst the latter is referred to as the *Satipatthana*.

Having achieved these visionary goals, the disciple is now prepared to embark on *bhavanamarga*. This equates with advanced meditation techniques, in Buddhism properly termed Repeated Meditative Cultivation. The object is to achieve the seven so-called Constituents of Enlightenment – the study of *dharmas*, energy, mindfulness, concentration, joyful zeal, aptitude and equanimity – and by doing so to address fully the second and third of the Noble Truths – those of origination and cessation. The mental discipline of *bhavanamarga*, freed at this level of devotion from all impurities, allows the ascetic to see with absolute clarity the origins of suffering and the sequence of causes which bring it about. Only with this sophisticated level of insight can the sequence be effectively reversed, bringing about the cessation of *dukkha*. This requires the elimination of impurities, identified as greed, hostility, pride, ignorance, false views and doubt, in all three realms in which *samsara* exists, although particularly in the latter two, those of form and no-form, which are referred to as the higher spheres. The process is assisted by the so-called Five Aids to Emancipation, namely faith, energy, mindfulness, concentration and wisdom.

The final stage, *asaiksamarga,* is largely a passive one in that

A BUDDHIST MONK IN CAMBODIA PRACTISING MEDITATION, ONE OF THE MEANS BY WHICH THE CONSCIOUSNESS IS FOCUSED IN THE SEARCH FOR ENLIGHTENMENT.

it carries the individual forward towards the ultimate, *nirvana*, driven by the momentum of the preceding stages. Rid of all impurities and passions, ignorance having been swept away, the journey of the disciple is complete, and to begin another cycle of material existence would have no meaning.

THE
MAIN
STRANDS
OF
BUDDHISM

Buddhism stemmed, in its entirety, from the teachings of Gautama Buddha in the fifth century BCE, but in the centuries after his death the disciples or monks in the religious communities elaborated the teachings and so paved the way for the development of various splinter sects and schools which eventually numbered 18. The first of the schisms came as early as the fourth century BCE when the existing community separated into two wings.

By that time the original disciples had established what became known as 'the doctrine of the elders' or *Theravada* and this was retained as the basis of teaching by the more conservative wing, the Theravada school. The breakaway group was more liberal and democratic in its assembly and was known as the Mahasanghika school, 'the Great Assembly'. It is generally believed that this wing eventually gave rise to the more familiar school of Mahayana, 'the Great Vehicle', which emerged in about the first century CE.

The languages in which the scriptures of the two wings of Buddhism are composed differ and this does little to narrow the divisions between them. The *Theravada* is composed in Pali, the ancient script of the Buddhist communities in India, whilst the writings or *sutras* of the Mahayana school are composed largely in the related but nevertheless distinct Sanskrit, the ancient language of the Hindu *Veda*.

The name Mahayana was coined by members of the school who considered their philosophy superior to that found in any of the older Buddhist schools of thought, including those following the more rigid Theravada discipline. The term was also applied to distinguish from Hinayana, 'the lesser vehicle', which was used as a derogatory nickname for the Theravada schools. In the early centuries, in spite of its inherent conservatism, Hinayana became the dominant and popular form of Buddhism in north India because its monasteries and temples were made accessible to the mass of the population. Eventually, though, Hinayana found its natural home in south India and expanded into Sri Lanka, Indonesia and Indo-China, whilst Mahayana spread northeast to embrace modern Nepal and from there to Tibet, China and Japan, under the title of Vajrayana Buddhism.

Western observers first learned of Buddhism through *pali* and therefore the conservative texts of the Hinayana school, although today the term 'Hinayana' is mainly used by western commentators who favour Mahayana philosophy as opposed to that of Theravada. Hinayana is the only one of the original 18 conservative Theravada schools to have survived to the present day.

MAHAYANA BUDDHISM

The Mahayana school developed in India between the first and third centuries CE and became the dominant Buddhist school

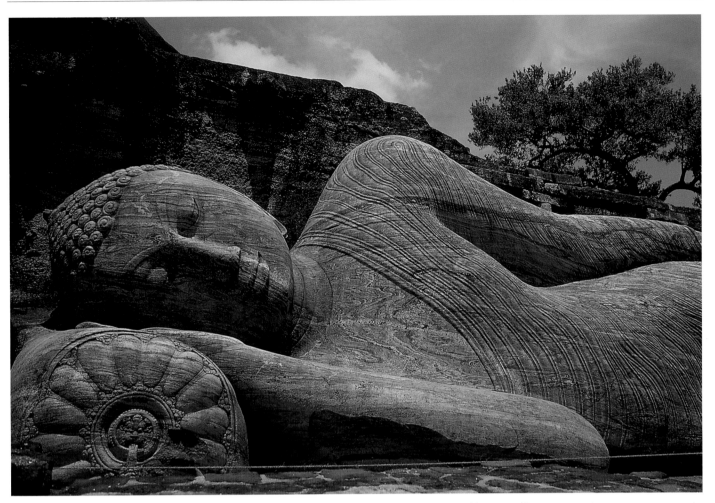

RECLINING *BUDDHA* SCULPTURE IN SRI LANKA, ONE OF THE STRONGHOLDS OF THERAVADA BUDDHISM.

between 300 and 500 CE. It developed out of the most powerful of the Mahasangika sects, the Sarvastivadins, who subscribed to a doctrine of *sarvastivada* which holds that 'all things are real'. Mahayana emphasizes individual interpretation of Buddhism and the supernatural or otherworldly nature of the *buddha* as the essence of all natural phenomena; it extols the salvation ideal inherent in the *bodhisattva* tradition and advocates the philosophy of *sunyata*, the elimination of all relative worldly elements to create a spiritual emptiness or void which, in contrast, the older Hinayana schools have supported. The liberalization of the rigid codes of the older schools allowed Mahayana disciples to travel more freely and expand their influence beyond the frontiers of India. Mahayana texts identify large numbers of *bodhisattvas*, all of whom can lend assistance along the difficult route to salvation, and this meant that a belief could flourish in the ability of the *bodhisattva* to use his spiritual powers to assist others in their quest for enlightenment. This is in contrast to the Hinayana philosophy's view that the Path can be travelled only with energies developed from within oneself.

The distinctions are down to differences in interpretation, and whilst Hinayana has remained loyal to the letter of the *buddha*'s teaching, Mahayana has tried to develop the underlying spirit of its message and to pursue the ideal that enlightenment is the doorway to the real strength of Buddhism, which is compassion. It is probably fair to say that Mahayana Buddhism is more difficult for a westerner to grasp in its diversity and constant adaptability, compared to the more stereotyped Hinayana form. Arguably it is largely through its adaptation and combination with other forms of belief in China and Japan that Mahayana Buddhism has survived, since in its birthplace, northern India, it is a minor player. On the reverse side of the coin, however, some notable reforming Mahayana thinkers – including Nagarjuna, a saint who lived in the second century CE, and Asanga, who was born in the fifth century – developed some excellent commentaries on the *sutras* which have aided their investigation and comprehension.

VAJRAYANA BUDDHISM

A number of splinter movements arose from the broad field of Mahayana Buddhism of which Vajrayana was the earliest, originating in north India in about the middle of the first century CE and adopting a doctrine that was both distinct and

MONKS IN A MAHAYANA MONASTERY IN TIBET.

the goddess and it therefore applies Left-hand Tantrism, that of the goddess who conventionally stands to the left hand of the god. It was this form of Mahayana Buddhism which led to the development of Lamaism in Nepal and Tibet and from there it spread to China and Japan where it became further adapted as Zen Buddhism. It is highly mystical in nature and therefore hard to define although some authors have pointed to limited similarities between Vajrayana Buddhism and early Christian Gnosticism.

Vajrayana philosophy advocates that the appearance of things is illusory and that, beyond the material plane, it is possible to identify the individual with the absolute. In order to achieve this transcendence of intellect it is necessary to follow certain specific techniques including the use of the *mantra* (see p.92).

The school of Vajrayana Buddhism, which is also less commonly known as Mantrayana Buddhism, earns its name from the *vajra* which has distinctly phallic connotations. The word means thunderbolt (see Symbols, p.94), but it is also the term used for the male genitalia. The *vajra* is worn as a symbol of the creative power of the *buddha*, although the sexual connotations which extend to forms of orgiastic worship have brought Vajrayana practices into disrepute amongst more mainstream schools of Buddhism.

LAMAISM

It is from Vajrayana doctrine that Lamaism developed as the dominant form of Buddhism in Tibet and subsequently spread into neighbouring countries in and around the southern Himalayas. The term *lama* was once restricted to a *guru* of great veneration but it became applied in more general terms to religious teachers and members of Tibetan monastic orders. In Tibet the ancient religion of Bon had flourished hitherto, based on a shamanistic hierarchy of magician priests and complicated rituals, but in the seventh century CE, amidst stiff opposition from religious conservatives, the Tibetan king Srong-btsan-sgam-po was converted to Vajrayana Buddhism by missionary monks from northern India.

It is to the credit of one of the most celebrated of all Buddhist scholars, Padmasambhava, in the eighth century, that

identifiably of Mahayana stock. The Vajrayana sect developed a Tantric school concerned essentially with magical manifestations; the word *vajrayana*, although correctly translated as 'the diamond vehicle', is perhaps more adequately understood as 'the magical vehicle'. The school follows a form of Tantrism, the ritualistic and magical doctrine based on a class of non-Vedic religious texts known as the *tantras* (see Mantras and Tantras, p.92).

Vajrayana Buddhism is, in many respects, comparable to Shaktism in Hindu belief, whose devotees pursue the worship of a merging of principles of the two religions was eventually achieved. Padmasambhava, a *yogi* of the Tantric school and a master of the occult, was instrumental in founding the first Tibetan Buddhist monastery, at Sam-yay. His work was furthered by an eleventh-century Indian scholar, Atisha, who rejected the sexual licence of Vajrayana Buddhism, whilst introducing strict celibacy amongst the *sangha* communities. Then, after some 200 years of expansion, and from a peak in the eleventh century, Lamaism entered a period of decline. This was partly attributable to politics and partly to the demands of celibacy. In the fourteenth century, however, Lamaism saw a fresh upturn in popularity, having been reformed by another leading figure of the movement, Tsong-kha-pa. It was at this time that the Tibetan version of the Buddhist canon was completed and, with the almost total obliteration of Buddhism in India, it became a key source of Buddhist scriptures.

Two of Padmasambhava's successors were believed to be reincarnations of the *buddha* Amitabha and the *bodhisattva* Avalokitesvara and from these, respectively, developed the separate roles of the Panchen Lama, who represents the spiritual figurehead of Tibet, and the Dalai Lama, whose successive reincarnations became the 'temporal' leader. In the seventeenth century, the fifth Dalai Lama was installed as absolute head of state by Mongol emperors, and this role continued until the exile in 1959 under Chinese communist rule of the most recent incarnation, the fourteenth Dalai Lama. When the present Dalai Lama was obliged to leave Tibet, the Chinese authorities replaced him with the Panchen Lama who was later stripped of his power for refusing to denounce his compatriot. He was the tenth reincarnation and died in 1989 at the age of 54.

A LAMA OF THE BON TRADITION, PRECURSOR OF BUDDHISM IN TIBET.

HINAYANA BUDDHISM

Hinayana, a derogatory term meaning 'the lesser vehicle', is not generally recognized by devotees of the school, who prefer the term Theravada Buddhism. *Theravada*, which means literally 'the teachings of the ancients' represents the most conservative form of Buddhism. Its followers adhere strictly to the teachings of Gautama Buddha, copied down by the first enlightened disciples, in contrast to the other schools which recognize a pantheon of *buddhas* and *bodhisattvas* and accept the validity of doctrinal texts other than those attributed to Gautama. Practised mainly in Sri Lanka, Burma and Thailand, the doctrine of *Theravada* is largely recorded in the authoritative texts dating from the first century BCE known as the *Tripitaka* (Sanskrit), *Tipitaka* (Pali) or 'Three Baskets'.

The school is believed to have originated in India at the time of the first Buddhist schism in the fourth century BCE. Tradition holds that Buddhism was introduced to Sri Lanka by the son of King Ashoka in the third century BCE, where it rapidly became the dominant religious doctrine, and by the fifth century CE had been established in southern India and various parts of south-east Asia. In Sri Lanka the main centre of authority was the Mahavihara temple at Anuradhapura where the Pali Canon is also believed to have been compiled. Written in the sacred mother tongue of Buddhism, it is the only complete text to have been preserved in an archaic Indian language.

Between the fifth and tenth centuries CE various notable monastic teachers, including Buddhagosa and Dhammapala, established a revised form of Theravada which became recognized as the 'classical school' still followed today. The adoration of icons and relics is discouraged and, whilst Mahayana Buddhism accepts divine assistance towards *nirvana*, in Theravada belief the responsibility for the struggle towards enlightenment is laid wholly at the door of the individual, with no recognition of help from above. This dogma very much follows the teachings of Gautama Buddha who insisted that the road to perfection was extremely difficult, required the ultimate in self-discipline and effort, and was to be achieved by very few.

MANTRAS
AND
TANTRAS

*T*he MANTRA *is a simple mystical sound device by which an ordinary person following either the Buddhist or the Hindu faith may achieve salvation. It is comparable with a Roman Catholic* NOVENA *in the sense that the user mutters the* MANTRA *repeatedly in a fairly automatic or mechanical fashion.*

MANTRA

Essentially a thought-form and magic formula combined, the *mantra* consists of a sequence of mystic syllables, sometimes a single syllable, which may or may not possess intelligible meaning. When written it may also be used as a charm, which is traditionally placed inside a hollow image: through the power of the *mantra* the image becomes the manifestation of the deity to whom the *mantra* refers. This is more commonly experienced in Nepalese and Tibetan tradition.

The *mantra* probably derives from a more expanded form of prayer, particularly used in Buddhism and known as a *dharani*. The latter is an apparently meaningless juxtaposition of syllables chanted as a magical device or charm. *Dharani* also refers to a group of 12 Buddhist saints, each of whom represents an idealized form of short and peculiar text, composed of meaningless syllables, which is believed to generate great mystic power.

A *mantra* may be included within a *dharani,* usually at the

A TANTRIC PAINTING AT ALCHI MONASTERY IN INDIA DEPICTING THE *DHYANIBUDDHA* AMITABHA IN MEDITATION.

beginning or the end, and there are various methods of utterance. It may be voiced aloud or 'throated' in a method known as *kanthika* or it may be uttered silently from within, in which case it is known as *ajapa* or non-uttered. Many types of *mantra* exist, of which those based on the OM syllable are perhaps the best known. A common form of *mantra* or *dharani* in Lamaist Buddhism is *om ma-ni pad-me hum* which is associated with worship of Avalokitesvara, the tutelary *bodhisattva* of Tibet, of whom the Dalai Lama is the living incarnation. Although in terms of language it is meaningless the *mantra* is generally interpreted to mean: Hail, the Jewel (*mani*) in the Lotus (*padma*), where *mani* reflects the *buddha* and *padma* is either the world or the flower from which Avalokitesvara was born. This may also have connotations of *yab-yum*, the male-female union of means and wisdom (see p.95).

Mantras may be restricted to a specified number of syllables. Thus the *pancaksara mantras* consist of five syllables and amongst the best known of them is one dedicated to the Hindu god Shiva: *om Si-va-ya-na-ma,* meaning simply 'praise to Shiva'. Others, termed *sadaksara mantras,* have six syllables, as in the *mantra* associated with Avalokitesvara, *om ma-ni pad-me hum.*

Mantras may also be generated to facilitate a specific purpose. Hence the *agniprajvalana* is a fire *mantra* with the object of kindling fire by mystical means, whilst the *brahmamantra* is believed to have the magical power to prevent the onset of decomposition in a corpse.

A MONK AT TRAKSHINDU MONASTERY IN NEPAL RECITING A *MANTRA* WITH THE AID OF PRAYER BEADS.

TANTRA

The *mantra* is not to be confused with a *tantra* although the two are closely related and *tantrism* was originally known as the *mantrayana*, the 'way of the mantras'. The *tantra* is also a mystical and magical device or formula found particularly in Buddhism where it evolved into two main strands referred to as Left-hand and Right-hand Tantrism. *Tantra* literally means stream or strand and refers to the ultimate wisdom said to embrace all human experience through the practice of perfection. Its objective is to reach into the subconscious mind and activate the spiritual and mystical powers which are latent in its depths. According to Buddhist tradition, *tantra* refers, in the tangible sense, to a series of ritual and magical texts which were originally devised by the *buddha* for the evocation of deities and, when used in association with *mantras,* to assist the disciple in acquiring occult powers. Tantric doctrine maintains that, through the repetitive use of the sound of the *mantra* in conjunction with other meditation practices, the *buddhas* and *bodhisattvas* can be directly contacted.

At first these Tantric texts were conveyed with considerable secrecy but after the fourth century CE they became more widely available in India and were promoted by the so-called '84 Perfect Ones', a celebrated group of Tantric scholars who were versed in mysticism and who later became canonized as saints.

Right-hand Tantrism involves the male deities of Hinduism and Buddhism, but more widely followed in Vajrayana Buddhism and Lamaism is the Left-hand form. Amongst the most famous pioneering exponents of this style of Tantrism in Tibet was the eighth-century *yogi* and founder of Lamaism, Padmasambhava. Left-hand Tantrism is also known as *vamacara* or 'left-hand practice' and focuses on the worship of the goddess who, by convention, stands to the left of the male deity. In Buddhism this female figure is the *tara*, meaning a 'star'. She is most often the *shakti* or female aspect of Avalokitesvara but may also be that of the various *dhyanibuddhas* such as Adibuddha or Amoghasiddhi. In Lamaism one of the most celebrated is Sitatara, the 'white *tara*', said to be the incarnation of a Chinese princess who became the consort of the Tibetan ruler Sron-btsan-sgam-po and was later reputed to be a manifestation of the *shakti* of Avalokitesvara-Padmapani.

There exists a special very brief form of *mantra* known as a *bijamantra*. This translates literally as 'seed *mantra*' and it is regarded as a basic thought-form which symbolizes the manifestation of a deity or deities. OM, used by itself, is undoubtedly the best known of the *bijamantras* of Buddhism and Hinduism and is applied at the beginning of all rituals and all holy books. It originated in India where it is known as the *brahmavidyabija*, AUM. This equates with OM in its utterance, although the three letters are said to represent the deities of the *trimurti*, where A symbolizes Brahma and creation, U is Vishnu and maintenance of the world, and M is Shiva, identifying destruction. In Buddhism the *trimurti* translates into the *triratna* or 'three jewels' which include the *buddha*, the *dharma* and the *sangha*. The *triratna* is represented by a triangular device known as the *trikona* or by the three-pronged *vajra*. In the same context *dharma* and *sangha* are sometimes worshipped as deities rather than being merely understood as abstracts or symbols.

SYMBOLS

*S*ymbolism plays a key role in Buddhism, much as it does in Hinduism, expressing commonly held beliefs which bind people together in faith but which are sufficiently abstracted to permit each individual to interpret them with a degree of personal latitude.

SYMBOLIC OBJECTS

One of the most significant symbols in Buddhism is the *vajra*. The meaning of the word and the exact origins of the *vajra* are unclear, but in its earliest form it seems to have been associated with lightning and with the trident device which represents lightning throughout much of the ancient near east. The *Veda* accounts for the *vajra* as a weapon. The god Indra wielded a *vajra* which is described as a club-like implement made, according to tradition, by Tvastar, the divine builder, from the bones of the sage or *rishi* Dadhici. In later Hindu belief the *vajra* became more closely linked with Shiva and with the god of war, Skanda, when it was generally depicted as a thunderbolt. In Buddhism it is defined as a 'diamond', an element which is indestructible but which is also capable of destroying through its extreme hardness. The *vajra* symbol has been used by Buddhists in an assortment of ways, particularly in association with magical rituals, which are strongly emphasized in the Vajrayana school.

The term *linga* is rarely encountered in Buddhism (see The Sects of Vishnu and Shiva in Hinduism, p.24) but *vajra* also comes to possess phallic connotations and, in this context, it may derive from the symbolism of the genitalia of the bull which was widely revered as an animal of great strength and virility throughout the ancient near east. In the wider sense the *vajra* is translated as the creative male principle in the cosmos.

SEEN FROM THE AIR, THE EXCAVATED BOROBUDUR TEMPLE IN JAVA SHOWS IN ITS PLAN THE GEOMETRIC SYMMETRY OF A *MANDALA*.

In Buddhist iconography the *vajra* is depicted as a double-headed staff terminating in prongs at each end, the tips of which are joined. The number of prongs varies between three, five and nine, all possessing different meanings. The *vajra* is usually carried in the right hand which refers to the notion in both Hinduism and Buddhism that the right side of the body is the honoured side. In the religious art of Lamaism the *vajra* is often found drawn in its own right and a *vajra* standing upright in a lotus or *padma* specifically symbolizes sexual union, although this combination has also been used to represent the five *dhyanibuddhas*.

The *vajra* is employed in a particular attitude or gesture known as *vajrahunkaramudra* in which the hands are crossed over the chest. The right holds a *vajra*, whilst the left grasps a *ghanta* or bell, representing the mystery of sound. The pose symbolizes the release from earthly passions and their associated suffering, which comes when the disciple has reached his destination on the Path of enlightenment. The symbolism is said to suggest the union between Wisdom and the Path.

Triratna, the 'three jewels', sums up the core of what it means to be a Buddhist and the symbol of *triratna* possesses great significance since it represents the *buddha*, the *dharma* or teaching of the *buddha,* and the *sangha* or community of disciples founded by the *buddha*. It is drawn as a triangle known as the *trikona* or as a three-pronged device which bears similarity to both the *vajra* and the *trisula*, a more conventional-looking trident originating in Hindu iconography.

The bell or *ghanta* in Buddhism stands for two distinct principles – impermanence and wisdom or *prajna*, a combination which reflects the teaching of the *buddha* that true enlightenment includes the understanding that nothing is permanent.

The *padma* or lotus symbolizes not only the family of *buddhas* but, more specifically, their emanations in the form of enlightened speech. The most celebrated figure of historical times was Padmasambhava, believed to be the emanation of the *buddha* Amitabha. Padmasambhava means 'lotus born', a title which refers to the myth of his birth on a lotus blossom. Buddhists regard the lotus as a flower of divine origin since it reproduces from its own 'womb' rather than in the soil, and the *padma* symbol is seen as a pledge of salvation. That the *buddhas* are born from the lotus indicates divine birth and in Vajrayana Buddhism the lotus also symbolizes the female principle or the female genitals. Thus in Buddhism it replaces the Hindu *yoni*.

SYMBOLIC ATTITUDES

Symbolism is also incorporated in attitudes. The *yab-yum* or 'father-mother' attitude is an extension of the *vajrahunkaramudra* gesture that is also to be found widely in Buddhism of the Vajrayana school. It depicts a god and his *shakti* in the position of sexual intercourse, symbolizing the male 'means' by which truth may be revealed, *upaya*, with the female *prajna*. The deities may hold a device known as the *vajraghanta*, a bell crowned with half a *vajra*, which reinforces the symbolism of the united male and female principles. It is considered that any member of a Vajrayana *sangha* can obtain esoteric knowledge in this way and that the route of sexual union is not restricted to deities.

In Buddhism the attitudes or gestures of hands, known as *mudras*, also possess precise symbolic meaning. One of the most celebrated is the downward pointing gesture of the *buddha* when seated, with the fingers of his right hand almost touching the ground. This *mudra* reflects the moment when Gautama Buddha was being ineffectually seduced by the demon Mara and, by tradition, he reached down in silence to touch the ground. As he did so a great earthquake shook the land and the demonic horde fled in terror.

SYMBOLIC PATTERNS

Geometric patterns may also contain symbolism. The *mandala* or magic circle, recognized in both Hinduism and Buddhism, is a geometric diagram which can be made on a piece of paper or by some other means. At its simplest, one of the most

AN EIGHTEENTH-CENTURY TEMPLE HANGING FROM TIBET, SHOWING AN ASSEMBLY OF SAINTS IN THE FORM OF A LOTUS FLOWER, A SYMBOL OF THE *BUDDHAS* AND THEIR EMANATIONS.

familiar *mandalas* is the symbolic offering made by a Buddhist each day with grains of rice which are spread on the ground as a gift to the deities. As a more detailed and ordered picture the *mandala* may include a precise pattern of figures, syllables or *bijas,* and shapes. The largest *mandalas* are created as architectural structures, often of considerable size, and in an extended sense a *mandala* is the geometric plan on which a temple may be constructed.

RITUAL

SELF-SURRENDER, PRACTISED HERE AT JOHANG MONASTERY IN TIBET, IS ONE OF A NUMBER OF BUDDHIST DISCIPLINES WHICH COMBINE PRAYER WITH ACTION.

Buddhism is a form of religion in which ritual adopts a comparatively minor role since it is essentially devoted to the teaching of DHARMA, the law, and the road to personal enlightenment. It is not the kind of organized religion in which ritual readily plays a part. However, long ago it was recognized that in order to attract a wider lay following, certain modifications were desirable and that these should include places of more conventional worship, or temples, and imagery placed in and around them upon which devotees could focus their acts of reverence.

DEVOTIONAL PRACTICE

Buddhist ritual, perhaps better described as devotional practice, is termed *puja* and is now an indispensable part of the religion, though its purpose is still strictly as an adjunct to enlightenment. *Puja* is a Sanskrit term for worship which is also applied in Hinduism, though in an accountably different way; Buddhist *puja* cannot be compared with the sacrifice-based ritual that developed from the *Veda*. The object of devotion in Buddhist worship is the image of the *buddha* and those who participate in Buddhist ritual are an integral and symbolic part of the process rather than a congregation coming together as an audience in the Christian sense. The ritual of Buddhism is something about which the principles can be taught and signposts can be indicated, but it can be fully understood only through personal experience and practice since it is concerned with the proper channelling or refining of emotional energies.

Whilst there is a short form of *puja*, the term more often refers to the Sevenfold *puja* since it generally comprises a sequence of seven distinct devotional aspirations. It is an exercise which is ideally carried out before an image or *rupa* of the *buddha*, although if a physical icon is not available, disciples may resort to mental imagery. In the guide given by the modern Buddhist teacher Sangharakshita, the Sevenfold *puja* based on the writings of the eighth-century-CE Buddhist master Santideva, the *Bodhicaryavatara,* includes (1) worship or *puja*, (2) obeisance or *vandana*, (3) seeking refuge or *sarana-gamana*, (4) confession of sins or *papa-desana*, (5) rejoicing in merit or *punyanumodana*, (6) transfer of merit or *parinamana*, and (7) self-surrender or *atmabhavadi-parityagah*. These seven disciplines are undertaken with a combination of action and prayer.

⋇

THE STAGES OF PUJA

At the outset of worship, lamps are lit to symbolize wisdom or enlightenment and offerings are placed before the *buddha* image. These may include flowers, rice, fruit or other produce, incense, jewels and water, and the offerings are varied according to the nature of the *buddha* or *bodhisattva* being addressed. The flowers not only beautify the place of worship but also symbolize the impermanence of nature, whilst incense is included because it is considered to have a calming and uplifting effect on the senses. These various offerings are essentially those that would be provided for an honoured guest – in this instance the *buddha*. In some Mahayana traditions the food is eaten after ritual by the worshippers, thus turning the *puja* into a religious feast.

During obeisance the aspects of the *triratna* are honoured – *buddha*, *dharma* and *sangha*. This takes place either by bowing down or by total prostration, face down on the floor, before the image and before the Teachers who represent the practice of *dharma*.

The seeking of refuge refers, once again, to the *triratna*. First the protection of the *buddha* is sought. He is the refuge through whom the disciple may overcome suffering. It also relates to the quest for *dharma* through which refuge may be obtained against the cycle of death and rebirth. Once the

LAMPS ARE LIT AT BODH GAYA AS AN INITIATION CEREMONY BEGINS.

disciple has found the transcendental Way towards total understanding, the bonds of *samsara* are progressively loosened and finally cast off. Refuge in the *sangha* means seeking the Way or gaining entry to the Stream with the help of the *bodhisattvas*. This aspect of ritual is a Mahayana rather than Theravada concept.

At this juncture in ritual the so-called Precepts or *sikkhapadani* may be uttered. Up to ten may be undertaken, although the number varies. The Precepts include an undertaking to abstain from the taking of life (*panatipata*), stealing or taking that which is not given (*adinnadana*), sexual relations (*kamesu micchacara*), telling lies or speaking falsely (*musavada*), intoxication of any kind (*surmeraya majja pamadatthana*), useless words (*samphappalapavaca*), slander (*pisunavaca*), covetousness (*abhijjha*), animosity (*byapada*) and falsehood (*micchadassana*). In Theravada tradition some of the Precepts are extended to include eating after noon, unseemly behaviour, use of high seats and beds, and handling money. Lay Buddhists in the Mahayana traditions undertake (1), (2), (4) and (5), listed above, and vary the third by abstaining from illicit or improper sexual relations rather than total abstinence.

Confession or *papa-desana* is less an unburdening of sins in the Roman Catholic sense than a coming-to-terms with one's own shortcomings, mainly those of ignorance and foolishness, which are obstructing the Path towards enlightenment. Rejoicing in Merit or *punyanumodana* is the converse and involves rejoicing in good deeds, whether those of oneself or others.

Parinamana effectively constitutes a positive attitude of mind and spirit that the merit earned in *punyanumodana* may be given over to help ease the sufferings and misfortunes of others who are less fortunate. *Atmabhavadi-parityagah* may be described as the poetic, inner sacrifice of the physical self and its pleasures, body, speech and mind, without remorse or sense of loss, for the broader fulfilment of all humanity.

The essential aim of Buddhist ritual is to achieve *bodhicitta*, the attitude of enlightenment which includes a sense of total altruism towards all of humanity. This, in turn, provides the route towards the ultimate of absolute *bodhicitta* which represents emptiness of mind and phenomena and the attainment of *nirvana*.

TEMPLES, SHRINES AND STUPAS

Buddhist holy places serve a number of functions — as places of devotion and ritual, as reliquaries and as monastic retreats. The oldest of them, inevitably, are to be discovered in the birthplace of Buddhism, northern India, although many of these have fallen into disrepair over the centuries and those which are more actively preserved and utilized tend to lie in lands to the east where Buddhism is the dominant religion. The Buddhist holy places in India are chiefly those which were first sanctified by the presence of the BUDDHA during his lifetime and were then venerated by his followers.

Essentially a monastic religion, Buddhism does not rely on temples in the sense of a Christian church where congregations assemble for communal worship, but rather on shrines for the performance of ritual and individual acts of devotion, coupled with monastic complexes and monuments known as *stupas*.

Of all the holy places of Buddhism, four stand at the pinnacle of veneration. These are the sites which the dying *buddha* listed to his personal attendant, Ananda, as being those which marked the essential moments of his life and which should, therefore, form an essential basis of itinerary for any Buddhist pilgrimage in northern India.

LUMBINI

The birthplace of the *buddha* as Siddharta, the prince of the Shakya clan, lies in the foothills of the Himalayas in Nepal, near the modern town of Rummindei. Named after Siddharta's maternal grandmother, it was originally a garden or park in which Queen Maya, by tradition, gave birth whilst touching the blossoms on a plaksa tree. During the third century BCE King

SCULPTURES AT VIENTIANE IN LAOS, WHERE BUDDHISM HAS BECOME ESTABLISHED.

Ashoka made a pilgrimage to Lumbini and sponsored the erection of *stupas* and a stone column topped by an equestrian statue. The latter was subsequently struck by lightning and broken in half but its remnants survived.

A description of the site was recorded nearly a thousand years later in the diary of a Chinese pilgrim named Hsuan-tsang, who noted the broken column surrounded by four *stupas*. The location appears to have been abandoned and lost, not to be rediscovered until the nineteenth century when a German archaeologist excavated the lower part of the column and was able to decipher Ashoka's inscription confirming Lumbini as the *buddha's* birthplace. Today the pillar has been restored (minus its horse) and the foundations of the *stupas* have been excavated, including a temple to Queen Maya, the walls of which bear carvings in bas-relief attesting to the birth of the *buddha*.

⋈

BODH GAYA

The spot where the tree stood beneath which the *buddha* achieved his enlightenment lies on the west bank of the river Nairanjana, a tributary of the Ganges. The original tree has long since died but it has given rise to an assortment of legends, including one that suggests it was hewn down and burnt by rival monks, whereupon a new bodhi-tree sprang up from the ashes and was diligently nurtured with the milk of a thousand cows. Successive trees have been planted down the centuries since the death of the original plant and it is recorded that the predecessor of the present tree became moribund in 1876. By the time Hsuan-tsang visited the site it was well established with a gated outer wall, *stupas* surrounding the bodhi-tree and an adjacent monastic complex.

Today the dominant feature of the place is the magnificent Mahabodhi Temple which is topped by a *stupa* containing relics of the *buddha*, beneath which are shrines for ritual and devotion. From an archaeological viewpoint it is not clear when the temple was built or by whom, only that it was in existence when Hsuan-tsang visited the place in the

seventh century CE. His description of a three-storeyed building standing about 170 feet high tallies with that of the present magnificent structure. The focus of devotion is the Seat of Enlightenment, the spot where Gautama is said to have rested beneath the tree. This now takes the somewhat more elaborate form of the *Vajrasana*, the Diamond Throne of the *buddha*, an object far removed in style from his original rustic seat.

By the early 1800s the temple had succumbed to neglect and was in a ruined state, but during the 1880s the British government undertook a restoration project and in 1945 the

THE SHRINE AT SARNATH MARKS THE PLACE WHERE THE *BUDDHA* DELIVERED HIS TEACHING TO THE COMMUNITY OF DISCIPLES.

entire site was entrusted to the Hindu government of India which later formally recognized it as a major religious shrine. Today a massive statue of the seated *buddha* occupies a commanding place in the central chamber and much of the earlier artwork has been restored.

SARNATH

The shrine commemorates the place where, in a deer park, the *buddha* is believed to have delivered his first teachings to the *sangha* community after enlightenment. This was the so-called Turning of the Wheel of Dharma. Sarnath lies a few miles from the ancient city of Varanasi (also called Benares) which developed an early reputation as a place of pilgrimage. By 300 BCE, Sarnath was a centre for *dharma*. It contained a complex of monastic buildings, *stupas* and shrines, mostly built during the reign of King Ashoka in the previous century. He erected one of his favoured commemorative pillars adjacent to the central shrine and topped it with a capital of four lions facing in different directions. Although the pillar subsequently collapsed, the capital was undamaged and now rests in the archaeological museum of Sarnath.

Between the fourth and sixth centuries CE Sarnath was extensively developed as an arts and education centre as well as a holy place, and by this time it included at least seven monasteries and a Jain temple around a central shrine.

Sarnath was sacked by Muslim invaders during the twelfth century but its ruins continue to attract pilgrims, who visit the massive brick and stone Dhamekh *stupa* with its distinctive, bluntly conical silhouette. Most of its carved stonework was removed during the eighteenth century to build a marketplace and today it stands 128 feet high as a stark but no less impressive reliquary. Another large *stupa*, the Dharmarajika, was totally destroyed with demolition charges during the same market-building programme although various precious objects and relics were salvaged.

In 1931 a modern Buddhist temple was completed in the deer park. It includes a large bell donated by Japanese Buddhists and many fine religious frescoes depicting the life of the *buddha*.

KUSINAGARA

Known as Kesavati during the *buddha*'s lifetime, Kusinagara was the capital of a small kingdom in northern India that obtained its sacred associations through being the place where the *buddha* completed his *parinirvana*, died and so entered into *nirvana*. One of the eight original *stupas* was constructed, according to tradition, over the place where the cremation fire had been lit and the *buddha*'s mortal body consumed. The site of this reliquary, known as Ramabhar Tila, lies on the east bank of the

Sonara river about a mile away from the main building complex of Kusinagara. The latter includes the striking domed *parinirvana stupa* and temple.

Ashoka built several *stupas* there, including one that reared a massive 200 feet into the air, and he accompanied them with pillars. But by the time the Chinese pilgrim Hsuan-tsang reached Kusinagara in the seventh century CE the place was largely in ruins, although there is evidence of further temple building in the eleventh or twelfth century, which was later destroyed by the Muslim invaders. The whole site remained abandoned until 1861 when a British archaeologist excavated the *parinirvana stupa* and its adjacent *nirvana* temple. Restoration work began in 1927

A *STUPA* IN THE NEPALESE HIMALAYAS, TYPICAL OF MANY SUCH MONUMENTS TO BE FOUND THROUGHOUT THE BUDDHIST WORLD.

the *stupa* later became a design of reliquary peculiar to Buddhism, although such commemorative cairns also find counterparts in other religions throughout the world. Tradition has it that after the *buddha* was cremated, his ashes were saved in a single urn and then divided evenly into eight portions which were distributed amongst the kingdoms represented at the cremation. Each portion, following the *buddha*'s personal request, was enshrined in a specially erected building. Eight *bodhi stupas* were built to house the relics, a ninth was constructed to hold the urn which had originally contained the ashes and a tenth was erected over the spot where the cremation took place.

The ubiquitous spread of *stupas* which took place subsequently in the Ganges basin is accounted for, in part, by the legend that King Ashoka took the relics from the original *bodhi stupas* and divided the material into 84,000 parts, equating to the number of atoms once believed to make up the human body. *Stupas*, however, became used for the ashes of other venerated Buddhists as well and in this way they came to be a familiar feature of Buddhist holy places throughout the world.

The design of the *stupa* is said to follow that suggested by the *buddha* when he folded his robe and laid it on the ground to represent the base, placed his begging bowl upside down on the robe to emulate the central chamber of the reliquary, and stood his umbrella on top to depict the spire.

The sites described here are the most venerated of Buddhist holy places in India, but the success of Buddhism throughout the oriental world is evidenced by the vast number of temples, *stupas* and monasteries, both ancient and modern, that exist for the worship of the *buddha*. These can be found wherever disciples have made their mark and converted populations.

Amongst the more extraordinary Buddhist monuments is that of Borobudur in Indonesia. Built in the ninth century CE, this enormous square pyramid with its many terraces surmounted by a spire represents a *mandala*. This is a style of *yantra*, an object of concentrated meditational focus which is itself a visual equivalent of a chanted *mantra*. The Borobudur *mandala* includes a geometric pattern of mystic figures and diagrams, *bijas*, and figures of deities incorporated into the plan of a temple, the walls of which are intricately carved with the *mandala* details.

In stark contrast, many of the Buddhist temples in Sri Lanka, where Buddhism was introduced as early as the third century BCE, possess a distinctly modernistic appearance and many are of twentieth-century construction. All the temples are accompanied by oversized figures of the *buddha*, often dwarfing the buildings, depicted in meditational or serenely benevolent posture.

and was completed on both buildings in 1972. Further archaeological excavation has revealed the foundations of many other *stupas* and four monastic buildings, attesting to the importance of Kusinagara as a Buddhist religious centre.

✄

TRADITIONAL STUPAS AND OTHER MONUMENTS

The *stupa*, in its original form, is a cairn of the type that was typically erected over the remains of emperors and other notables in ancient India. Through its traditional association,

BUDDHIST MONASTICISM

In much of Buddhism it is recognized that the student undergoing discipline as a prerequisite for priesthood must be segregated into a non-secular environment. The Buddhist monastic societies originated in India and the style of monasticism developed, in some degree, as a reaction against Hindu BRAHMANISM which was focused on the religious discipline applied to lay people rather than monks and nuns.

Effectively founded by Gautama Buddha after his first teachings in the deer park at Benares, Buddhism enjoyed a 'honeymoon period' for several centuries from the time when the original five *arhats* or ascetic disciples came together. Its popularity then waned in India during the medieval period whilst, at the same time, it was becoming established throughout much of the rest of Asia. As the religion was disseminated, so it also became separated into a number of schools and then into smaller sects, each of which developed its own distinct monastic tradition.

THERAVADA MONASTICISM

The oldest school, the Theravada or 'way of the elders', is based on the doctrines contained in the ancient Pali texts and is mainly active in Sri Lanka, Burma, Thailand, Cambodia and Laos, though in the last two countries it has experienced serious repression recently under communism. The community of disciples within a monastic order is known as the *sangha*; this may be a *bhikkhu-sangha*, which consists solely of monks, or a *bhikkhuni-sanga*, which is made up of nuns. When both types are combined they are known as an *ubhatosangha* or 'twin community'.

Each noviciate to Buddhist monasticism abandons wealth, worldly possessions and family ties, irrespective of age, when joining. The Orders tend to recruit their entrants at an early

NOVICE MONKS IN THAILAND ARE INITIATED INTO A MONASTIC ORDER.

stage of life and many are little more than children. The belief is that children are more able than older individuals to acquire the five essential principles of speaking, assimilating, comprehending, teaching and memorizing.

Although Buddhist monks originated as wandering mendicants, travelling the roads of northern India in an essentially nomadic existence without any permanent abode, it became apparent that they needed more settled places of residence during the monsoon rainy season when the roads became impassable. Whilst on the roads they tended to spend nights or longer periods of time in deer parks, which were often set aside for them by wealthy sponsors, and in other temporary hostels, but these were far from suitable for more permanent housing. Monastic retreats first originated as small cells, often self-built, that were capable of housing one or two monks, but later, as the *sangha* communities grew, larger houses were needed and these, again, were provided or financed by landowning Buddhist patrons. Thus the great Buddhist monasteries were founded, built on sites that were accessible from the major towns and cities yet separated

THE FOURTEENTH DALAI LAMA, SPIRITUAL LEADER OF BUDDHISM IN TIBET, HAS BEEN IN EXILE SINCE THE CHINESE INCURSION IN 1959.

sufficiently to allow them to operate, uninterrupted, as places of quiet contemplative life.

The ancient Pali texts provide a detailed view of the ideal way of life for Buddhist monks and nuns. In modern times some of the rules of Theravada have changed and other schools of Buddhism follow noticeably different paths but, for many, life is still much as it was originally ordained. Within the monastic walls the monks are not expected to live in extreme austerity. Following the Middle Way expounded by Gautama Buddha, they are entitled to a reasonable range of furniture, including beds with mattresses, chairs, tables and even cotton carpets, although beds and chairs may not have legs more than 8 inches high and ornate soft furnishings are forbidden. All property is deemed to be in the common ownership of the *sangha* and any deviation from the property rules – largely detailed in the *Vinaya pitaka*, the *Theravada* texts within the *Tripitaka* specifying monastic discipline – is an offence which demands confession or *pacittiya*. These rules include keeping the monastic buildings clean and tidy.

Within the *Sutta-pitaka*, the discourses of the *buddha* which include the so-called 'five collections' or *Niyaka*, there is frequent reference to the type of dress to be worn by monks and nuns. Robes are described as *kasaya*, which means ochre-yellow, but there is little further detail about style. Tradition has it, however, that the *buddha* spent many years of his ascetic life dressed in rags, and therefore the robe, according to the *Vinaya-pitaka*, should be sewn from rags collected from various places including burial grounds. It is believed that for many decades Buddhist disciples wore such rag-robes as an obligation. Later, however, it became accepted that the *buddha*, in his Middle Way

policy, adopted the wearing of garments made from new material and so the tattered style of dress was largely abandoned in favour of better-made clothes, often fabricated from expensive material including silks, although always sewn from several pieces of cloth in deference to the original tradition.

In the first years of the *sanghas* Buddhist monks and nuns were not allowed to work for a living and were permitted only to eat food that was provided for them by benefactors. Furthermore the storing and cooking of food within the monastery was strictly forbidden, as was the consumption of alcohol. Monks and nuns were not allowed to obtain or possess money under Theravada rules. Begging by members of monastic orders was considered entirely respectable and the monk seeking alms with his begging bowl has been a familiar sight in many parts of Asia. Nor, under these rules were monks and nuns allowed to indulge in sexual intercourse: abstinence was considered *de rigeur* and any lapse resulted in immediate expulsion from the community.

LAMAISM

This school derives from Vajrayana and therefore Mahayana Buddhism, and has much in common with the traditional conservativism of Theravada. It is essentially a monastic style of Buddhism practised mainly in Nepal and Tibet. In Tibet, though now suppressed by the Chinese communist regime, its popularity and adherence has been enormous, evidenced by the statistic that about one in four of all Tibetan males used to follow the life of a Lamaist monk. Prior to the communist incursion in 1959, when the spiritual head of Lamaism, the Dalai Lama, was exiled and Buddhism was outlawed, the Tibetan countryside also bore witness to general religious fervour by its many prayer wheels and prayer flags. Thousands of these devices dotted the landscape, inscribed with prayers, since they were believed to bring spiritual blessing when the wheels were turned or when the breeze set the flags fluttering. For an individual to hang prayer flags was to accrue merit in the eyes of the deities.

Lamaism was once summarized as 'an external practice of the Hinayana, an internal practice of the general Mahayana and secret practice of the esoteric Vajrayana' and, in many respects, Lamaist monastic life echoes that of the Theravada tradition. Thus its monks wear the ochre robes made of several pieces of stitched material and celibacy is considered highly important. But the liberalization of teachings has resulted in the proliferation of a great many sects which, at times, have sought both spiritual and political dominance in Tibet.

Much is based on the teachings of the *guru* Atisha who introduced his style of Buddhism to Tibet in 1042 CE. This became known as *Lam Rim* or 'Stages on the Path' and it has been incorporated into the monastic life of various Orders, including Geluk, Kagyu and Shakya. The Geluks (*dGe lugs*) represent the famous 'yellow hats' Order, so-called because they wear yellow headgear, distinguishing them from the red hats of other Orders, and in the sixteenth century their influence was such that they gained the support of the Mongol overlords, persuading them to establish the Dalai Lama as the Tibetan spiritual and political authority. Successive reincarnations of the Dalai Lama have all belonged to the Geluk Order.

The *Lam Rim* teaching was popularized largely through the writings of the third Dalai Lama, Gyalwa Sonam Gyatso, which are entitled the *Essence of Refined Gold. Lam Rim* subscribes to all the essentials of classical Buddhism, including the close working relationship with a spiritual master which leads to accomplishment of the discipline of Tantric *yoga* and final enlightenment. The cultivation of correct attitude between disciple and scholarly master, who is handing down the teachings of the *sutras* and *tantras*, is regarded as being of great importance and the *guru* is expected to have attained the more advanced training including discipline, the serenity of meditative concentration, and the deeper levels of truth. He must also be able to explain the practices of *dharma* without distortion or error, be able to perceive the true emptiness that lies beyond materialism, and must generally possess a greater degree of learning than his pupils. The disciple learns from the master the techniques of practising contemplative meditation, firstly on the words of the great dissertations and then on the themes encompassed by those words. The disciple monk is not generally required to trawl through vast tomes of Buddhist written works, however, but to learn through the *Lam Rim*,

which is essentially devised as an oral teaching method. Designed to suppress the negative aspects of the mind and develop a spiritual awareness, this oral basis of learning accounts for much of the importance attached to the student-teacher relationship.

For his part the student is required to have a sincere spirit of enquiry rather than a passive acceptance of his vocation. He must also possess what the present Dalai Lama has described as 'critical intelligence, a sense of curiosity, without which it is like leading a monkey on a chain ... when we lack inquisitiveness we are not able to determine how to apply the specific instructions to our own stream of being'. The student is urged to acquire qualities of mindfulness, mental alertness, conscientiousness, humility and modesty, working to improve the world by ethical means. Errant forms of behaviour include anger and impatience, both of which are regarded as being strongly negative attitudes. The Lamaist disciple must, in other words, pursue 'goodness' and avoid improper activities through self-discipline.

The young Lamaist monk will first seek to attain basic or novice initiation into the Order known as *upasika*. After this, intensive study begins and the disciple undergoes a sequence of Tantric initiations which introduce him to various *mandalas* and other esoteric practices, including traditions leading to longevity. His daily life will include prayers to various sacred images within the monastery, *sadhana* or invocation of the deities, teaching sessions with his master, periods of meditation based on *yoga* methods, meals and domestic duties. On a less frequent basis he will undertake pilgrimages to other holy places.

MAHAYANA MONASTICISM

Outside of monastic Lamaism the Mahayana school of Buddhism, which has been spread predominantly into China and Japan, has adopted an accountably different monastic path since it is geared much more closely towards the layman and

AT SIKKIM IN INDIA, PRAYER FLAGS CONVEY DEVOTIONAL MESSAGES.

its disciplinary rules are more liberal. The notion of entering a monastic order to lead a solitary and celibate existence, with the entire focus of life resting on personal salvation, is not overtly encouraged and, in Japan, monks and nuns have been allowed to marry since the mid-nineteenth century when the Meiji Restoration rejected celibacy.

The priesthood, particularly in Japan, is there to serve the lay following and Mahayana Buddhists are frequent visitors to temples. Shrines are erected in all Buddhist homes and simple offerings are made on a daily basis to include flowers, tea, cakes and incense. For most of the sects, other than those of the Tariki school, meditation is also a vital part of the religious discipline. Nonetheless many Zen monasteries have been established in Japan and these constitute significant centres of religious activity for those who wish to pursue a quiet contemplative life.

MODERN BUDDHISM

*I*n common with Hinduism, from which it evolved in the sixth century BCE, Buddhism is a dynamic 'living' religion, currently believed to possess about 500 million followers, and therefore these two strands of faith are amongst the world's oldest continuous demonstrations of religious belief. Although Buddhism has largely been abandoned in India for many centuries, it was once far more influential in the sub-continent. Between about the second century BCE and the eighth century CE, it was probably the dominant religious movement in southern India, but over a period of time it became marginalized by Hindu reformers.

WAT PAH CITTAVIVEKA IS AN ACTIVE THERAVADA COMMUNITY BASED IN WEST SUSSEX.

Despite this decline, in modern times about 5 million Indians who do not belong within the Hindu caste system, or the 'scheduled classes', have allied themselves with Buddhism. These people, for whose rights Mahatma Gandhi fought passionately, are known as *harijan* or 'God's people'. Their leader, Dr B. R. Ambedkar, himself a member of a scheduled class or *mahar*, broke all ties with the caste system and in doing so alienated many of his countrymen, including Gandhi who was a staunch supporter of the caste system.

DEVELOPMENT OUTSIDE INDIA

There have also been a number of areas of the world, such as east Turkestan, in which Buddhism gained an initial following only to fall victim to the spread of Islam. Today Buddhism is practised mainly in its Theravada and Mahayana forms. The latter includes many varieties of which the best known is probably Zen, practised chiefly in Sri Lanka, Burma, Thailand, Indo-China, Nepal, Tibet, China and Japan, though it is also gaining a steady following of converts in the west. Particularly within its Mahayana division, Buddhism has become vastly diverse, crossing both national, ethnic and religious boundaries. It is a curious truth that wherever Buddhism has flourished in the world it has generally done so with the support of rulers who became sympathetic to its tenets, underwent conversion, and patronized its establishment in their domains. Arguably one of the main factors in its success, however, not only as a religion, but as a philosophy and a cultural way of life, remains its adaptability and its willingness to compromise with other beliefs. Not least for this reason, it has been able to expand as a major influence into Tibet and China (notwithstanding communist suppression) where it has largely become syncretized with Bon and Taoism respectively, and into Japan where it co-exists with the Shinto religion.

In Tibet today, the Buddhism which still survives under communist rule largely owes its shape to two great spiritual figures of the past, the eighth-century philosopher Santaraksita and the Tantric scholar Padmasambhava, and the work of

MILTON KEYNES HAS A PEACE PAGODA BUILT BY MONKS AND NUNS OF THE NIPPONZAN MYOHOJI ORDER.

these pioneers continues to be regarded as exemplary by monks who follow the Nyingma school of Tibetan Buddhism.

Zen Buddhism was established first in China then in Japan, but in the 1960s it was exported to Europe by way of a monk named Taisen Deshimaru who travelled the Trans-Siberian railway to Paris. His movement, the Mission de Maitre Taisen Deshimaru, now claims 200 cells throughout the world, of which 90 are established in France.

BUDDHISM IN BRITAIN

An attempt, largely unsuccessful, was made to introduce Buddhism to England in 1908 through the mystic Allan Bennett, who was a friend of the celebrated pagan and black magician Aleister Crowley, and who founded the Buddhist Society of Great Britain and Ireland. Others who had previously been initiated into Buddhism in the east, subsequently tried to re-establish *sanghas* in Britain, though again with limited success. In 1954 one of these converts, named William Purfurst, whose Buddhist name was Bhikku Kapilavaddho, set up a monastic cell which moved around various private house locations in London. Although Kapilavaddho never truly succeeded, one of the London addresses was later taken over by a Thai Buddhist, Ajahn Chah, who revitalized the small moribund *sangha*. By chance, in 1978, this community was able to purchase a run-down Victorian country house in Sussex, near the village of Chithurst. Today the community, known as the Wat Pah

Cittaviveka, is flourishing and it follows the disciplines of the so-called Forest Tradition of Theravada.

This term originated in Thailand where 'forest monks', whose interest was primarily in achieving *nirvana* through austerity and reclusivity, became distinguished from 'town monks' who effectively served as local priests and teachers. During the 1940s Ajahn Chah wandered the remote areas of his homeland as a mendicant and became increasingly devoted to the Forest Tradition. In the 1950s he was active in promoting this through missionary activities in Thailand. He established a forest *sangha* which he named the Wat Pah Bong and then turned to exporting his style of Buddhism to visitors from the west. In 1974 he founded the Wat Pah Nanachat monastery which was devoted to training European and American noviciate monks and three years later he came to England, subsequently to set up a headquarters at Chithurst.

A style of Japanese Buddhism has also been established in England, based in Milton Keynes, where, in 1980, a peace pagoda was created under the banner of the Nipponzan Myohoji monastic Order. This movement was inaugurated, in the aftermath of the atomic devastation at the end of the Second World War, by Nichadatsu Fujii. He subscribed to the ideas of peace, based on the *Lotus sutra*, put forward by a Japanese scholar named Nichiren, the thirteenth-century founder of the Nichiren Shoshu sect of Buddhism. It is the doctrinal basis on which the largest of all the lay religious sects in Japan, the Soka Gakkai, was founded in 1937. This part-religious, part-political cult claims 10 million devotees worldwide and has more than 60 members elected to the Japanese parliament.

JAINISM

🔹 ❋ ❋ ❋ ❋ ❋ ❋ ❋ ❋ ❋ ❋ ❋ ❋ ❋ ❋ ❋ ❋ ❋ ❋ 🔹

Jainism evolved out of Hinduism at about the same time in history as Buddhism and, in part, for similar reasons. Although the two faiths pursued different paths, their ultimate objective was, and still is, the release from the cycle of death and rebirth attributable to *karma*. Like Gautama Buddha, the sixth-century-BCE founder of Jainism, Mahavira, wished to reform away from certain Hindu practices. These did not include the caste system, which Jains regard as valuable, but both leaders rejected the Vedic tradition of animal sacrifice, believing that violence towards fellow creatures and the taking of life in whatever form was a sacrilege. Mahavira's teachings provided a strong allure to the *kshatriya* or warrior class of nobles from whose martial principles he himself had withdrawn when still a comparatively young man. He was, however, still conventionally attuned in his social roots.

Jainism was, and still is, essentially an Indian religion, largely though not entirely monastic, with a following of both sexes that is variously claimed at between three and six million. Like Buddhism, it evolved in northern India in an era of political and social unrest – an ideal climate for the emergence of new faiths to which people could look for social and moral guidance and support.

At first Jainism was centred in the Ganges valley but it saw a shift in its centres of influence as politics and patronages changed. During the third century BCE the Jain community migrated to Gujarat and Rajasthan in western India, where it established a new monastic base from which to extend its influence. Later Jainism became increasingly popular in southern India and Jains were at the forefront of literary and scientific effort. Indeed a number of influential rulers actively supported their aims and beliefs. From the sixth century onwards, however, an increasing proportion of those in secular authority were converted back to Hinduism.

Jain monks, forbidden to bathe lest they destroy waterborne life, became notable for their ascetic lifestyle, a visible demonstration of their extreme devoutness in abandoning physical care and attention in the quest for inner spiritual purity.

MAHAVIRA

The founder of Jainism was born at Kundagrama in Vessali, one of the many ancient tribal kingdoms which once existed in north-east India. The archaeological site is near modern Patna in what is now Bihar state. Legend tells that Mahavira was the son of a BRAHMIN named Rishabhadatta and Devananda but that he was transferred, as an embryo, from the womb of Devananda to that of Trisala, the wife of a KSHATRIYA or military ruler named Siddharta (no relation to the Siddharta who became the historical BUDDHA), to whom he was born as the second son. His date of birth is claimed to have been in about 540 BCE and he was therefore slightly older but otherwise a contemporary of Gautama Buddha.

There is some comparison between this myth of 'two mothers' and that of the Hindu deity Balarama, the elder brother of Krishna, who was transferred from the womb of his true mother Devaki to that of Rohini, and it implies a divine birth that somehow places the individual apart from ordinary mortals. Although he is best known to Jain followers as Vardhamana or Mahavira, the 'Great Hero', he is recorded in some Buddhist texts as Nigantha Nataputta and this is now accepted as one of his epithets.

※

THE SEARCH FOR ENLIGHTENMENT

Like Gautama Buddha, Vardhamana grew up in the affluent lifestyle of a prince amongst the ruling warrior class of *kshatriyas* and, according to some traditions, wed a princess named Yasoda who bore him a daughter Anavadya. At the age of 28, when his parents died, he renounced materialism and deserted his family in favour of the life of a wandering mendicant and ascetic in the lower reaches of the Ganges valley, hoping to secure release from *samsara*, the wearying cycle of death and rebirth. When he achieved enlightenment at

the age of 42 he became known as the twenty-fourth of the great teachers or *tirthankaras* in the present aeon of Jainism, the so-called 'Makers of the Path'. According to tradition, he was following in the footsteps of an illustrious predecessor, Parsva, who is said to have lived during the eighth or ninth century BCE. All previous listed *tirthankaras* are, however, probably in the realms of myth and Vardhamana effectively initiated the historical Jain religion.

Unlike the compromise or Middle Way lifestyle that was settled on by Gautama Buddha, Vardhamana elected to pursue extreme asceticism. It is said that, although during the first years of his wanderings in search of salvation he was equipped with a single loin-cloth or *dhoti*, he eventually discarded this and went naked for the rest of his life. In some respects he and Gautama Buddha followed similar ideals in that they represent independent-minded reformers who rejected aspects of Hindu Vedism that they considered unacceptable, including animal sacrifice which they believed to be undesirable. They agreed on non-theism, but differed in their view of the caste system which Gautama Buddha regarded as unacceptably elitist. Together they also probably derived some of their doctrines from the ancient *sramanas* or 'labouring' religious teachers who diverged from the style of the orthodox *brahmins* by arguing that salvation was possible through non-theism and asceticism. The religious pioneering of the *buddha* and the *mahavira* may, to a degree, have stimulated positive advances within Hinduism and been seen as a united counter-movement. On the other hand, the Buddhist scriptures account Nigantha Nataputta as one of the principal opponents of the *buddha* and suggest that he was advised not to permit any of his disciples to hear the words of the 'deceiver Gautama' lest they were attracted by the charms of the rival teacher.

※

FOUNDING THE NEW MOVEMENT

Vardhamana achieved full enlightenment, having wandered fasting, arguing, studying and contemplating for some 13 years amongst other ascetic philosophers of his time. In doing so he became an *arhat* or saint, recognized as *tirthankara*, the acclaimed leader of the new order of Jains, properly known as *jinas* or conquerors, 'those who overcome', so-called because they have overwhelmed the negative *karma* which binds them to *samsara* and the material world. He gained his converts

AN IMAGE OF MAHAVIRA, THE FOUNDER OF JAINISM, IN KOBA JAIN TEMPLE IN GANDHINAGAR.

largely from his own *kshatriya* class in Bihar and not only developed monastic communities for both monks and nuns but encouraged a sizeable lay following. For the remaining 30 years of his life he led the Jain community, extolling a life of extreme austerity and spreading the Jain doctrine of passionless detachment which can be gained only through the most severe and rigidly disciplined of self-mortifying lifestyles, personally applied without any outside help from gods or past *tirthankaras*.

Very little accurate information is available about his life and the limited amount that exists is mostly a formalized part of the mythical tradition. It is believed that he pursued self-mortification to the end and that his death came from voluntarily imposed starvation or *samlekhana*, which he promoted as a final act of ascetic discipline, at a place called Pava, now Pavapuri, near modern Patna. Tradition has it that he died in 527 BCE, the beginning of the era recognized by Jains and known as *virasamvat*, the 'Year of the Hero', although this date is disputed and scholars now believe that his death occurred in 468 BCE.

There are claims that Vardhamana, rather than the *buddha*, was actually the first of the breakaway heterodox teachers to form a monastic community or *sangha* in India. The earliest texts of Jainism are, however, lost and no certainty can be placed on the argument. In common with the historical *buddha* as the last in a line of *buddhas*, the *mahavira* is regarded as being at the end of the current succession of *tirthankaras*. His teachings are preserved by the Jain movement, therefore, as the focus of their ongoing faith and practice.

ANCIENT JINAS AND TIRTHANKARAS

*A*lthough the Jain doctrine recognizes the existence of deities who live in heaven, none of these is able to achieve perfect enlightenment. They are tied to the laws of SAMSARA, the Wheel of Existence, and must therefore die and be reborn. Freedom from this eternal round of suffering is available only to those human beings who have broken free from the limitations imposed by KARMA or action in life, achieved the spiritual summit of perfection and become TIRTHANKARAS.

Tirthankara is a difficult word to translate but it is interpreted as the 'Maker of the River Crossing', since *tirtha* in Sanskrit means one who finds a ford and *kara* implies a maker. It means, therefore, one who has discovered and then taught the way to cross the stream of existence between *samsara* and *nirvana*, the painful reality of mortal existence and ultimate, blissful enlightenment. The term is largely synonymous with *jina*, meaning 'one who vanquishes or overcomes' and from which the title Jain is a corruption. It is, however, distinct from the Hindu concept of a *brahmin* and Vardhamana preferred to call his disciples *sramanas* or 'strivers' who were required to leave the domestic life and go forth, having renounced conventional social values and become part of the family of ascetics.

The historical *tirthankara*, Mahavira or Vardhamana, is described as the twenty-fourth *tirthankara*, indicating that there have already existed a previous 23 who are regarded as the saints or salvation-teachers of the faith of Jainism. None of these earlier *tirthankaras* has any confirmed basis in history,

WORSHIPPERS MAKING AN OFFERING TO AN ICON OF THE HISTORICAL *TIRTHANKARA*, MAHAVIRA, IN SITAMBRA TEMPLE, CALCUTTA.

although there is some suggestion that the penultimate name in the list, Parsva, may have been a historical person living in the eighth or seventh centuries BCE, in which case he may be owed the credit for founding Jainism. All, however, are believed to have been born into the warrior class of *kshatriyas* and subsequently experienced a calling from the gods to renounce the material world, become great spiritual leaders and to guide their disciples across the stream between *samsara* and enlightenment. They are the *jinasvaras*, or Lords of the *jinas*, whose souls have destroyed *karma* and who, through practising meditation, have died in perfect understanding so that their souls have become wholly liberated to live on in a state of disembodied bliss.

THE PRESENT SERIES OF TIRTHANKARAS

Each aeon is believed to have produced 24 *tirthankaras*, of which only the present series, a momentary fragment in the overall span, is identified. Each succession of 24 has the obligation to maintain the Jain *triratna*, the 'Three Jewels' of correct faith, understanding and activity. The names of the *tirthankaras* describe various abstract principles to which the Jain teacher, and by implication each disciple, should aspire in order to uphold the Three Jewels. They begin with Rishabha(natha), said to be identical with a minor bull incarnation or *avatara* of the Hindu god Vishnu which may indicate that, at one time, there was a Hindu attempt to absorb Jainism. Rishabha(natha) is followed by Ajita, representing the unconquered, Sambhava (origin or birth), Abhinandana (praise or salutation), Sumati (wisdom), Padmaprabha (the splendour of the lotus), Suparsva (having beautiful aspects), Candraprabha (the moonlight), Suvidhi (good ordinance), Sitala (the cooling protector against heat), Sreyansa (auspicious), Vasupuyja (the son of excellence), Vimala (one who is bright and pure), Ananta (the infinite), Dharma (the teaching), Santi (tranquillity), Kunthu (the jewel), Ara (the spoke of the Wheel), Malli (the act of holding), Munisuvrata (he who fulfils the vows of the saints), Nemi (protector of the rim of the Wheel), Aristanemi (the rim of whose Wheel is unhurt), and Parsva, followed by Mahavira who proclaimed himself the successor to the series and modelled himself on the practices attributed to Parsva.

Of the earlier *tirthankaras*, Nemi was allegedly a cousin of the Hindu *avatara* Krishna who appears as a major character in the *Mahabharata* and the *Bhagavad Gita* and, again, this may represent a political move to bring the two beliefs into some form of union. The suffix *natha* is usually added to the names as a term of respect or reverence since it means Lord. To the list of 24, the Digambara Jains add the name of Gommata, the son of Rishabha, who became regarded as a Jain saint.

This array of *tirthankaras* is represented by a series of icons or statues which repose in Jain temples and their worship is the essence of the first of the eleven 'higher vows' of

A SYMBOLIC PAINTING DEPICTS ONE OF THE JAIN *TIRTHANKARAS* SEATED ON AN ELABORATE THRONE.

obedience that a Jain layman takes when he wishes to embark on the more advanced journey towards freedom from *samsara*. The number 24 has also taken on a mystical arithmetical significance as a *sankhya* or symbolic figure.

The figures of the 24 vary, however, in physical stature. It is believed that during *avasarpini* (see p.118) the *tirthankaras* achieve massive size, but as *utsarpini* evolves, and the quality of human existence diminishes, so not only does the stature and lifespan of the *tirthankaras* diminish but so does the interval between their successive births. Hence Rishabha and Ajita were of gigantic proportions, lived for vast periods of time and were separated by equally long duration, whilst Parsva and Vardhamana lived for a hundred years or less, their births were separated by only two hundred and fifty years, and they grew to more or less normal human size.

JAIN PHILOSOPHY

SPIRIT AND MATTER: A JAIN SVETAMBARA NUN WALKS ALONG A DESERT ROAD IN NORTHERN INDIA.

*J*ainism is essentially a non-theistic, monastic religion deeply concerned with ethics and with the Path towards freeing the soul from sensual stimuli, passions and emotions, thereby reaching the perfect state where human suffering, death and rebirth no longer exist. In this it follows a similar course to Buddhism but differs in the philosophy and nature of the enlightenment through which liberation from the Wheel of Life may be attained, and also in that it carries an intrinsic pessimism about the chances of success in conquering SAMSARA (material existence).

The philosophy largely ordains the practice and at the core of Jain conduct is the principle of *ahimsa* which demands following a way of life wholly opposed to violence of any sort against living creatures. It is for this reason, amongst others, that former Hindu devotees, disenchanted with animal sacrifice of the Vedic religion, have been attracted to Jainism. It also requires, to a far greater extent than with Buddhism, that the mind becomes isolated from the world and that the untempered and wilful thought processes become suppressed. The state of perfect isolation and the supreme knowledge that comes with this isolation is known as *kaivalya*, which compares approximately with Buddhist enlightenment or *bodhi*.

Jainism recognizes differences with Hinduism and Buddhism on a cosmic scale although it also includes unusual elements of spiritual nationalism. Integral with the Jain concept of the world is the *jambu* or 'Rose apple tree' *Eugenia jambolana*, which equates with the notion of a world tree that is part of mythology the world over. An enormous specimen of the *jambu* grows, according to tradition, on the summit of Mount Meru, the mythical Himalayan mountain of the gods lying in the centre of the continent of Jambudvipa (India), around which the seven other continents are arranged.

PERCEPTION OF THE UNIVERSE

Within the wider canvas, the Jain universe is eternal, without beginning or ending, and through the symbolism of a turning wheel it is destined to a repeating cycle of ebb and flow, rise and fall. The destiny and fortunes of humanity or *manusyaloka* are reflected in the cosmic cycles and, in the present era, we are caught up in a negative, downward phase. This concept of the Age of Kali is one which Jains share with Hinduism. Not all, however, is fatalistic, for whilst the cosmic cycles are predetermined and inflexible, the destiny of individuals within the universal canvas is more self-determined. It is down to each and every one of us whether or not we achieve personal salvation and freedom through enlightenment.

Within the Jain universe there exists a dichotomy – an infinite number of substances which are divided in nature, representing, on the one hand, souls, the spiritual components of the cosmos, and on the other the material elements. Those of the spiritual dimension are termed *jivas*, whilst material elements or non-souls are *ajivas*. Within the dichotomy between spirit and matter, each component further possesses an infinite number of individual characteristics. This myriad of substances exists wholly independently and unaffected by our perceptions. In other words, unlike Buddhism which argues that all things perceived through the senses are illusory, Jainism claims that they truly exist and is therefore based on realism. This realism also possesses a chilling and pessimistic downside in that, since it recognizes an infinite number of *jivas* crowding the universe, it argues that most of them are destined to an eternity on the Wheel of Life, never to be freed from *samsara* and the misery of mortal death and rebirth.

Jain philosophy is largely expounded in the discursive texts which analyse the traditional doctrines or *Agamas*. The major Jain authors include Kundakunda who lived in the first or second century CE and wrote a detailed philosophical overview of the *Agamas*; Umasvati, the compiler of the *Tattvartha-sutra*, again based on the *Agamas*, and the first Jain scholar to write in Sanskrit as distinct from Prakrit; and Hemacandra, the twelfth-century author of the *Pramana-mimamsa*, a classic and comprehensive work on Jain philosophy. The philosophical discussion, however, is closely allied with Jain logic, a discipline which was first elaborated by Siddhasena, a seventh-century-CE scholar and thinker whose notable works include the *Sanmatitarka* and *Nyayavatara*.

KNOWLEDGE

At the heart of Jain philosophy is knowledge or *svaparabhasi*, the analysis of its detailed nature, and the relationship between knowledge and self. Knowledge is classified either on the basis of the philosophy contained in the *Agamas* or on that of the logic school. The *Agamas* divide knowledge into five types, two of which, known as *abhinibodhika* and *sruta* (that which is learned), are based on the senses and three, *avadhi*, *manahparyaya* and *kevala* (those of the ascetic), are transcendental. Logicians, by contrast, argue two main types of knowledge – *pratyaksa*, which includes *avadhi, manahparyaya*

IN RANAKPUR TEMPLE, A CARVING OF THE TURNING WHEEL SYMBOLIZES THE ETERNAL NATURE OF THE UNIVERSE.

and *kevala*, and *paroksa*, which includes *abhinibodhika* and *sruta*.

Pure knowledge provides the key to transcending beyond the Wheel in both Buddhism and Jainism, but in Jain philosophy *prama* is more accurately defined as judgemental knowledge – in other words, being able to make the proper judgement about the nature of an object. The source of this valid judgemental understanding, the means whereby it is obtained and which allows us to accept or reject an object, is *pramana*. Siddhasena describes it in the *Pramana-mimamsa* as 'knowledge which is self-revealing and object-revealing and which is free from contradictions'. According to his understanding, there is a somewhat ambivalent relationship between knowledge and self in that the two are neither wholly different nor wholly linked but rather the one is the essential quality of the other. This gives knowledge an eternal quality because self is eternal and, irrespective of whether liberated or

AN ICON SKILFULLY REPRESENTS THE LIBERATED SPIRIT OF SELF OR *JIVA* WHICH CONSISTS OF PURE KNOWLEDGE.

116

bound by *karma*, self cannot exist without knowledge. By contrast, knowledge is also ephemeral or perishable when it is based on experience. Perishable knowledge appears when its object is present and disappears when its object is absent.

Like Buddhists, Jains accept that knowledge is self-revealing in that it does not require any other ingredient before manifesting itself. Unlike Buddhists, however, they recognize that knowledge is also object-revealing. Knowledge reveals an object – for instance, a light bulb – only whilst revealing itself. When the mind knows what the words 'light bulb' mean in terms of shape, texture and colour, one automatically knows that one knows the light bulb when one sees it!

The two main types of knowledge identified by logicians, *pratyaksa* and *paroksa,* form part of a philosophical argument known as the Theory of Perception. *Pratyaksa* is described by the early Jain philosophers as the clear knowledge which is derived from the *aksa* or self, alone, something distinct from knowledge that is not born of the self, which is identified as *paroksa*. *Pratyaksa* itself is differentiated into the knowledge which is gained through the organs of sense, *samvyavaharika pratyaksa*, and that superior source which is non-sensory, *mukhya pratyaksa*. Sensory knowledge is of five types based on the nature and function of the external sense organs (touch, taste, smell, sight and hearing) and each is gained on two levels – one which is physical, *dravyendriya*, and one which is psychic, *bhavendriya*. In addition to the five external senses there exists an internal sense, the mind or *anindriya*. According to Jain belief, the mind is capable of understanding and recognizing everything and is not bound in the way that the external senses are limited to understanding only a particular kind of object. In other words, the sense of touch, for instance, cannot understand an aroma whilst the mind can absorb both.

LEVELS OF EXISTENCE

The self or *jiva*, as an isolated and liberated spiritual essence, consists of pure knowledge and understanding. However, when the soul transmigrates into a new body at mortal birth it becomes associated with, and adulterated by, material things. These exert an adverse influence on its purity and totality of consciousness which varies in its severity according to the level the soul adopts when it takes on its temporal, though not necessarily human, existence. Of the five levels the one adopted is determined by the sum of the *karma* pursued and accumulated during previous earthly lives.

At the highest (fifth) level, which includes *devas*, human beings, infernal beings and the more sophisticated members of the animal kingdom, the spirit may call on five senses – touch, taste, smell, sight and hearing. At the fourth level, including most of the more dynamically active and distinctive insects, the soul has access to four senses – touch, taste, smell and sight,

with the omission of hearing. At the third level, including the more lowly insects, the soul has three senses through which to experience the world – touch, taste and smell. At the second level, including worms and molluscs, the soul has only two senses at its disposal – touch and taste. At the first and lowest level of entry, the soul can rely only on touch. This level includes the whole of the plant kingdom and the elements of earth, air, fire and water.

From this list it becomes apparent why the Jain disciple cannot adopt or condone violent conduct towards other forms of life and why he or she must follow the path of *ahimsa*, including, for example, a strictly rationed vegetarian lifestyle, since even destroying plant life is injurious to the lowest grade of *jiva*. To a dedicated Jain disciple the highest motto may be *ahimsa paramo dharma*, meaning non-violence is the highest religious law, and it encapsulates the essence of a religion which demands total pacifism.

For a Jain monk or nun this pacifism and extreme respect for life takes on fundamental and day-to-day reality. Initiation (see p.124) includes making the *mahavratas* or 'Great Vows', of which there are five. These are designed to permit the disciple to achieve inner purity, but the machinery is focused. Essentially there is only one vow – that of non-violence – with the others arising from it:

1. To reject the killing of all forms of life and to repent and avoid violence, either administered directly or through encouragement to another. This must include care when moving about the countryside in order to avoid damage to living things, even down to diligence over where an alms bowl is laid and ensuring that no life forms are present in food and drink. The vow also necessitates a regulated 'retreat' during the four months of the rainy monsoon period when plant and animal life is at its most abundant and vulnerable, and the undertaking to control mind and speech lest they act to encourage violence.
2. To abstain from lies and false speech through deliberation and to reject anger, greed, fear and amusement.
3. To abstain from taking the property of others or 'not to take what has not been given'.
4. To abstain from all sexual conduct, mental or physical, by distancing oneself from any member of the opposite sex, avoiding impure thoughts and consumption of stimulants such as alcohol.
5. To renounce all material possessions and any objects which act upon the senses.

To these five has been added a sixth vow – to abstain from eating and drinking at night. A seemingly curious addition, it was included because to do otherwise would necessarily involve wandering about after dark seeking alms which would make it impossible properly to observe the first *mahavrata*.

MYTHOLOGY
AND
SYMBOLISM

*A*lthough Jainism is a non-theistic religion which rejects the belief in a divinity in the form of a single god or DEVAS constituting a pantheon, nonetheless it does recognize a divine presence, the PARAMATMAN, pervading the universe. The eminent Jain author Hemacandra, who lived from 1088–1172 and who was a member of the Svetambara sect, was willing to call PARAMATMAN 'god' and to argue that it is this omniscient being alone to whose total enlightenment the JINA aspires. He emphasized that in no way could this being be equated with any of the gods of Hinduism, who regularly demonstrated passions and worldly behaviour and were, therefore, thoroughly tainted with KARMA.

Officially Jainism rejects the entire notion of the Hindu pantheon but, seemingly in paradox, it has also permitted a mythology to develop, much of which clearly owes its origin to Hindu belief and the reality is that whilst it is vehemently antagonistic towards the sensual and sexually charged Shiva, it is more tolerant of Brahma and Vishnu. All but one of its sects allow the inclusion of statues of deities and demigods, standing in addition to the 24 *tirthankaras* or saints of Jainism, as focuses of worship within its temples.

⇒⊂

MYTHOLOGY OF ORIGINS

In respect of the teachers or *tirthankaras*, it claims a vast backward-projecting lineage almost all of whom lie wholly within the realm of myth. Although in historical reality Jainism began in north-eastern India in the sixth century BCE with the reformist ascetic Vardhamana, Jain mythology asserts that the movement extends to the origins of human existence and beyond. The overall history of the world is believed to be divided into aeons, in each of which the 'Wheel of Existence' makes either upward or downward turns, known respectively as *avasarpini* and *utsarpini*, and each aeon lies under the spiritual responsibility of 24 great enlightened teachers or *tirthankaras*. Mythical history, according to Jain tradition, is described in the 'Deeds of the Sixty-three Illustrious Men', or 'Universal History' as it is generally known, and it is without beginning or ending. Most is merely recognized, in passing, as a *fait accompli* but the current aeon is recorded in some detail and it identifies by name a succession of *tirthankaras* and their contemporaries. Thus Vardhamana is seen not as the founder of Jainism but merely the last in line of current succession. In this idea of a mythical succession of teachers Jainism shares a common belief with Buddhism.

In Jain mythology the *tirthankaras* are the only individuals who are able to break free from *samsara* and painful susceptibility to death and rebirth. Residing in the heavens, however, is an assortment of *devas* and their *shaktis* who *are* subject to *samsara*, many of whom owe their origins to Hinduism and were probably retained in order to boost the attraction of Jainism for potential Hindu converts.

Each *tirthankara* is ministered to by an assortment of retainers and messengers. Amongst these are attendant demi-gods known as *yaksas* who may have a protective or guardian function – the word literally means 'ghost' in Sanskrit – and who are included in a group known as the *vyantaradevatas*. They often appear as deformed dwarfs with pot-bellies and are registered in two somewhat divergent lists of 24, one being recognized by the Digambaras, the other by the Svetambaras (see p.120). In addition, the *tirthankaras* may also be attended by other celestial figures known *sasanadevatas*, which translates approximately as 'deities of government or order'. These are

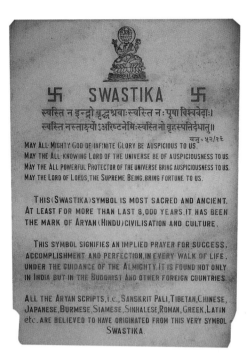

THE ANCIENT SYMBOL OF THE *SVASTIKA* SIGNIFIES AN IMPLIED PRAYER
FOR PERFECTION AND SUCCESS.

female counterparts of the *yaksas* and, as with the *yaksas*, the list of personalities detailed by the Digambara sect differs from that of the Svetambaras, although both sects account for 24 *sasanadevatas*.

Jainism has also adopted a number of mythical characters who bear strong resemblance to Hindu deities. They include a series of nine demi-gods known as *baladevas*, each of whom possesses the same attributes as the elder brother of Krishna, one of the most significant Hindu incarnations or avatars of Vishnu.

Another group of deities are the *bhavanavasi*, the 'dwelling in places', who possess the appearance of young men and who are separated into ten categories known as *asura-kumara, naga-kumara, suparnakumara, vayukumara, dvipa-kumara, udadhi-kumara, dik-kumara, vidyut-kumara, stanita-kumara* and *agni-kumara*. Several of these, again, resemble Hindu gods.

Jainism also shares with Hinduism and Buddhism the notion of deities who guard quarters of the sky. These are the *dikpalas* or 'Regents of Direction' whose role it is to protect the world against demons. In Jainism there are eight, known as the *astadikpalas,* whose number include the four guarding the compass points plus an additional four in the north-west, the north-east, the zenith and the nadir.

Some of the sets of *devas* are identified as having female aspects or *shaktis*, another tradition borrowed from Hinduism. Amongst the best known are the *astamataras* or 'Eight Mothers', listed as Brahmani, Mahesvari, Kaunari, Vaishnavi, Varahi, Indrani, Camunda and Tripura, most of whom can be easily identified with Hindu gods or their *avataras*.

Some groups of Jain deities, in contrast, have arisen quite independently of Hinduism. Amongst these are the *vyantaradevatas* mentioned above. They are lesser *devas* who attend on the more important gods and saints and whose number includes eight categories – *kinnara, kimpurusa, mahoraga, gandharva, yaksa, raksasa, bhuta* and *pisaca*.

SYMBOLISM

Hinduism, Buddhism and Jainism share similar symbols in their iconography. The *tirthankaras* display the familiar gesture of reassurance and fearlessness, the *abhayamudra*, where the right hand is displayed palm outwards and turned towards the worshipper with the fingers pointing upwards. The *cakra* or wheel symbolizes the spoked Wheel of the Law or *dharma*, often bearing eight spokes representing the Eightfold Path promoted by the *buddha* in his teachings. In addition, the *svastika* or angled cross, which is also a frequent talismanic symbol in Jainism, is common to all three religions as a lucky or auspicious object, although its interpretation may differ according to whether the angles of the cross turn clockwise or anticlockwise.

ONE OF EIGHT *ASTAMATARAS* HOLDS ATTRIBUTES OF CAMUNDA,
A FORM OF DURGA.

THE SECTS OF JAINISM

During the first two hundred years or so after the death of its founder, Mahavira, the Jain movement remained comparatively small and cohesive with its monastic communities restricted to the lower parts of the Ganges valley in Bihar state in north-eastern India. The movement had been effectively placed on a viable footing during his lifetime by the conversion of 11 BRAHMINS from Hinduism who became known as the GANADHARA and who were destined, after the death of Mahavira, to become the leaders of the ascetic Order of JINAS.

Towards the end of the fourth century BCE Jainism received a considerable boost to its popularity in the form of the conversion of the emperor Chandragupta (circa 321–297 BCE) who not only joined a monastic Order but abdicated his reign as the founder of the Mauryan dynasty in the northern Indian state of Magadha.

This coincided with a major famine in northern India which resulted in large parts of the population, including many Jain monks under the leadership of the *acarya* or teacher Bhadrabahu, emigrating south in search of food. Most became concentrated in Mysore. Meanwhile those elements of the Jain *sangha* communities which had remained in the north under the leadership of another *acarya*, Sthulabhadra, underwent a number of reforms away from the extremes of asceticism laid down by the founder. In particular they abandoned the practice of going naked and, probably from about the fifth century CE onwards, adopted a dress of white robes consisting of three simple garments.

WOMEN ARE MORE COMMONLY ACCEPTED IN THE MONASTIC ORDERS OF THE SVETAMBARAS OR 'WHITE CLAD'.

FORMAL DIVISION
INTO TWO SECTS

After some twelve years in Mysore the leader of the southern Jains returned to Bihar and found that the practices of the two communities had diverged considerably. In consequence it was decided that two sects effectively existed. These divisions were formalized at the Council of Valabhi which took place in the mid-fifth century CE and they have continued to the present day. At about that time in history the original *sangha* community in Bihar also migrated towards the western part of India where their main concentration developed and became permanently established in the Gujarat province. Those ascetic monks or *munis* living mainly in southern India, who follow the more austere discipline of Mahavira, and who have in the past gone naked, are known as the Digambaras, which means 'sky clad', whilst the other group, concentrated in Gujarat, the major sect in terms of numbers of devotees, are distinguished as the Svetambaras or 'white clad'.

Although there is some indication that Mahavira and his contemporaries went nude, it also appears that a certain latitude was allowed since at least two of the early texts, the *Acaranga* and the *Sthananga*, merely advise against wearing too many garments, suggesting that nudity during the summer months is a form of penance and indicating that a monk may wear clothes, voluntarily, to avoid embarrassment. Nowadays Digambaras do not go naked but wear coloured robes to distinguish them from the Svetambaras.

In terms of ideology the differences between the two groups are largely down to fundamentalism. According to tradition, the leader of the Digambaras, Bhadrabahu, was the only living *acarya* to have properly memorized the oral teachings of his founder which had been passed down from generation to generation but somehow became lost to other *acaryas* at the time of the schism. After Bhadrabahu's death, an attempt was made by pupils to write down these teachings and they were subsequently incorporated as the basis of a Jain

LIKE MAHAVIRA, WHOSE EXTREME ASCETICISM THEY FOLLOW, JAIN MONKS OF THE DIGAMBARA SECT MAY STILL GO NAKED.

canon. Ironically this canon was accepted by the more liberal Svetambaras but rejected by the Digambaras, who claimed that the resulting text was impossible to authenticate and, especially, that certain aspects were clearly apocryphal. In particular, they found themselves unable to accept the story of Mahavira's transference as an embryo from Devaki, his true mother, to the womb of Rohini, and his marriage to Yasoda, which contradicted their strict rule of celibacy.

For the Svetambaras such religious licences as taking reasonable nourishment and using the material comfort of an alms bowl were much more acceptable than to the Digambaras. Another major sectarian distinction lies in the recruitment of women nuns, given that there is overall a mysogynistic Jain view of female enlightenment. One of the cornerstones of Digambara belief lies in nakedness which, for both sects, has been regarded as unacceptable in women for social reasons. Thus, although there is evidence that Mahavira's *sangha* not only included women but that their numbers substantially outstripped those of men, female members of the Digambara community are discouraged and, today, there are less than 100 Digambara nuns. Women are more readily accepted into the Svetambara community.

The two major sects have not been at loggerheads with each other to the exclusion of mutual activity and there are records from the medieval period of Digambaras and Svetambaras going on joint pilgrimages. Furthermore, in spite of efforts to dislodge it, one of the holiest places of the Digambaras is a *tirtha* (see p.129) at Mount Girnar in Gujarat in the midst of Svetambara influence.

SUBDIVISIONS

Inevitably the large sects have attracted a welter of smaller divisions based on local practices and idiosyncrasies. In more recent times, however, the Svetambaras have become split with two more accountable ideological sub-divisions, the Sthanakavasis and Terapanthis, both of which deny the worship of icons. The majority of Jains, both Digambara and Svetambara, accept images in their temples and shrines but during the seventeenth century the Sthanakavasis, under the leadership of a merchant called Lavaji, decided to revert to the principles laid down in one of the old scriptural texts, the *Dasavaikalika*. This text details monastic rules, including the rejection of icon worship as an echo of Hindu theism. Some of their monastic community mounted an ideological rebellion during the nineteenth century and elected to break ranks, reverting to the image-worshipping ideals of the Svetambaras, but the Sthankavasis still maintain an identifiable presence in India. Recently there has been an attempt to reconcile their various splinter groups into a single, more cohesive body, but the proposal for a congress failed due to reticence about using microphones, since it was argued that there was a risk that they might damage small airborne forms of life.

The not-dissimilar Terapanth sect was founded in the eighteenth century by an *acarya* named Bhiksu, who originated from Rajasthan. Terapanthis share many of the ideological views of the Sthanakavasis, but the sect considers itself wholly autonomous. Bhiksu was originally influenced by a Sthankavasi teacher named Raghunathji but later distanced himself from the Sthankavasis, claiming that they were building liaisons with local business communities and power-broking families which conflicted with the true spirit of *ahimsa* (non-violence). Bhiksu maintained that strict adherence to the teachings of Mahavira was essential and that regular and severe fasting must be applied as part of the ascetic code. He took the arguments about the investment of souls in the lower forms of life literally and even developed rigorous rules about non-violence towards plant life. He also argued that the only merit in religious practice lay in that which was transcendental and that the entire purpose of non-violence was in the discipline which led to purification of the soul, rather than any strict sense of compassion for other life forms. Terapanthism is thus the most severe and extreme of all the Jain ideologies. Partly for this reason its activities carry a high public profile in the Indian press and media.

One of the most striking outward characteristics of both the Sthanakavasis and Terapanthis is the wearing of the *muhpatti* or 'mouth shield', a practice which seems to have originated sometime during the medieval period. The *muhpatti* is a square or rectangle of cloth which is permanently worn across the lower part of the face and tied behind the ears. It acts as a protective screen, though not in the sense of the veil worn by Islamic women but rather as a furtherance of *ahimsa* since it is designed to minimize injury or destruction of insects and other minute forms of life by filtering them from the air that is breathed in and out. Other Svetambaras own and wear the *muhpatti* but only to a limited extent, such as during readings from the religious texts and when preaching.

At least one sect, the Ajivikas or 'Followers of the Way of Life', which evolved from Jain origins is considered heretical. Its founder, Maskarin Gosala, was a contemporary of Mahavira and one of his pupils until he abandoned the teachings and led a break-away movement. He is attributed with having learned certain magical powers from Mahavira and given himself the spurious title of *jina*. It is alleged in the Jain orthodox texts that Gosala recanted before his death and acknowledged that Mahavira was the true spiritual *tirthankara*, but the Ajivika sect did not promptly fade away and there is evidence that in southern India its members were still active as late at the end of the thirteenth century CE. Its ideology remains vague since it left no doctrinal or canonical texts and there is some suspicion that its heretical nature was more attributable to orthodox Jain propaganda than real schism.

Eventually though he became an unofficial follower of the Digambara sect, having been deeply influenced by the writings of the early Jain philosopher Kundakunda, and in 1934 he broke with the Sthankavasis by publicly discarding his *muhpatti* during the *Mahavir Jayanti* festival. He reverted to the life of a Digambara layman, took up residence in the town of Songadh near Satrunjaya in Gujarat and began preaching as a Digambara *acarya* with an emphasis on the necessity for a true understanding of the nature of the soul in order to achieve enlightenment and freedom. Correct knowledge and practice could not function without this essential prerequisite.

In 1937 Kanji built the *Digambara Svadhyaya Mandir* temple complex in Songadh as his spiritual headquarters and as a religious educational establishment in which to house his fledgling *sangha*. He ordered that the sayings of Kundakunda be inscribed in gold leaf on the walls, claimed that in a previous incarnation he had lived as a contemporary and student of Kundakunda, and directed his disciples to follow the teachings of the ancient *acarya* since these, he argued, reflected the most valid commentary on the philosophies of Mahavira.

FOLLOWERS OF THE STHANAKAVASI AND TERAPANTH SECTS WEAR A *MUHPATTI* OR MOUTH SHIELD TO AVOID INHALING AND KILLING INSECTS.

MODERN DEVELOPMENTS

Amongst the most recent twentieth-century Jain sects is the Kanji Svami Panth. Kanji was an ascetic who had grown up in a Sthankavasi family and taken monastic initiation in 1913.

From the Songadh spiritual power-base Kanji proselytized his version of Digambara Jainism throughout much of India and achieved a popularity that is probably unparalleled elsewhere amongst the Jain communities. The sect has also successfully 'networked' within lay communities and built up substantial financial resources which it has reinvested, to an extent, in new temples. The Kanji Svami Panth may be said to represent the popular and liberalized face of a religion that otherwise displays an unprepossessing and austere image.

ASCETICISM AND RELIGIOUS DISCIPLINE

Jainism is a way of life closely identified with extreme forms of asceticism, particularly in its more advanced levels of adherence, and there is a popular image of the Jain monk, emaciated, dirty, seated and with the meditation pose of DHYANAMUDRA (both hands lying in the lap, palms up and fingers extended), symbolic of total absorption of thought.

Along the way to becoming a venerable teacher or *arhat* it is necessary, however, to pass through 14 stages of quality or *gunasthana*. According to the Jain canon the early stages are known as *ksullaka*, meaning 'small'. They approach their culmination with initiation as an ascetic, which opens the way to achieving the ultimate enlightenment through renunciation of all passions, destruction of *karma*, meditation and adoption of a life of extreme austerity.

WORSHIP AND MEDITATION

For lay persons and non-ascetics, worship includes, most importantly, *agrapuja* or 'Chief Worship' with the offering of fruit, rice, sweetmeats, incense and lamps before the images of the *tirthankaras*. As part of the ritual these icons may be smeared with a paste made from sandalwood which is the main ingredient of incense or *dhupa* and which is kept in a small metal bowl known as a *laghupatra*. Worship also includes *bhavapuja* or 'devotion through the disposition of the mind', demanding the chanting of praises in honour of the *tirthankaras* and meditation.

In common with most other eastern religions, meditation forms part of the way of life of the Jain disciple, whether monastic ascetic or lay person. Meditation is designed to focus the mind and to clear it of unwanted and obstructive emotions or passions, yet in Jainism meditation has different connotations. The contemplative Buddhist is concerned to channel the consciousness, whilst the Jain wishes only to empty the mind of all thoughts. It seems likely that at an early stage of Jainism there existed a more positive form of meditation to

A PLAQUE RECORDS THE NINE INVOCATIONS, KNOWN AS THE *NAVAPADA*, USED TO AID MEDITATION.

rid the body and mind of *karma* but it became part of the Jain argument that the mind was inextricably linked with the body and, therefore, *any* mental activity carried considerable risk. Jains did not, in the past, put forward any coherent solutions about how to control the mind against its instinctive wanderings and therefore they have tended to place meditation as a secondary discipline, with more emphasis on devotional activities and fasting.

There is, however, a certain reliance on the utterance of *mantras* and *bijamantras* in order to achieve tranquillity and gain benefit from their magical powers. Jain *mantras* are composed in Prakrit, the Sanskrit-related dialect of the ancient texts and the whole *mantra* system in Jainism fits into an abstract pattern known as the *navapada* or 'Nine Stages' which is based on the *siddha* 'Wheel of Perfection', a spoked device like a Hindu *cakra* that symbolizes the 24 *tirthankaras*. The best known of the Jain *mantras* is the *paramesthimantra* or 'Teacher *mantra'*, also referred to as the *pancanamaskara* or 'Five Homages', and is addressed to the five central figures of Jain asceticism, the superior or chief gods known as the *paramesthins*. It is repeated daily: *namo Arihantanam, namo Siddhanam, namo Ayariyanam, namo Uvajjhayanam, namo loe savva-Sahunam*, meaning 'Hail to the *arhats*, hail to the perfect ones, hail to the masters, hail to the teachers, hail to all the monks of the world'. Other *mantras* are used in more specific circumstances. A ceremony known as *santi* requires, for example, the utterance of several *bijamantras* referring to different parts of the body in order to suppress the physical senses.

DUTIES OF THE LAY PERSON

For Jain lay persons, whose overall discipline is less far-reaching than for ascetics, there are six obligatory duties or *avasyaka* which must be performed each day in the form of ritual. These not only demand a regular confirmation of the Jain disciple's devotion and rejection of harm to other forms of life but also provide a common form of ritual binding together of the monkish and lay arms of Jainism. The obligations include *samayika*, the restraint of equanimity, *caturvinsatijinastuti*, the act of praising the *tirthankaras*, *vandana* or reverence to the *guru* or teacher, *pratikramana* or repentance, *kayotsarga* or laying down the body, and *pratyakhyana* or abandonment.

In more detail, *samayika* involves standing motionless for a period of time, conventionally set at 48 minutes, during which all binding emotions and thoughts are suppressed and a sense of benevolence to all living creatures is advanced. The act of praising the *tirthankaras* is believed to be an aid to liberation from *karma*, the activity which binds one to *samsara*, the Wheel of Life. The act of homage to the teacher is a largely ritualized act requesting forgiveness and asking after his welfare. At the core of *avasyaka* is repentance which, for the ascetic, must be

COCONUTS, BANANAS AND OTHER FRUIT ARE AMONGST THE OFFERINGS THAT FORM PART OF JAIN WORSHIP.

A Jain monk rests on the steps of Sitambra temple in Calcutta.

performed twice daily before the teacher and is generally preceded by *alocana* which translates more or less accurately as an 'acknowledgement of faults', not so much a confession in the Christian sense but a promise to strive harder towards proper conduct. The ritual of *pratikramana* includes the recitation of six formalized expressions of fault and includes repentance for injury caused to any living thing, however inadvertent, since each life form possesses a soul. So an insect or even a green plant crushed by a passing footfall will require an apology. The Jain declares: *I ask pardon from all living creatures. May all creatures pardon me. May I show friendship to all creatures and enmity towards none.*

Kayotsarga requires the disciple to assume a prescribed standing posture, motionless with the arms extended straight down though not touching the sides of the body, and it is intended to symbolize the life of austerity. This attitude is the familiar one in which *tirthankaras* are depicted in Jain iconography. The final obligatory action, *pratyakhyana*, is a further undertaking to abandon, in the future, those weaknesses and faults which were repented in the sense of action past, in *pratikramana*.

THE ASCETIC'S LIFESTYLE

Those students of Jainism who pursue the more basic teachings with total dedication are destined to become members of the ascetic community, the *sangha* of would-be *jinas*. The mendicant members of the *sanghas*, like those of Buddhist monasteries and nunneries are known, respectively, as *bhiksu* and *bhiksuni*. The male members are also referred to as *munis* and their female counterparts are *sadhvis*, but although they are loosely defined as monks and nuns they do not live in monastic establishments. By contrast most are homeless and live out their lives as wandering mendicants, answering to their tutor monk or *sripujya* and becoming involved with the lay community, although they may also stay temporarily in cult centres or refuges known as *upasrayas*, particularly during the monsoon season. This period of retreat is known as *caturmas*. Those Jains who live permanently in temple environments are termed *yatis* and are not considered ascetics.

For the monk, the lifestyle demanded by Mahavira is severe. In order to achieve the level of ascetic an individual is required to abandon all possessions and family ties and to possess a deep spiritual commitment. The ascetic directs the following confirmation to the teacher: *I perform the rite of equanimity, I abandon all improper activity for the span of my life, threefold by threefold, in mind, body and speech. I undertake not to perform, nor approve of anybody else who performs, any improper action. I repent of it, Master, I censure, reject and abandon myself.* In modern times it has been recognized that this can involve considerable distress to a family and some Svetambara sect teachers now demand an agreement from the person's next of kin before initiating them.

Jain initiation is known as *diksa*, a term whose roots imply self-sacrifice, although the principles of sacrifice as such are rejected and it is also to be seen as the shedding of old ties to enable a bonding with new ones within the community of ascetics. There is, incidentally, some evidence that young women may enter a Jain community in order to avoid commitment to a conventional secular marriage.

The rite of initiation takes place after a probationary period that can last from a month to two years and varies between the Digambara and Svetambara sects, that of the latter being a more complicated affair. Digambara initiates bid goodbye to their families, cast off their clothes, tear out their hair, take the solemn vows of *ahimsa* or non-violence, accept a new name and are given their only permitted material possessions, a whisk and a water jar, after being adorned with religious symbols including the angled cross or *svastika*.

Once initiated the Jain disciple is committed to an ascetic life aimed at eliminating *karma* and thus liberating the soul, by controlling and subduing the material senses. This is achieved only through adherence to great austerity and restraint, coupled with intense mental discipline. The mendicant Jain ascetic confirms *avasyaka* on a daily basis but is also committed to keeping the Great Vows taken at initiation, which are more far-reaching. Austerity does not mean, however, that the Jain ascetic lives as a recluse shut off from outside influences and avoiding the lay community. On the contrary, with missionary and preaching activities, the mendicant monk or nun goes out to meet the secular world whilst at the same time retaining the strict principles of the vows. This intense discipline is helped in several practical ways, through three restraints and five more positive actions.

Gupti (The Three Concealments)

The word translates as 'protected' or 'hidden' and this is a general self-discipline which refers to self-restraint concerning three distinct aspects of personal existence, the mind, the body and the speech, since the unguarded or overt use of any may result in a failure to uphold the Vows.

Samiti (The Five Careful Actions)

This translates as 'effort' and the actions are more specific. The first *iryasamita* or 'care in motion' is a clear elaboration on the principle of the Great Vows to avoid damaging other living things, through using great diligence whilst walking about, and to avoid any other action which is violent, or could result in, violence. The second requires control of speech to avoid harsh or thoughtless words and to maintain reasonable sobriety since excessive merriment is regarded as an undesirable demonstration of emotion.

The third *iryasamita* requires careful selection of food provided as alms so that the disciple does not consume anything containing meat or animal products. The fourth requires that the ascetic takes great care when placing objects on the ground in order that no small life forms are damaged through inadvertent violence. The fifth requires the same diligence towards the well-being of small creatures before defecating on the ground.

To assist the monk in avoiding damage to living things he may carry a *khakkhara*, otherwise known as a 'beggar's staff'. This device includes a number of metal rings attached to a long wooden handle which strike each other, making a loud noise, and it has been used both to announce the presence of a begging mendicant and to warn animals of the approach of a monk so that he may avoid harming them inadvertently.

The most extreme and final conduct of the Jain ascetic is that of *samlekhana* or *sallekhana*, the so-called 'religious death', which Jain philosophy vehemently denies is an act of suicide since the latter involves an emotionally charged state of mind and reliance either on equipment or a deliberate and positive act such as drowning or jumping from a bridge. *Samlekhana* involves self-mortification through passivity, by voluntary denial of food. The disciple literally and deliberately starves to death in a controlled manner. The argument for this method of dying is that the soul is freed from all the negative factors imposed by the body and its needs, and is able to focus wholly on the spiritual quest in the final months and days of life. The act is also known as *samthara* or the 'death bed'.

Until about the twelfth century CE there is historical evidence that from time to time lay members of the Jain community practised *samlekhana*, but from that period onwards the incidence was largely restricted to the monastic community. When the practice was at its height, particularly amongst Svetambara disciples, it was considered the ideal way for an individual at the peak of mental and physical abilities to end their bodily life, but as time went on it became an extreme act restricted more to elderly members of the *sangha* community. *Samlekhana* is still continued, however, and there are records that as recently as 1989 a Jain nun starved herself to death at the age of 87.

FESTIVALS
AND
PILGRIMAGES

*A*lthough having an essentially monastic appearance, Jainism embraces a substantial lay following both inside and, particularly, outside India. So, not least in order to maintain links with the secular world, it follows an extensive diary of seasonal festivals which are usually based on some person or event from the movement's history.

MAJOR FESTIVALS

The most important of the public events that take place during the Jain religious year coincide with the end of the monsoon season and its accompanying retreat known as *caturmas*. Each of the major sects, the Digambaras and Svetambaras, hold celebrations which are, respectively, the festivals of Dasalaksanaparvan and Paryusan. The first in the calendar is the Paryusan or Festival of Abiding which spans eight days in the year of Svetambara monks and which is centred on the recitation of the *Kalpa-sutra* of Bhadrabahu. This is a venerated

MAHAVIR JAYANTI, MARKING THE BIRTHDAY OF MAHAVIRA, CULMINATES IN A PROCESSION AND IS CELEBRATED BY BOTH MAJOR SECTS.

scripture which relates the life of Mahavira and, briefly, that of other *tirthankaras*, including Rishabha, Nemi and Parsva. It provides an authoritative source for ascetics concerning ritual or *kalpa*. During the festival all lay members of the Jain community are urged to live the life of an ascetic for at least one day but, overall, Paryusan includes fasting and confession and ends with a communal declaration of remorse about injury to living creatures during the previous period and a request for forgiveness. On the day following the festival the local communities get together for a modest thanksgiving meal.

Dasalaksanaparvan, which means Festival of Ten Religious Qualities and which lasts for ten days, is held by the Digambara sect shortly after Paryusan but omits recitation of the *Kalpa-sutra* since this constitutes a Svetambara scripture that is not recognized as authentic. Instead it relies on the *Tattvartha-sutra* composed by the philosopher Umasvati. This falls into ten chapters, one for each day of the festival, and these deal with forbearance, gentleness, uprightness, purity, honesty, restraint, austerity, renunciation, abandonment of material possessions and chastity. Towards the end of the festival, devotees undergo a period of fasting followed by *kasmapana* or 'Asking for Pardon'.

The Jain festivals are marked by their sobriety and lack of colour and in this they contrast sharply with those of Hindus. Jains strictly shun any Hindu celebrations, such as the spring rite of Holi, which possess sexual undertones. Even the Mahavir Jayanti, which marks the birthday of Mahavira in March or April, and which is incidentally the only festival held concurrently by both major sects, involves fasting and confession and its sole concession to festivity is a procession at the close.

The Jain religious year ends with a celebration of the equivalent of the Hindu Diwali or Festival of Lights which marks the moment when death and final liberation from *samsara* came to Mahavira and which takes place in mid-October. It also more or less coincides with the Buddhist commemoration of the enlightenment of Gautama Buddha and includes *puja* (see p.96), though it is not a widely observed fast. Tradition has it that the local rulers in the states of the Ganges plain where Mahavira had travelled, lit lamps to symbolize the enlightenment that accompanied his earthly death.

Other significant festivals include those which honour the scriptures and which include dusting, repairing and updating holy books. The Digambaras celebrate Srutapancami or Scripture Fifth in May/June, so-called because it is held on the fifth day of the Indian month of Jyestha. Similarly, the Svetambaras hold their Jnanapancami or Knowledge Fifth, its title derived from the *Jnanapancamikatha* scripture of Mahesvara, on the fifth day of the Indian month of Karttika, which bridges October/November. The Svetambaras also celebrate a Day of Silence in November/December which is devoted to calm contemplation and inward prayer.

PILGRIMAGE TO HOLY PLACES

Some of the festivals are linked with holy places or *tirthas* of Jain tradition. They therefore involve pilgrimages which are undertaken by monks and lay Jains alike and which attract considerable attendance as devotional 'days out'. That of Aksayatritaya, which commemorates the enlightenment of the first *tirthankara*, Rishabha, and which takes place in April/May, includes visits to one of several *tirthas*. Mount Satrunjaya in Gujarat is recognized as the holiest Svetambara *tirtha* in India and is one of five holy mountains. Tradition claims that Satrunjaya was visited by Rishabha and that his grandson, Pundarika, and his son, Bharata, died there. In a curious mixing of traditions it is also the place where the five Pandava heroes of the Hindu *Mahabharata* epic achieved salvation. A temple, dedicated to Rishabha's attendant *sasanadevata*, Cakresvari, stands with others at the summit.

Other ancient and holy places, dedicated to Rishabha, include Abhanagari in the Jaipur district of Rajasthan, Mount Abu in the Sirohi district, and Ayodhya, an ancient town in northern India which also has great religious significance for Hindus.

Other pilgrimages honouring *tirthankaras* take place from time to time to Jain holy sites across India.

HOLY SITES OFTEN FORM THE FOCUS FOR FESTIVALS.

MODERN JAINISM

*T*oday Jainism claims a membership in India of about three and a quarter million, whilst beyond the sub-continent there exists an additional following of rather less than a million whose SANGHAS have become established in Europe, North America, Africa and, to a lesser extent, elsewhere in Asia. But the fortunes of Jainism fluctuate and during more than two and a half millennia of its existence it has enjoyed a see-saw popularity.

After a medieval period marked by persecution, Jainism became more peaceably established in the two main areas where it remains dominant today, in Gujarat and Rajasthan in western India (predominantly Svetambara), and in Mysore further south in the Deccan region (predominantly Digambara). Traditionally a highly conservative movement, Jainism in these places has reformed very little in modern times although there has been some attempt to move from a strongly ascetic focus to one which favours the lay membership. In south India in the twentieth century there has been a policy of school building within Jain communities, though this appears to have been as much concerned with transmitting traditional Jain values as with broadening the scope of secular education.

JAINISM'S INFLUENCE ON MAHATMA GANDHI

Its doctrine of *ahimsa* or non-violence has attracted some notable figures, not least amongst whom was Mahatma Gandhi, the spiritual leader and politician to whom are attributed the most far-reaching modern social reforms India has known. He promoted its peaceful principles throughout his life although, ironically, his devotion to them contributed to his assassination.

JAINISM IS FLOURISHING IN PARTS OF INDIA TODAY.

Gandhi was a lifelong Hindu and was concerned to preserve his faith as a way of life. He was deeply influenced by the *Bhagavad Gita* which he regarded as an allegory on the struggle between personal aspirations and divinely ordained duty, but certain aspects of Jainism appealed to him greatly and he modelled much of his lifestyle on its ethic of non-violence. Originating from Gujarat province, where Jainism exerts its greatest influence, Mohandas Karamchand Gandhi was born in 1869 at Porbandhar and in his youth he formed a brief but highly impressionable relationship with the Jain mystic, Srimad Rajacandra whom he met in Bombay in 1891 after his return from law school in England. Two years older than Gandhi, Rajacandra grew up with a Hindu father whilst his mother was a practising Jain so his view was somewhat catholic — a point that was probably not lost on Gandhi who had by then developed a keen interest in other religions, including Christianity, and had even dabbled with atheism.

Gandhi was a firm advocate of the caste system, although he also believed that the 'outcastes' of India whom he called the *harijan* or 'God's People' should be accepted as the fifth caste and he fought passionately for their rights. Rajacandra, schooled into a rigid caste observance, urged him to observe the duties and obligations of his merchant caste as 'a necessary

130

THE JAIN DOCTRINE OF NON-VIOLENCE IS EVIDENCED BY THIS HOSPITAL FOR THE CARE OF BIRDS IN DELHI.

adjunct to correct moral behaviour' but at the same time to pursue asceticism and the non-violent Jain ethics of *ahimsa* and this was advice that Gandhi seems to have followed closely.

Having spent time in South Africa, where he had experienced racial discrimination at first hand, Gandhi developed a community or *ashram*, based on truth, love and passive resistance, which became known as the Satyagraha *sangha*. To these principles he added the discipline of non-violence which had been expounded to him by Rajacandra in Bombay. He also regularly indulged in periods of starvation which approached self-mortification or *samlekhana* and whilst he believed in their efficacy for purification and redemption of the soul there is little doubt that he also used them to his political advantage. Much of his celebrity status in the west is attributable to these well-publicized 'fasts to the death' in passive protest against British imperialism and Islamic encroachment on Hinduism.

DEVELOPMENT OUTSIDE INDIA

In spite of its austere image Jainism has been exported to various other parts of the world. At the end of the nineteenth century immigrant groups of Svetambaras, usually bonded by caste, moved to East Africa to begin new lives and eventually the sect built temples at various sites in Kenya, including Nairobi and Mombasa. It is said that these emigré devotees today understand little of the true concepts of Jainism and their devotional practices are largely carried out to maintain a link with their former homeland and its traditions. There is no monastic community because Svetambara ascetics are not permitted to travel beyond the borders of India, and lay members abroad adopt more liberal attitudes including a tolerance of eating meat.

Parts of the East African community migrated again, during the 1960s and 1970s, setting up small communities in Britain and other parts of Europe, again based on caste links. In England the most prominent cell was established in Leicester where it evolved into a community association in 1973 and within 10 years had set up similar nuclei in European countries. These communities are significantly different from those established in India because of the absence of ascetic monks with whom they would otherwise interact. They have tended to become 'westernized' in their attitudes, whilst maintaining those aspects of orthodox Jainism which are deemed logical within a technologically sophisticated modern environment. They extol the virtues of vegetarianism, non-violence and frequent meditation.

Jains follow approximately the gloomy Hindu view of the future, envisaging a continuing downward spiral in the quality of human life until the remnants of population live in caves and scavenge for food. The apocalypse will come, they believe, with a global fiery holocaust, then, with the world cleansed of its old taints, the new aeon will begin. The Wheel will renew its upward cycle and Mahapadma, the first of the next succession of 24 *tirthankaras,* will be born.

CHINESE PHILOSOPHY

*C*hinese understanding of the world and its spirituality has, in common with that of other cultures, stemmed from ancient traditions of animism and shamanism. During the course of thousands of years it has been moulded not only by the diversity of the country and the wide variety of its people but by the effect of alien religions, most particularly Mahayana Buddhism. The Chinese mind is both enquiring and open to fresh ideas and, therefore, beliefs have emerged with a somewhat cosmopolitan flavour. Nonetheless what evolved down the centuries has remained quintessentially Chinese.

China's native belief is known as Taoism, which may be summed up as the 'Way', the achievement of understanding of the absolute essence pervading the universe. Like Buddhism, Taoism is not merely a religious belief, it is also a philosophy. China has nurtured some of the world's most outstanding minds, amongst whom Lao Tzu, Confucius and Mencius are some of the best known. They have paved the way to advancements in art, philosophy and science which have exerted a profound influence on western culture, yet Chinese beliefs also include elements that would seem anachronistic in a modern western cultural setting – alchemy, divination, talismanic magic and ancestor worship. Taoism also maintains a strong focus on the promotion of longevity and good health.

The cultural process is an ongoing one. Both Taoism and the Chinese mentality encourage cross-fertilization of ideas, and Taiwan in particular has also seen an upsurge of interest in western religions and philosophies. Whilst in the past Hinduism and Buddhism have exerted a profound effect on religious trends on the mainland, it is predictable that western ideologies will penetrate there to a greater extent as liberalization continues. Travelling the opposite route, philosophical Taoism, and particularly the *I Ching*, has also aroused considerable recent interest, along with Zen Buddhism, in the west.

THE
BEGINNINGS
OF CHINESE
RELIGION

he earliest religion in China evolved in prehistoric times in the so-called era of the Sage Kings and so only the scantest detail is known of its belief and practice. Any evidence that might have existed for archaeology to unearth has not apparently survived the passage of time and so it lives on largely in myth and legend.

It is known only that the religion was based on nature and the seasonal cycles and, in common with early Vedic Hinduism and the Magi-based beliefs of ancient Persia, it recognized a pantheon of deities or nature spirits and practised animal sacrifice as the principal means of invoking and appeasing its gods. It lost popularity, in effect, because it had not evolved and developed a religious philosophy capable of satisfying the up-and-coming intellectual breed of Chinese who appeared in about the seventh or sixth century BCE, among whom was the great pioneering mind of Confucius.

AT THE MERCY OF THE RIVER

This early religion was animistic, typical of tribal hunters who have not yet developed agricultural techniques and who are often nomadic, following wild herds of animals and living in temporary camps. Archaeology records that at some time during the third century BCE such people first inhabited the flood plain adjacent to the Huang He, the 'Yellow River' which runs its muddy course through northern China past modern

HUANG HE, THE 'YELLOW RIVER', IN TRANQUIL MOOD.

Beijing. If an earlier indigenous population existed in China it has left little or no record of its passing. It is known that the immigrant tribes hunted and fished, then began to husband small domesticated herds of animals and eventually to plant and grow simple cereal crops of millet and wheat, but their harsh existence would have been dominated constantly by the river and its vagaries. Beyond its alluvial plain the country of northern China becomes a cold, windy and dry plateau which would have been virtually uninhabitable for people with such limited resources, so the settlers were committed to life along the river banks with all its attendant dangers. Once called 'China's Sorrow' because of its toll on human life, in the twentieth century the catastrophic power of the Huang He has been only partially ameliorated by the installation of modern flood barriers.

The early tribal settlers would have revered the Huang He as a deity and would have formulated a religion based on the river, the wild animals and plants which inhabited its banks and, above their heads, the presence of the sun by day and the moon and stars in the night sky. In this they would have shared a common view of nature and its spirituality with other primitive tribes the world over.

SHAMANISM

Within this environment shamanistic beliefs developed. A primitive tribesman generally sees the world as having both earthly and spirit form. He comes to an understanding that his own being has a twofold nature and he applies this logic to the rest of nature so that every living thing possesses a personal psyche capable of overcoming the hurdle of death. The logic goes a stage further, however, and argues that everything, animate and inanimate, is part of a huge and constantly varying chain. Each object in nature is a link in the chain but the links are fluid and can drift one into another. This means that nothing seen or felt through the senses is necessarily what it seems. It is possible for a mountain to be a sleeping deity, for a cloud to become a bird, for a stick to become a serpent, all according to the whims of the spirit guardians. Everything is at the disposal of the spirit world and one of its members may, in an instant, become a rock, a tree, a raging flood, a sighing breeze or a morning mist.

This belief that life exists in all aspects of the natural world and that everything which exists has feelings and powers is the essence of animism and it is regulated through the discipline of shamanism, the 'touchstone' of which is that if a spirit is offended by some human action it must be placated by a member of the tribe equipped for the purpose. If it is likely to be offended by some future action, an insurance premium must be paid to guard against its hidden powers, and the placation and the insurance premium alike are generally met through ritual and sacrifice.

To the Wu hunter-gatherers of ancient China the spiritual powers of the river and the animals they hunted must have been highly significant. To kill a bear, a deer or a fish would have risked bringing down the wrath of its spirit guardian. There was also the additional risk of slaughtering something or someone disguised as the prey! Thus a strong spiritual chemistry developed between hunter and hunted, river and settler, and a correct relationship between man and the animal world around him became fundamental to life.

Amongst the most important rites to a hunter-gatherer is that of sacrifice, which is envisaged as satisfying two related needs. Although it may appear to be an excuse for wild bloodletting there is a more profound reasoning behind the ritualized killing of an animal. It is, in part, a sincere effort to appease the spirits with offerings of life and food. The spirit world of the hunters is believed to possess essentially similar needs to that of human beings in as much as it eats, drinks, sleeps, has sexual intercourse, goes to the lavatory and experiences a gamut of similar emotions to our own – pleasure, sorrow, benevolence, aggression, triumph and fear. Many early societies develop myths explaining that the spirits placed us on the earth for little more reason than to provide labour and sustenance for a pantheon which has become tired of doing its own menial chores.

There is, however, another function to sacrifice which the early hunters and fishermen living beside the Huang He probably recognized. There is a belief that ritual slaughter is a formal enactment of the climax of the hunt and that by creating it in a controlled and reverential setting it is possible to minimize the potential dangers of the 'real thing'. There exists a genuine concern that without proper ritual, the bear or water buffalo in its next life will seek revenge against the hunters who are setting out to take its life.

It was from these simple beginnings that Taoism, the great religion and philosophy of China, was to take shape.

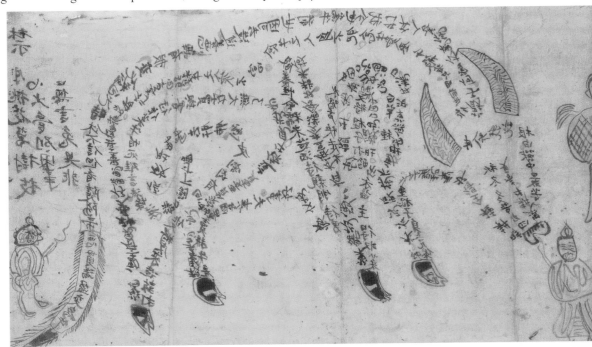

A NINETEENTH-CENTURY DEPICTION OF A WATER BUFFALO, COMPOSED OF A POEM AND SURROUNDED BY THREE TAOIST PRIESTS.

THE WU PRIESTHOOD

*T*he religious fraternity of ancient China was that of the Wu priesthood but unfortunately, for reasons which have been explained, remarkably little is known of its beliefs and practices. The word WU means shaman, the earliest style of priest, seer and magician who is characteristic of the religious beliefs of hunter-gatherers. This is usually a member of the tribe who possesses an above-average intellect and is reputed to have supernatural abilities.

The shaman sees that which ordinary people are unable to see and has the mental agility to transmit these inner visions into words and actions. It is the shaman who mediates with the spirit world and with the birds, animals and trees but who also claims certain mastery over the natural world by magical means. It was the Wu shaman who provided the only defence against the damaging caprices of the Huang He river, who underwrote the fortunes of the hunt, and who interceded against blight, famine, infertility and human sickness, all of which were brought about at the hands of the spirits.

SHAMANS OF LEGEND

The legendary archetypal shaman of China was a tribal chief named Shun who, it is said, learned his arts from the daughter of an unnamed predecessor. The most celebrated ancestor amongst the Wu priesthood, however, came from the succeeding generation and was named Yu. According to tradition his father was also a shaman, named Kun, who was given the ill-fated responsibility by Shun of interceding with the spirits to control the seasonal inundation of the Huang He plain. The river flood was devastating crops, herds and the human population alike. When Kun failed in his task he was slaughtered and his corpse left on a hilltop as an offering to placate the spirits of the river. Unbeknown to the tribe, however, Kun was carrying a son inside his body and thus he remained, lifeless, for three years until the spirits restored him in the form of a bear. With his claws he ripped his belly open and gave birth to Yu and tradition has it that, throughout his life, Yu constantly shifted shape between human and bear. Even when in human guise the shaman often exhibited bearlike traits in his movements and subsequently, for hundreds of years at least, until the later part of the Chou Dynasty in the third century BCE, priests were dressed in bearskins and adopted the shuffling gait of a bear.

Yu is said to have succeeded in taming the waters of the Huang He and causing them to abate because he had access to a secret text containing magical formulae and known as the *Shui-ching* or Book of Power over Waters.

It is believed that, through his communication with the spirit world and with animals, Yu was privy to the secrets of the universe and that these were revealed to him in the patterns on the back of tortoise described as the *Lo-shu pa-k'ua*. From this occult knowledge were derived the divinatory arts of later Taoism. As a great tribal shaman, Yu was believed to be able to fly to the heavens to communicate with the celestial spirits and this passage was achieved by Yu and his successors through a dance, probably assisted by hallucinogenic drugs creating a state of ecstatic trance, and known as the Steps of Yu. The dance includes a number of components, the first of which, the Steps of the Celestial Ladder, transports the shaman to the sky. The next is a spiral dance which starts at the periphery of a circle and moves clockwise, gradually turning towards the centre, and represents a journey from the outer margins of the galaxy towards the Pole Star. This series of steps has been emulated by Taoist priests and followers of the martial arts in China down to the present day.

THE ROLE OF THE PRIESTS

From these beginnings and the activities of the mythical Yu, a class arose in ancient China known as the *wu* priesthood, whose magical and occult attributes were claimed to be as powerful as those of their archetypal founder.

The religion of Wu was effectively abandoned throughout large parts of China during the Chou Dynasty when the feudal structure of society also broke down. It is, however, from the Chou period that the activities of the Wu priests are largely recorded in texts. This was a time of change, with constant warring between factions before the country was split up into more stable small kingdoms, but it was also a period of Chinese history when philosophy began to flourish. The impact of Confucianism made the primitive beliefs of the shamanistic society appear passé and they became largely redundant, although the old religion persisted in parts of the south-east, particularly in the three ancient kingdoms of Wu, Ch'u and Yueh, centred on the Yang-tze valley and its estuary. This region was considered rustic by the more sophisticated northerners and it retained many elements of shamanism in its beliefs and religious activities. Some of the elements were to find their way into the Taoism which came in the wake of the Wu religion.

The *wu* priests were deeply involved in divination, reading omens, making predictions about the course of events and advising on whether activities were or were not auspicious. They were also called on to interpret dreams which were considered to be messages sent directly from the spirit world, cast out demons from the sick through administration of herbal remedies, and curb the excesses of nature be they in the form of tempest, flood or drought. In the latter respect rain-making was, and still is, an important

A TAOIST PRIEST OUTSIDE THE SHANGQING GONG TEMPLE AT THE TOP OF QINGCHENG MOUNTAIN.

function of the priest in China, a country regularly plagued by long periods without rain. The priest also took on the duty of encouraging the spirits to visit the temporal world and take temporary residence within his mortal frame. This spiritual occupation was manifest in various ways, including ecstatic trance, unintelligible mutterings, spasmodic movements and more regulated dancing.

THE
TAOIST
PANTHEON

China is a vast country with a history extending back over thousands of years. Before the time of its unification under the Ch'in Dynasty, which followed that of Chou, it was fragmented into a number of independent states. It also experienced influences from many other cultures, both before and after its unification.

Not least because of the complexity of its background, the gods and goddesses who staff the celestial Chinese heavens are of mixed race and origin. They have stemmed from its old indigenous nature religion of Wu, from the more sophisticated Taoist concepts of a celestial population, and from imported elements of Hinduism and Buddhism. Under the Taoist heaven, irrespective of the origins of its deities, the earthly population was governed by a court, at the head of which stood the 'Jade Emperor', Yu Huang, and the 'Empress of the West', Hsi Wang Mu. That the Taoist deities retained their seats of power is a remarkable achievement , in some respects, since many of the Chinese emperors were strong patrons of Buddhism and it indicates the extent to which Taoists were prepared to adapt their own religion and amalgamate certain elements in order to make the overall doctrine politically acceptable.

The broad span of Taoist mythology, which developed in parallel to the Confucian philosophy, came to pervade all aspects of life in China before religious belief was suppressed under Communism. The make-up of the pantheon and its personalities is seen as equating to that of an earthly government, so the Jade Emperor employs a Prime Minister, named Kuan Yu, and a host of lesser ministers, each responsible for their own areas of administration. They, in turn, rule over bureaucracies down to the level of local celestial administrators and city gods. Each profession and every trade enjoys its patron

deity and, at the domestic level, each family has its image of Tsao Chun, the Kitchen or Stove God.

The names given to Chinese deities may seem confusing since an individual described both in history and in myth may be allotted more than one name. Part of this complexity is due to the convention of substituting the family and given names of a mortal personality with a celestial name or, in the case of emperors, by his 'reign name' once they become deified. The last emperor of the Shang Dynasty is named, historically, Chou Hsin, but after his deification he becomes Chou Wang, where Wang means 'king'. Likewise the warrior hero who fights against him in the earthly Battle of Mu is named Fa Ch'ang, but in his immortal form as one of the mythical characters in the Battle of Ten Thousand Spirits, he becomes Wu Wang. Names may also be spelled differently as English attempts to match the Chinese sounds, according to whether the Wade-Giles or the less familiar Pinyin systems are followed. Under the more modern Pinyin standards Peking thus becomes Beijing. Most of the mythological characters are probably better known by the Wade-Giles anglicization and so this is the form adopted here.

THE CELESTIAL HIERARCHY

Chinese mythology recognizes two categories of deity according to whether they have existed from the beginning, since before the formation of the cosmos, or whether they are individuals who have once lived on earth but been granted immortality because of their exemplary conduct. The first category are known as the Earlier Deities of Heaven and the others as the Later Deities of Heaven. The spectrum of celestial beings, with their antagonists in the form of demons and *kuei* or foreign devils, is interwoven with an essential principle of Taoism that two opposing forces exist in the universe, *yin* and *yang*, and that these create a dynamic tension which results from the one balancing the other (see p.180).

A TENTH-CENTURY PAINTING FOUND IN DUNHUANG CAVES SHOWING THE DEITY KUAN YIN BEING WORSHIPPED BY THE PAINTING'S DONOR.

is also described as Yuan Shih T'ien Tsun, the god of time. Ling Pao T'ien Tsun, the god of the sacred spirit, occupies the Great Pure Realm of T'ai Ch'ing. The third member of the triad, Tao Te T'ien Tsun, the god of virtue, lives in the Azure Palace of High Purity, Shang Ch'ing.

Beneath these beings, illustrious but largely remote from the lives of earth-bound people, come the Jade Emperor, Yu Huang, also known as Shang Ti or Yu Ti, and the Empress of the Western Heaven, Hsi Wang Mu, both of whom are more closely involved with the human condition and its fate (see p.144).

DEITIES OF CREATION

In terms of creation mythology of the more material kind, the god P'an Ku stands as the mythical embodiment of the universe, an improbably dwarfish figure wearing a leaf skirt or a bearskin. Engendered by himself within a cosmic egg floating in the void, he grew over a period of 18,000 years at a rate of 6 feet a day, hacking out the structure of the universe as his frame expanded until one day he was able to smash the eggshell. When it broke, its two halves formed heaven and earth and the light flooded in. From the body of P'an Ku came the structure of the world: his head formed the mountains, his teeth and bones the rocks, his eyes the sun and moon, and his breath the winds, whilst the stars hung suspended in his beard.

A few highly revered deities in the Taoist pantheon can be seen to have made their way from India via Buddhist missionaries. Kuan Yin, the 'Hearer of Cries', who derives from the Buddhist *bodhisattva* Avalokitesvara, is a benign guardian goddess of great popularity, although she is not provided with normal offerings of food and wine by Taoists. Her name is invoked if danger threatens and she is also a goddess of fertility to whom newly-weds pray for children. Introduced into China as a male deity, her change of sex was undertaken between about 600 and 1100 CE. Some authors claim that she is a manifestation of the goddess Tou Mu, the 'Mother of the Bushel of Stars' (see p.145). Kuan Yin usually sits on a lotus, holding a willow branch and a flask filled with the dew of compassion.

Dragon mythology constitutes a significant part of Chinese tradition. The Dragon Kings hold an important place in popular celebrations as fearsome guardian deities which breathe fire and bring good fortune including, as a bonus, the occasional spitting of pearls! Each is known generally as a Lun Wang or 'King of the Dragons'. On the mainland of Hong Kong, the city of Kowloon is properly named Chiu Lung, meaning 'nine dragons'. This refers to the eight hills of Kowloon which are believed to be resting dragons. The ninth dragon is the emperor. The most important individual deity amongst the Dragon Kings is Ao Kuang whose son, Ao Ping, was slain by Li No Cha during the fabled Battle of Mu.

A DRAMATIC INTERPRETATION OF SOULS BEING TRIED AT AN INFERNAL COURT OF JUSTICE.

Within the group known as the Earlier Deities of Heaven the most illustrious deity is Lao Tzu, the founder of Taoism, the essence of the primordial beginnings and the source of all life, whose apotheosis from the third century CE onwards became known as T'ai Shang Lao Chun. Immediately below him, close to the apex of the pantheon, stands a triad of deities known as the San Ch'ing or Three Pure Ones. Their names include the Chinese word for the sky or its embodiment, *t'ien*, and this is coupled with *tsun*, meaning Lord. Hence they stand as the Celestial Lords of Creation ruling over the Three Realms of Heaven – Jade Purity, Great Purity and High Purity. Wu Chi T'ien Tsun, the god of infinity, is generally accepted as the occupant of Yu Ch'ing, the Realm of Jade Purity, although he

PORCELAIN FIGURINES OF CHINESE DEITIES: INCLUDING THE EIGHT IMMORTALS OR PA HSIEN, MOST HIGHLY REVERED OF THE LATER DEITIES.

One of the most extraordinary aspects of Chinese mythology rests in the personality known as Nan Chi Hsien Weng, 'Old Man of the South Pole'. At the time when he was first envisaged in the minds of philosophers, the Chinese perception of the world was limited to India to the west, inhospitable mountains to the north and oceans to the east and south, yet Chinese astronomers recognized that the earth possessed an axis and that there was a rotation of the heavens around the Pole Star which, paradoxically, lies above the northern hemisphere Pole in the constellation of Ursa Minor. They were unable to comprehend the South Pole as a place of ice and snow and so they envisaged it in highly mysterious terms ruled over by an aged figure responsible for determining the lifespan of human beings. Nan Chi Hsien Weng is believed to live in the Pole Star, known as the Shou Hsing, and to visit his earthly realm once a year at the beginning of the ninth month.

Special attention is also paid to the god of the dead, T'ai-i T'ien Tsun, whose name means Celestial Lord of the Great Beginning. Also known as Ti Tsang Wang, he is regarded in China as a compassionate deity who looks after the well-being of the soul in life and in death equally, although he may be portrayed in art attended by demonic-looking spirits. He is distinct from the Lord of the Underworld, Yan Lo or Yan Wang, who represents a deity borrowed from Hinduism by way of Buddhist missionaries, his Chinese name being an adulteration of Yama, the Hindu god of the dead. Yan Lo is an altogether more ferocious individual drawn as a green-skinned demonic character dressed in red robes and attended by an assortment of retainers.

At a domestic level the most important deity has been Tsao Chun or Tsao Wang, the Kitchen or Stove God, who is usually represented by a small clay icon resting in a niche in the kitchen of the household and sometimes by little more than a paper effigy placed above the stove at the time of Chinese New Year. He probably evolved out of a form of shamanistic ancestor worship into a more generally recognized deity. By convention, invocation of Tsao Chun is conducted by the male head of the family and at New Year his worship may include offerings of food and drink, after which the paper image is ceremoniously burnt.

LATER DEITIES

Amongst those figures who are deemed to be the Later Deities of Heaven, the Pa Hsien or Eight Immortals are the most revered (see p.146) but others feature strongly in Chinese myth. Fu Hsi is claimed to have been the first emperor of China, reigning from 2953–2838 BCE and subsequently deified. The story of his birth tells that his mother became pregnant through the breath of heaven, carried her son in pregnancy for twelve years, and that he was born near the city of Hsian. When he grew to adulthood Fu Hsi became a great shaman who discovered the *ho-t'u* or 'Diagram of the River Ho' which became elaborated into the *pa-k'ua* pattern of the Earlier Heaven that accounts for the organization of the nature of things and has become a fundamental tool of divination. Tradition has it that Fu Hsi was responsible for bringing civilization to the people of China and is the patron god of the arts of divination.

The consort of Fu Hsi is Nu Kua who, according to some myths, reigned as the mortal Empress Nu Huang after his death. In separate mythology it is suggested that she arose as a creator goddess, the mother of humankind, and was only subsequently allied with Fu Hsi. Various other traditions place her as the daughter of the water god, Shui Zhing Tzu, or as the final creation of the primordial creator god P'an Ku. In later times she became the patron goddess of wedlock and is often depicted in paintings with the head and upper torso of a beautiful woman but a lower body consisting of two intertwined snakes.

EARLY MYTHOLOGY OF CHINA

*T*he understanding of Chinese mythology in the west is hampered by the comparative lack of translated material, hence Chinese deities and myths are relatively unfamiliar in Europe. In reality the mythology of China is rich and varied and recognizes a vast number of deities who are individually responsible for everything that occurs in the temporal world, be it tangible or even an abstract thought. The earliest mythical traditions, however, are known only in the most fragmentary way since few were written down as conventional texts. Most of the information about Wu mythology comes from two sources dating to the third century BCE.

The *Annals and Books of History* includes the writings of the early Chinese historian Ssu Ma Ch'ien. His lifetime work has provided most of the information we have on myth and legend in Chou dynastic China, although it covers 'historical' traditions and details events and characters about which it is largely difficult to determine whether they are fact or fiction.

EVIDENCE OF THE BANNER OF SOULS

Understanding of mythology was greatly increased in 1972 after a tomb was excavated in the Hunan province of southern central China. The archaeological burial site, known as Ma Wang Tui, has been dated to about 202 BCE and has yielded paintings including a banner detailing many of the oldest known Chinese myths. This invaluable piece of third century BCE artwork predates Ssu Ma Ch'ien's text by as much as 50 years and it has become popularly known as the Banner of Ma Wang Tui, or the Banner of Souls.

Amongst the scenes included in the Banner of Souls are some which are clearly animistic in nature. Animals are depicted which must derive from the earliest form of mythology in China constituting aspects of the old Wu nature religion. The rabbit or hare features in the Banner and although it is regarded as the fourth animal of the Chinese zodiac, involved mainly in the preparation of the elixir of immortality, it appears that it was once the central character in the myth of the Hare in the Moon. Its details are lost but the story was probably also animistic.

Another of the animal characters on the Banner, whose exploits were popular during the Chou Dynasty, is the three-legged toad. This creature was formerly a woman named Ch'ang O who fled to the moon to escape the wrath of her husband, the Celestial Archer, when he discovered that she had drunk his elixir of immortality. Because she was not entitled to the magical draught she became immortal but only as a grotesque beast. She is believed to live in the moon and to consume it during eclipses.

REALMS OF PARADISE

In common with the course of mythology in many other cultures, the vague animistic spirits of the hunter-gatherers evolved into a more clearly defined pantheon with human characteristics as communities became more settled. The Banner of Souls concentrates on myths of the afterlife in the two realms of Chinese paradise, the Western Heaven and the Eastern Heaven. The Western Heaven, ruled by the Queen of the West, Hsi Wang Mu, is said to be ascended by way of the

A DETAIL FROM THE BANNER OF SOULS SHOWS SOME OF CHINA'S MYTHOLOGICAL ANIMALS.

mountain of K'un Lun. The place remains in the realms of myth, but tradition has it that the mountain lies in the Kunlun Shan range which forms part of China's western border with both Tibet and the Altai.

The Eastern Heaven, ruled by the Jade Emperor, is on the mythical islands of P'eng Lai. The Banner depicts these islands which are reputed to lie somewhere in the China Sea and which, in Taoist times, became the home of the Eight Immortals. It is recorded that, during the Han dynasty which followed that of Ch'in, sailors were commanded to seek out these islands but never returned and this added to the mystique. It was alleged that the islands were surrounded by a magical sea, the *ju shui*, on which no worldly vessel could float and that they were the abode of gods and goddesses who drank the elixir of immortality from fountains of magical water.

Also included in the detail of the Banner is the Queen of the Western Heaven who, in Taoism, is the goddess of longevity, but who is also one of the oldest deities known in China. She is thought to have originated as a plague goddess with feline fangs and a tail but in the Banner she is depicted as a more benign personality with other key figures of her supernatural retinue, including the hare and the toad. Hsi Wang Mu is claimed to have visited both the Chou emperor Mu Wang, whom she met at the legendary Lake of Gems in 985 BCE, and the Han dynasty ruler, Wu Ti, sometime during the second century BCE. Some texts also identify her as the mother of the celestial tortoise on whose back are inscribed the secrets of the universe that were revealed to the archetypal priest Yu.

IMMORTALITY
AND THE
JADE
EMPEROR

A mongst the early mythological characters who make their appearance on the Banner of Souls — the third-century-BCE discovery made recently at Ma Wang Tui near the modern city of Xi'an in Shensi Province — the Jade Emperor is a notable exception. He is a 'late' mythical character who was not introduced until the era of the emperor Chen Tsung who reigned from 998 until 1023 CE. Before this time an ancestral deity was recognized, named Shang Ti, the High Lord of Heaven, who almost certainly evolved from a tree spirit in the Wu religion. The Jade Emperor, known variously as Yu Huang and Yu Ti, then underwent a process of elevation which was to make him synonymous with Shang Ti.

Tradition claims that Chen Tsung was visited by Yu Huang in order to confirm his own celestial authority on earth and it was Chen Tsung and his successor, Hui Tsung, who named this deity the Jade Emperor. He is believed to live in a star named Tzu Wei in the celestial heights accessible only by way of the Jade Mountain which rests at the centre of the mythical islands of P'eng Lai. In Taoist mythology the Jade Emperor is also regarded as an incarnation of the Celestial Lord of the Great Pure Realm, Ling Pao T'ien Tsun (see p.140). Although not the highest deity amongst the gods and goddesses of the Earlier Heaven, he nonetheless rules the celestial realm and is in control of human destiny.

THE IMPORTANCE
OF JADE

The use of the title 'Jade Emperor' is not without significance. Jade is a hard, greenish, semi-precious stone, much of which comes from river valleys in Thailand where it occurs as loose rocks and boulders, and from ancient times it developed a reputation in Chinese alchemy as a key ingredient in the elusive elixir of immortality. When the tombs at Ma Wang Tui, including that of the third-century-BCE emperor, Hsi Huang Ti, were unearthed they revealed some remarkable details. Several of the bodies were completely enclosed in suits that had been intricately fashioned from a large number of joined plates of jade. In each sarcophagus jade was also inserted into the bodily orifices and a disc of jade, known as the *pi*, was placed over the heart. When the remains were examined they were found

ABOVE: A *PI* RING CARVED IN JADE, ONE OF MANY FOUND IN ANCIENT TOMBS.

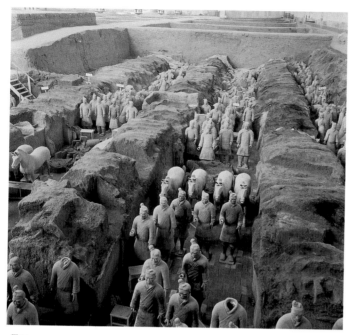

THE NOW FAMOUS TERRACOTTA WARRIORS EXCAVATED AFTER 2000 YEARS OF BURIAL AT XI'AN.

peak in the Kunlun Mountains and she also owns a garden in which grows the tree yielding the mysterious Peaches of Immortality. Another goddess, Tou Mu, whose origins are Buddhist and who derives from Marici the Mahayana goddess of the aurora, is the provider of the elixir of immortality. She is the Taoist patron of physicians, frequently invoked by alchemists to help them complete the formula of the elixir. Known as the Mother of the Bushel of Stars, she holds the sun and moon which also identify her as the goddess of celestial bodies.

Considerable mythology has grown around Hsi Wang Mu and her Peaches of Immortality and the wood of peach trees is valued in China for making powerful charms and talismans. Each of the mythical fruit takes a thousand years to form and another three thousand to ripen, at which time Hsi Wang Mu celebrates her birthday by eating one of the peaches. Her palace, constructed of pure gold with walls 333 miles in circumference, was built by Hou I, the Heavenly Archer, in

to contain a high, and probably lethal, level of powdered jade.

Hsi Huang Ti, whose capital during the Han dynasty was called Chang'an, pursued the myth of immortality literally to the death. Convinced that he could live forever, he prepared his body through an elaborate ritual of consuming pills containing quantities of ground-up jade, apparently believing that this material would slowly replace his more vulnerable organs and tissues. When it finally became apparent that he was approaching death, no doubt hastened by the quantity of jade in his vital organs, he ordered that his body be encased wholly in the stone and he had built for himself an extraordinary subterranean mausoleum. Intended to replicate his kingdom it included fabulous riches, a lake of mercury and a ceiling covered with the stars of heaven. He also commanded to be fashioned and buried close by, the astonishing life-sized and fully armed terracotta soldiers which replicated his living forces. The many hundreds of figures, excavated in 1974 from the trenches where they had lain for some 2000 years, were to provide him with an army in his life beyond death.

ASSOCIATED WITH IMMORTALITY, PEACH BLOSSOM HAS A SYMBOLIC SIGNIFICANCE IN CHINESE ART.

THE EMPRESS OF THE WEST

The Taoists became obsessed with finding the alchemical secrets of longevity and it is the celestial co-regent with the Jade Emperor, the Empress of the Western Heaven, Hsi Wang Mu, who is believed to be the divinity holding the key to eternal life. Accompanied by Jade Maidens it is she who grants or denies immortality although she does not actually dispense the elixir. Her home is a palace on the summit of a mythical

return for whose labours she gave him a gift of the elixir. She placed a condition on this offering, however, that Hou I was to fast for a year before drinking the elixir. For safe keeping he placed the potion in the roof of his house where it remained until, one day, his wife discovered and drank it. She found herself floating upwards through the window of the house and, fleeing ever faster from her irate husband, eventually she reached the moon. Having neither been entitled to the potion nor completed the necessary prerequisites, she was denied immortality in human guise and turned into the famous three-legged toad which lives in the moon (see p.142).

THE EIGHT IMMORTALS

*A*mongst the most important of the deities beneath the supreme triad are the Pa Hsien, the so-called Eight Immortals. They conveniently sum up much of the essence of Chinese myth and have gained great popularity to the extent that many people carry charms or amulets which symbolize one or more of the group. The Pa Hsien were once mortal beings who achieved immortality through their exemplary life-styles and now live on the mythical paradise islands of P'eng Lai.

They have been deliberately chosen to represent a cross-section of the population. They are of both sexes, though predominantly male, or ambivalent in their gender, of varying affluence and social position, young and old. Why they became grouped collectively is unclear since each is from a different period, none lived contemporaneously, and only three apparently have any claim to historical existence. All appear, however, to originate from a time no earlier than the late medieval period. The following list of eight does not necessarily represent the order in which the Pa Hsien are alleged to have achieved immortality, nor their seniority.

(1) Han Hsiang Tzu was said to have lived under the Tang Dynasty in the ninth century CE and studied with a philosopher named Han Yu who was said to be his great uncle. He then became a disciple of another member of the Pa Hsien, Lu Tung Pin, who directed him to the top of the Sacred Peach Tree, the symbol of longevity, from whose branches he fell into immortality. He represents culture and his emblem is a flower basket.

(2) Ho Hsien Ku, the only female member of the Eight Immortals, was also born during the Tang Dynasty, in about 700 CE, during the reign of Empress Wu. As a girl she was given a lotus blossom with magical properties by Lu Tung Pin. Later, following premonitory dreams, she was directed to the Pearl Mountains near her home where she was instructed to grind up and swallow a semi-precious stone to achieve immortality, upon which she became the goddess of housewives or, alternatively, unwed maidens. Her emblem is a lotus.

(3) T'sao Kuo Chiu was the brother of Empress Ts'ao who reigned during the eleventh century CE. He was implicated in the slaying of a student whose life was brutally cut short by T'sao Kuo Chiu's younger brother, Ching Chih. The latter had become infatuated with the student's wife which led to the killing. The spirit of the student, however, returned to demand vengeance

A NINETEENTH-CENTURY PAINTED TILE SHOWING THE EIGHT IMMORTALS WITH THEIR TRADITIONAL EMBLEMS.

and T'sao Kuo Chiu urged his brother to have the wife slain in order to eliminate potential witnesses to the original crime. The wife was saved and the murderous plot was revealed. The younger brother was executed and T'sao Kuo Chiu incarcerated. The empress then used her influence to have him released under an amnesty and he became a reformed recluse living in the mountains. During the sojourn which occupied the remainder of his life, the other immortals taught him the way to achieve self-perfection. He represents the nobility and his emblem is a writing tablet.

(4) Lan Ts'ai Ho is depicted as being either male or female, wandering as an itinerant beggar and wearing rags. It is said that one day he died of alcoholism and became the guardian deity of the poor and needy. His emblem is a lute.

(5) T'ieh Kuai Li was tutored in the ways of achieving perfection by the triad of supreme deities and is depicted walking with an iron crutch. The story goes that when the time came for him to rise to heaven he instructed his brother to cremate his corpse if he failed to return within seven days. Distracted by the imminent death of his mother, however, the brother incinerated the body on the sixth day. T'ieh Kuai Li returned and, finding that his body had gone, adopted that of a dead mendicant whose deformed frame required the support of a crutch. Subsequently he became the god of the sick and infirm. His emblems include the iron crutch and a flask of medicine.

(6) Lu Tung Pin was born into the family of a local governor during the Tang Dynasty in 755 CE. As a student, visiting an inn he encountered one of the other immortals, Chung Li Ch'uan. Whilst asleep he experienced a prophetic dream of a future life in which he was to rise to a position of authority before being disgraced. So moved was he by the experience that he asked Chung Li Ch'uan to school him in the ways of perfection and when he achieved immortality he became the patron of scholars. His emblem is a sword.

AT A TAOIST TEMPLE IN PENANG, MALAYSIA, EACH ROOF COLUMN IS CARVED WITH AN IMAGE OF ONE OF THE IMMORTALS.

(7) Chang Kuo Lao lived during the seventh century CE, became a hermit and died at the age of more than 100. According to tradition, he was called to the court of the Empress Wu but died on the steps of her palace. His corpse failed to decompose and he was miraculously restored, after which he went to live a monastic life in the mountains until his death. When his tomb was opened subsequently it was found to be empty.

(8) Chung Li Ch'uan is said to have lived in the first century BCE, become a senior figure in the government of the Han Dynasty and then converted to life as a hermit, during which he discovered the secrets of alchemy. One day a fissure at the back of his hermit's cave opened and revealed a jade casket which contained the formula for the elixir of immortality and he was carried to P'eng Lai on the wings of a stork. He is the patron of the military and his emblems include the Peach of Immortality and a fan of stork feathers.

THE EPIC BATTLE OF MU

Virtually every culture of the world develops its epic myths and legends which frequently take place in a 'once-upon-a-time' period of the fabled past. They are set in the heroic age of a nation's early pre-history when the absence of reliable records allows romance and imagination free rein. These epic tales serve as exemplary stories, as a focus of national pride and, since they are timeless, as a means to link the cultural legacy of a people's pioneering past with its present and future.

The Chinese Battle of Mu, otherwise known as the Battle of Ten Thousand Spirits, claims its place in history having first been sustained through oral tradition and then by way of art and text. But the actual event, if the records are to be taken as being in any way reliable, became transmogrified over many centuries and developed into a conflict between mythical heroes and villains whose celestial war mirrored that of the earthly forces.

The battle in 'history' is noted in the official Shi Zhi records and in the texts of the historian Ssu Ma Ch'ien who was, in fact, writing in the second century CE, some one thousand years later during the time of the Tang Dynasty, and was therefore hardly an authoritative observer. According to the official records the battle took place in 1122 BCE at Meng on the Huang He (Yellow River) and marked the overthrow of an old, allegedly corrupt regime, the Shang Dynasty (1766–1121 BCE), and the triumph of the incoming Chou (Zhou) Dynasty. An archaeological discovery in 1976 goes some way towards corroborating the account. A commemorative bronze bowl was excavated which included in its decoration the actual date of the battle detailing the year, month and day.

THE BATTLE IN MYTHOLOGY

The mythical version is recorded in various Taoist religious texts, including the *Book on the Making of Immortals* and the *Catalogue of Spirits and Immortals*. These serve not only to elevate the battle to mythical status but also explain, in model fashion, how many of the deities of the old Shang order became redundant, giving way to new names and personalities.

The last emperor of the Shang Dynasty is named as Chou Hsin and tradition casts him as an evil tyrant, although his concubine, T'a Chi, was probably even more notorious in her cruelty to their subjects. In mythology Chou Hsin becomes Chou Wang who is also identified in the role of god of sodomy. He was ousted by a warrior hero named Fa Ch'ang (1169–1116 BCE), deified as Wu Wang, whose father Hsi Peh, deified as Wen Wang, reputedly founded the Chou Dynasty. Wu Wang is, incidentally, accredited with completing the authorship of the *I Ching*, a Taoist text which had been begun by his father whilst incarcerated by Chou Hsin.

Other main characters of the conflict on the winning side include Chiang Lu Shang, a general who had changed sides from the Shang to the Chou camp to fight on behalf of Wen Wang. He is alleged to have been a descendant of Huang Ti, the Yellow Emperor who ruled China in mythical times during the third millennium BCE, and he became deified as Chiang Tzu Ya. After his mortal life Chiang Tzu Ya was himself able to order the deification of slain battle heroes, a capacity which accounted for many of the gods of the new dynasty. Fighting alongside Chiang Tzu Ya was an extraordinary figure named Li No Cha who appears to have been entirely of mythical origin. He was 60 feet tall with eight arms, three heads each with three eyes, an earth-shaking voice and breath that appeared as blue smoke. He possessed magical weapons and devices made of gold including a bracelet and a 'wind-fire machine' which saw off many of the opposing side.

Fighting in the camp of the Shang emperor were two paramount generals: Feng Lin, whose deified form was the star

Tiao Ko, and Chang Kuei Fang, deified as the star Sang Men. At the climax of the battle Chang Kuei Fang confronted Li No Cha in combat but was defeated by the magical power of the golden bracelet.

Many personalities make their appearance in the narrative of the battle though none are perhaps more bizarre than the Keng San Ku Niang, three sisters of one of Chou Wang's slaughtered generals who are otherwise known as the Three Ladies of the Imperial Lavatory. In imperial China the attendants of the emperor's toilet were highly regarded members of court since the quality of the motions passed was carefully scrutinized each day and provided the basis of a prognosis of the ruler's health and well-being. Each lady wielded weapons in the form of golden scissors and her lavatory bucket, referred to as the 'Golden Bushel of Troubled Origins'. This fighting trio of matrons caused considerable mayhem until their devices were rendered impotent by Li No Cha with his wind-fire machine. After the battle Chiang Tzu Ya magnanimously elevated the three to the ranks of immortals where they became midwife goddesses.

The battle is described in great detail in the mythical texts and it draws towards a decisive outcome when the efforts of the god of thunder and rain, Lei Ku – in mortal life Wen Zhung Dai Shih – who provides one of the most formidable weapons in the arsenal of the Shang forces, fails to kill Wen Wang with a strike from a lightning bolt. Facing defeat, Lei Ku retreats but is confronted by a trio of generals from Wen Wang's side who eventually incinerate him with his own lightning. This permits Wu Wang to advance his forces and overrun the remnants of opposition, so clearing the way for the rise of the Chou dynasty.

ONE OF THE WARRIOR GODS OF TAOISM.

THE
JOURNEY
TO THE WEST

*A*mongst the most popular myths of China is a truly epic tale which also illustrates the profound impact that Mahayana Buddhism has exerted on Chinese beliefs. The story of Sun Hou Tzu, the Monkey King, and Hsuan Tsang, a Buddhist monk with a mission to recover the religious texts of Buddhism from India, has remained an important part of Chinese tradition. It is partly a vicarious and humorous entertainment, an adventure story akin in certain respects to the Hindu epic of RAMAYANA, but also, like RAMAYANA, a moral tale of the finer aspects of human endeavour which come to prevail over those of a less worthy nature.

Like most myths, the Journey to the West began as an oral tradition long before it was established in the literary repertoire and, during its long history, it has no doubt been altered in some of its details but the overall flavour and intent probably remain intact. It is believed to possess a genuine historical foundation in that the monk Hsuan Tsang did make the journey at some time during the Tang dynastic period (618–906 CE). Sun Hou Tzu is, however, of wholly mythical origin and bears no relationship to the military strategist Sun Tzu who lived during the Classical Period. The period in which the myth is set is one during which many of the old-established theories of Taoism, including the efficacy and power of alchemy, were becoming passé amongst intellectuals, and people were finding an increasing interest in Buddhist philosophies against which they began to view Taoist magical beliefs as ineffectual and naive. Clearly the myth was compiled

THE MYTHICAL JOURNEY TO INDIA INVOLVED CROSSING SOME OF CHINA'S MOST FORMIDABLE MOUNTAIN RANGES.

THE TALE HAS INSPIRED AN OPERA ENTITLED *THE MONKEY KING*, PERFORMED
HERE BY BEIJING OPERA AT THE DZUNG HE THEATRE IN BEIJING.

from the viewpoint of Buddhist sympathy and underlines the increasing importance attached to the arrival of Buddhist *sutras* in China.

Sun Hou Tzu is also known in some versions as Sun Wu Kong but his title, as the 'Monkey King', was conferred upon him by the Jade Emperor, Yu Huang or Shang Ti. According to tradition he emerged from a rock on a mountain known as Hua Shan (Grand Mountain) in Shensi province. It was there, incidentally, according to the *Hua Shan Chi* (Chronicles of Hua Shan), that the famous Wu Chi diagram on which the idea of the Taoist cosmos is based also appeared, magically engraved on a rock face.

THE STORY

The story goes that, when still young, Sun Hou Tzu developed both a wanderlust and an exaggerated opinion of his own importance which was exacerbated when he was given a magical weapon by the Ryujin Dragon King named Ao Kuang. He soon began to abuse the powers of this device and the Jade Emperor elected to punish him by giving him the menial job of groom in the Celestial Stables. Sun Hou Tzu rapidly became disenchanted with this role and made his way back to the Hua Shan where he got up to more mischief whilst his conceit grew larger. Improbably, he was given the task of guarding the Peaches of Immortality for the Empress of the Western Heaven, Hsi Wang Mu, but only managed to eat them himself.

Eventually Sun Hou Tzu's escapades came to the attention

of the celestial court which decreed that he must be executed. However, since Sun Hou Tzu had eaten all the Peaches of Immortality, the punishment was good only in theory. The *buddha*, his patience close to exhaustion, demanded to know what would satisfy his craving for power and glory, to which Sun Hou Tzu replied that nothing less than being 'Ruler of the Universe' would suffice. The *buddha* agreed, though only if Sun Hou Tzu could jump beyond his reach. The Monkey King leapt so high that he touched the limits of the universe, where he signed his name to prove he had been there but, on his return, the *buddha* revealed the signature written on his palm and Sun Hou Tzu was forced to admit defeat.

The *buddha* decided to put Sun Hou Tzu's craving for adventure to more constructive use and instructed him to protect the monk Hsuan Tsang on his sacred mission. The journey was clearly destined to be both long and arduous and the pair soon met their first adversaries which included a ferocious black bear, a giant and a villainous beast named Chou Pa Chai. The latter was once an official at the Jade Emperor's court but was discovered attempting to seduce the emperor's daughter, executed and reincarnated as a pig. Having eaten his parents he took to living on a mountain, which was in the path of Sun Hou Tzu and Hsuan Tsang, where he attacked passers-by. All three adversaries, however, were persuaded by the goddess Kuan Yin to join the pilgrimage and rise out of their base ways.

In one chapter of the journey there is an unfamiliar indication of conflict between Taoists and Buddhists. A group of Taoist priests are reported to have intercepted the travellers and forced them into menial labour. Sun Hou Tzu, however, slew three demons which had been bothering the priests, whereupon the provincial overlord conferred on the party the status of Taoists and gave them safe passage.

The myth takes on a moral tone in various episodes. At one stage the party was tempted to divert from its sacred mission by the attentions of seductresses but managed to stay true to the intended course. The group of missionaries also negotiated volcanic mountains, became temporarily imprisoned by demons, and even sank into a morass of rotting fruit from which they were rescued by the pig, now reformed, who used his snout to clear a safe path.

Eventually, after a trek that took them through nine kingdoms and lasted for fourteen years, the party reached India where Hsuan Tsang obtained 5048 volumes of the sacred texts of Buddhism. He returned with them to China, accompanied by Sun Hou Tzu, and presented the scriptures to the emperor Tai Kung.

LAO TZU

*T*he most important name in the development of early Chinese spiritual philosophy is that of Lao Tzu, the founder of Taoism although, like his philosophical successors, Chuang Tzu and Lieh Tzu, he exists more in tradition and legend rather than through any historical certainty. Lao Tzu is believed to have been a contemporary of Confucius, born sometime between the early sixth and mid fifth centuries BCE though one of the popular dates for his birth is given as 604 BCE. He lived, therefore, in the troubled times towards the end of the Chou dynastic period.

POLITICAL UNREST

In the political and historical record of China, the time from the early eighth century to the late third century BCE was marked by the collapse of the old established political and social structures and by the country becoming wracked by civil war. The span of some five hundred years is identified in two distinct periods, the first of which is known as the Spring and Autumn Period, lasting from about 770–476 BCE, when the local barons were jostling and fighting for supremacy in a constant ebb and flow of power. At the outset a number of semi-autonomous states existed, run on strictly feudal lines, at the forefront of which stood the so-called Five Warlords, Ch'i, Ch'in, Chin, Ch'u and Sung. The emperors of the Chou Dynasty had effectively set up these local tyrants with lands and resources in gratitude for past military and political support and, during the next three centuries, their noble houses succeeded in reducing the number of fiefdoms from almost 150 to 44 through petty conquest.

The Spring and Autumn Period was followed by that of the Warring States when the still comparatively large number of fiefdoms, including the small remnant of the imperial Chou kingdom, became further reduced, initially to seven and then to a single united structure. The military strategist Ch'in, after whom the country is named, defeated all opposition and become the first supreme ruler of China.

In Taoist terms this time of strife is known as the Classical Period, the era when the great philosophical texts were composed. Ironically, out of chaos and unrest, emerged some of the world's most outstanding and enduring philosophers and thinkers. These intellectual giants were set to advance theories on a range of topics from military strategy to the law and other aspects of wisdom.

LAO TZU'S WORK AND INFLUENCE

Lao Tzu was born, if tradition is to be believed, during the Spring and Autumn Period. Like Confucius he viewed the old remnants of the Wu priesthood, with their elaborate rituals and sacrifices, as being anachronistic and out of touch with the new and more sophisticated culture developing in northern China. There were, however, major differences between Lao Tzu's philosophies and those of Confucius, to the extent that the latter is said to have found him 'incomprehensible'. Confucianism developed as a secular philosophy seeking to improve the quality of life in a strictly material world with the ultimate aim of becoming a sage. Taoism, the 'Way' of the universe, is directed more towards the metaphysical and the transcendental. Through meditation, yoga and alchemy its devotee seeks to rise above human existence and to gain immortality.

Lao Tzu's most influential text, and the standard classical work of Taoism, is claimed as the *Tao Te Ching*. Unfortunately it has not been possible to date this or confirm its authorship with any certainty but, from reference or lack of it in other commentaries, the text is believed to have been in existence at least between 350 and 300 BCE and, by convention, it is given the alternative title of the *Lao Tzu*. The Confucian student Meng Tzu, better known as Mencius, who was a contemporary of Chuang Tzu and Lieh Tzu and who lived between 371 and 289 BCE, does not mention the *Tao Te Ching*. On the other hand the later Confucian writer Hsun Tzu, who was born in about 300 BCE, comments on the text at some length and this narrows the window of probability regarding its dating.

AN EIGHTEENTH-CENTURY PAINTING DEPICTING SHAKYAMUNI, LAO TZU AND CONFUCIUS.

he disagreed with the militaristic and brutal attitudes which pervaded the royal court.

Scholars of the *Tao Te Ching* now agree that its authorship is a composite which was probably assembled over a period of many decades during the Spring and Autumn Period. The mythology offers a more romantic account of its origin. In his disenchantment with the ruthlessness of the Chou rulers and the other warring feudal lords, Lao Tzu elected to seek enlightenment and to pursue a gentler alternative. He became a contemplative itinerant making his way towards the western borders of China, perhaps attracted by the lure of Buddhism. On reaching the frontier with Tibet, he persuaded one of the border guards to write down a dictated essay of some 5000 words which expounded alternatives to the endless warring that plagued the country. These included a greater reliance on political initiatives and the benefits of living in harmony with the natural order. Having delivered his philosophy Lao Tzu disappeared, never to be seen again. The essay was the *Tao Te Ching* and the border guard, Wen Tzu, dedicated himself to proselytising the message of Lao Tzu who had become an immortal or *hsien*.

Lao Tzu's successors, Chuang Tzu and Lieh Tzu, modified his original teachings by advocating a Taoist path of

It is suggested that Lao Tzu was born into an upper class family, as Li Erh, in the Ch'u kingdom in southern China. As a young adult he was employed as an archivist in the service of the imperial government but began to find increasingly that remaining detached from political affairs and living in harmony with oneself. Through the personal changes which would follow, and the understanding which would come out of them, changes in society as a whole would also evolve.

OTHER CHINESE RELIGIOUS PHILOSOPHERS

CHUANG TZU

In addition to Lao Tzu, the builder of philosophical Taoism and its quest for the 'Way', Chuang Tzu was one of the three great thinkers of the Classical Period from whose collective philosophy, *Tao Chia*, was to arise the religious branch of Taoism known as Tao Chiao. Historical records are vague but Chuang Tzu is said to have lived during the fourth century BCE in the so-called Warring States Period. He was a contemporary of Meng Tzu (Mencius) the successor to Confucius. He developed a form of mysticism on which he wrote extensively, and his philosophy forms the basis of one of the major religious works on Taoism. Many of the Chinese philosophers also lend their names to the titles of the texts attributed to them. Hence the main thesis of Chuang Tzu is also called the *Chuang Tzu*, although only the early part is believed to be of his personal authorship. His collected works, under the title of the *Nan Hua Ching*, are available in modern English translation and reveal that his views conflicted sharply with those of Confucius, whose goal was essentially one of perfection through secularism or worldly activities.

Chuang Tzu's writings advocate a more personal form of mysticism than that of Lao Tzu's *Tao Te Ching*. He achieved a widespread following, particularly in southern China, during the T'ang Dynasty when he received the patronage of the Emperor Hsuan Tsung, although, as a way to discover the secrets of Tao, he rejected involvement in government or administration. In common with his fellow philosopher, Lieh Tzu, he was particularly interested in health and longevity and is said to have subscribed to a philosophy of non-involvement or *wu wei*, arguing incompatibility between politics and the pursuit of longevity, and extolling the need to distance oneself from world affairs. Elements of the old style of shamanic religion also pervade his works, although his view is somewhat ambivalent. He argues that the more superficial form of shamanism is staffed by little more than charlatans but that the true sage possesses immense supernatural powers. He also modified the principle laid down in the *Tao Te Ching* that Tao is benign in nature, arguing the view that Tao is a strictly neutral source of existence.

Chuang Tzu also developed some curious personal beliefs, rejecting the idea of burial or cremation and insisting that his earthly remains be left to decay exposed to the air. His overall theories contributed to the development of the *fang-shih* or *fa shih*, the so-called 'masters of the method', who specialized in the magical arts. Some of these masters applied talismanic magic in healing and were the forerunners of the Celestial Teachers (also referred to sometimes as Central Orthodox Taoism), whilst others concentrated their skills on developing techniques to encourage longevity.

LIEH TZU

The third author of the great classical texts of Taoism is thought to have been an approximate contemporary of Chuang Tzu who lived during the Warring States Period of the fourth century BCE, although the text attributed to his authorship, the *Lieh Tzu*, was not compiled until about 300 CE and lacks the literary style of the Chuang Tzu writings. Both Lieh Tzu and Chuang Tzu nonetheless developed essentially similar philosophies about the need to care for the body as a prerequisite to longevity. Emulating Chuang Tzu's philosophy of non-involvement, he too believed firmly that the pursuit of longevity and politics do not mix.

Also in common with Chuang Tzu he incorporated elements of the old Wu-style shamanism into his arguments, endorsing the power of the wise man or sage over animals and natural forces and his ability to perform supernatural feats, but at the same time warning of the existence of charlatans using spurious claims of powers to further their own interest. Lieh Tzu himself was believed to have extensive powers, including those of levitation, and in paintings he is often depicted floating above the landscape.

CHANG TAO LING

Born in 35 CE at T'ien Mu Shan in Che Kiang province, he was also known as Chang T'ien Shih and is considered to be the founder of magical Taoism. When a young man, Chang Tao Ling travelled as an itinerant student of alchemy and, according to tradition, discovered the formula for the elixir of immortality as well as developing a philosophy on the nature of disease. Illness, he claimed, was caused through sin and the way to restoration of health was through a combination of confession and immersion in a sacred lake. Apparently he developed a keen commercial approach to his treatments and used the revenue for undertaking public works and purchasing private estates on which he built temples and spiritual retreats. At the age of 60, wishing to prolong his earthly life rather than become an immortal immediately, he took only half the required dose of his elixir, regained his youth and lived to 123. He is said to have died in 157 CE. His descendants are the hereditary leaders of modern religious Taoism.

T'AO HUNG CHING

Living the life of a recluse, T'ao Hung Ching established a centre in the Mao Shan mountains in south-east China and formalized Shang Ch'ing Taoism. Born into an aristocratic family in 456 CE, he received an extensive schooling in a wide

AN EIGHTEENTH-CENTURY WATERCOLOUR PORTRAYAL
OF CHANG TAO LING.

range of subjects and, at one time, was appointed librarian to the imperial court. He elected to retire from political life and became a hermit who devoted much of his time to collecting texts of Shang Ch'ing Taoism (see p.156) and producing a documented plan of the celestial hierarchy, including biographical profiles of its members, its ranks and organization.

From his catholic knowledge of theosophy and philosophy, T'ao Hung Ching developed his own interpretation of Shang Ch'ing which became known as the Mao Shan school. This is wholly distinct from the Mao Shan sect of magicians which emerged some thousand years later during the Ming Dynasty. Mao Shan Shang Ch'ing recognizes a strong pantheon and applies principles of both internal and external alchemy in its approach to health and longevity. It uses herbal medicines and meditation techniques. In the centuries following the death of T'ao Hung Ching the philosophy was promoted through the establishment of monasteries and training centres.

TAOIST TRADITIONS

*A*s Taoism evolved it did so along a number of distinct lines. What began as a philosophy became a religion and with this came a proliferation of sectarian views which focused on mysticism, magic, alchemy, divination and ceremonial, all of which seek, in their own manner, to offer a route towards understanding of and unity with Tao, the invisible and undefined force of the universe. Overall, three traditions developed – those of Ling Pao (talismanic), Shang Ch'ing (mystical) and T'ai Ching (alchemical), although various schools and sects have incorporated elements of some or all the traditions.

TALISMANIC OR LING PAO TAOISM

Founded by Chang Tao Ling, who was also the founder member of the Celestial Teacher sect, this tradition properly dates from about the second century CE during the Eastern Han Dynasty. It was originally employed in Magical Taoism, by the members of the Celestial Teacher, Mao Shan and Kun Lun sects, to ward off malevolent spirits and for healing purposes, but was later employed by the Mystics to aid them in travel to the celestial realms and by alchemists in their quest for the formula of the elixir of immortality. A talisman in China consists of words and symbols, sometimes including the name of the deity being invoked, usually written on yellow paper using red ink, but sometimes inscribed invisibly in the air. Those employed by Kun Lun and Mao Shan sorcerers are written in modern Chinese, whilst those of Celestial Teachers, Shang Ch'ing, and Ling Pao followers are rendered in an archaic script known as Ancient Seal.

The preparation of talismans, believed to possess considerable powers, is permitted only to initiates and is accompanied by strict rules of ritual. The writer must present offerings of food and drink to the deities involved, abstain from stimulants, sexual activity and eating meat in the twenty-four hours prior to composing the device, and make incantations. When the talisman is written the work must be carried out only at certain times of the day and the month.

MYSTICAL OR SHANG CH'ING TAOISM

This tradition is said to have been founded during the Western Chin Dynasty (265–316 CE) by Lady Wei Hua T'sun, a woman of aristocratic birth who had fled the barbarian invasions, and in the early days its members were all related, stemming largely from the aristocratic families of south-east China. It was, however, allegedly formalized earlier in the first century CE by the Taoist hermit T'ao Hung Ching (see pp.162–3). It relies, unusually, on a combination of shamanism and mysticism. Shang Ch'ing promotes the view that the body is inhabited by an assortment of spirits, some good, some evil. Those that are benevolent protect various parts of the body from illness and decay but when they abandon their charge, a trio of more demonic inhabitants takes over and the person dies. In this microcosm of the universe within our bodies the highest deity is called The One and is synonymous with Tao, the essence of immortality which keeps us alive. Lady Wei Hua T'sun elaborates the doctrine of 'Keeping the One', preserving the guardian spirit that resides within us, in her written work known as the *Shang Ch'ing Huang T'ing Nei Ching Yu Ching*.

There are three important guardian spirits inside the human frame, each controlling an aspect of energy and known as the Three Ones. The highest of these resides between the eyes in the Celestial Realm of the body and is termed the guardian of spiritual energy, controlling the activity of the mind. Below, in the area of the heart, the Terrestrial Realm, is the guardian of vital energy, manifested in the breath. The third guardian

A EUROPEAN INTERPRETATION OF CHINESE 'SORCERERS' PRACTISING THE MAGICAL ARTS.

controls generative energy from the Water Realm which lies in the abdominal region. Ranking beneath the Three Ones are the five spirits which control the viscera – heart, lungs, liver, spleen and kidneys.

The demons which oppose these benevolent spirits are depicted either in human guise or as strange beasts which reside at three points along the spine and which are nourished by our desires. The locations are perceived as gateways to the realms occupied by the Three Ones. If the gates are closed, the Three Ones are themselves deprived of energy, so the objective is to starve out the demons by ridding the mind of desire or other negative stimuli on which they might feed.

ALCHEMICAL TAOISM

This form of peculiarly Chinese wisdom has nothing to do with the conventional western notion of transforming base metals into gold, although it does involve transformation. It is an alchemy of the physiology and functions of the body, refining it to a high degree of health and from a mortal to an immortal state. This, according to Taoist belief, can be achieved in one of two ways. The formulation and concoction of pills and potions allegedly provides an elixir of immortality and is known as external alchemy, whilst the disciplining of change within the mind and body, including meditation and other techniques, though without recourse to the use of external devices, is known as internal alchemy.

The trained practitioners of alchemy have been known as the Fang Shih or 'Masters of the Formulae' and their art is based on an archaic text known as the *Tsan Tung Chi*. This was supposedly compiled by an early alchemist, Wei Po Yang, who is attributed in mythology with having discovered the secrets of immortality which he shared with his dog and a faithful student. External alchemy requires the incorporation of two elements, water and fire, which symbolize the creative sexual principles of *yin* and *yang*, and involves esoteric substances being heated, compounded and refined to produce powerful energies. Internal alchemy claims similar ingredients but they are perceived to exist within the 'cauldron' of the living body.

TAOIST SECTS

ects, in one form or another, have existed in China since prehistoric times. This was probably inevitable in a country of such vast size and touched by so many different religious and philosophical influences. Largely, however, the individual movements seem to have developed without animosity towards one another of the kind that has bedevilled religion in the west. It has been claimed that 'in Taoism there are no heretics, only sects'.

Religious sects in China largely proliferated during the Ming Dynasty (1368–1644 CE) when state-sponsored religion was abandoned and a climate of social and political liberalization resulted in a wide diversity of popular religious practice and belief. This was also the period during which 'foreign' religions and philosophies became firmly established in China and there was, in particular, a movement towards melding the disciplines of Taoism, Buddhism and Confucianism. In Taoist religion the concept of the *chen-jen* or 'realized being' was developed to reflect the high regard in which leaders of the sects and other outstanding thinkers came to be held. At the close of the Ming Period, China was riddled with sects of every character and size. Most were destined to a brief flowering but their priestly leaders were also highly influential in imperial circles, often replacing experienced secular administrators, and this led to levels of corruption which, in part, were responsible for the downfall of the Dynasty.

MAGICAL ARTS

Many of the sects owe allegiance to more than one discipline or influence but those focusing on the magical arts probably derive from the oldest origins. The principles to which they subscribe were first established by the shamans of the archaic Wu religion who relied on invoking supernatural powers in the natural world for the benefit of the community by means of intercession, sympathetic magic and ritual. Many of the magically orientated movements have vanished over the course of time but today three sects are recognized as still being significantly involved in magical Taoism.

Mao Shan Sect

Recognized mainly in southern China and parts of South-East Asia, its sorcerers are the chief exponents in the art of talismanic magic. They are also strongly reliant on divination, but it should be made clear that they are both distinct and separate from the members of the Shang Ch'ing Mao Shan mystical sect. Highly secretive in its activities, the Mao Shan selects noviciates only through personal recommendation of senior sect members and is chiefly concerned with the exorcism of evil influences. Mao Shan magicians are called upon to offer protection against natural disasters and personal misfortunes by drawing on the benevolent influences of minor guardian deities and other spirits of a kind that are rejected by Celestial Teachers (see below). Members of the sect rely on the effect of talismans and other magical devices, including bells and mirrors, and on the powers of the spirit entities who are invoked to enter their bodies temporarily.

T'ien Tsun Sect (Heavenly Master or Celestial Teacher)

Although its origins lie with the arts of sorcerers, this is one of four major branches representing orthodox Taoism in China today. The movement evolved from the Five Bushels of Rice Society founded by Chang Tao Ling (see p.164) and effectively represents the beginnings of religious Taoism. Chang Tao Ling compiled a biographical reference work, the *Auspicious Alliance Canonical Register*, which included a substantial number of deities and spirits whom he listed by name and function and he

Kun Lun Sect

Unlike the previous two magically orientated sects, the Kun Lun practitioners draw heavily on Buddhist Tantric magic which has been imported from Tibet, although they also rely on invoking the powers of Taoist deities. The movement originated in the mountains of north-western China, from which it takes its name, and its members are known as Fang Shih or 'Masters of the Laws' which distinguishes them from the Tao Shih. They rely on a combination of talismans and *mudras*, the hand gestures which derive from Hindu iconography, to provide similar services to the Mao Shan magicians and Celestial Teachers and are active in similar areas of southern China and South-East Asia where magical and divinatory powers exert the strongest influence.

ALCHEMICAL ARTS

As well as those which are magically focused, China has produced a plethora of sects whose interest lies in alchemy. In Chinese terms this does not refer to the refining of base metals into gold but rather the transformation of the physiological structure and functions of the body. Such change was pursued through two forms of alchemy, external and internal,

IMAGES OF TIGERS, THIRD ANIMAL OF THE CHINESE ZODIAC, EMBLEM OF AUTUMN AND THE WESTERN HEAVEN, ADORN THE WALL OF A TEMPLE IN TAIWAN.

was instrumental in transforming Taoism from a philosophy into a religion. Chang Lu, one of the grandsons of Chang Tao Ling, was responsible for extending the political influence of the movement into central China and, since then, the sect has become based on Lung Hu Shan (Dragon and Tiger Mountain) in south-east China.

The Society effectively became an organized religious sect with the emergence of a text entitled *T'ai P'ing Ching* (The Book of Peace and Balance), the authorship of which was attributed to divine hands and which constitutes the first known scriptural discourse of Taoism.

Chang Tao Ling's successors were also sorcerers practising a mixture of talismanic and divinatory arts and their influence has remained strong. They work for the benefit of the community, exorcising malevolent influences and keeping evil spirits at bay, offering their services as healers, guiding the spirits of the dead, and officiating in rain-making ceremonies. They rely on talismans and incantations which were revealed to their founder, Chang Tao Ling, by various deities. Invocation of underworld gods and the old spirits of the nature religion is denied.

the principles of which were frequently used in combination. The external involves the ingestion of elixirs and other substances in order to induce longevity and, ultimately, immortality. The internal form relies on ingredients found inside the body, which becomes its own crucible, to achieve the same ends. Irrespective of which form was adopted, the alchemists relied, as an adjunct to their conviction that immortality lay within reach, on a combination of physical exercise, sexual techniques and meditation.

Many of the Chinese emperors, already steeped in belief about their own divinity, were obsessed with finding the key to cheating death and remaining in their earthly bodies for an eternity. This was particularly true of those who ruled during the T'ang Dynasty (618–906 CE). Against their faith stood a complete lack of evidence that it was possible to produce a 'pill' that would bring immortality, coupled with the sobering reality that too many prominent alchemists had died from experimentation with ingesting such lethal substances as lead, mercury and jade. This finally resulted in some radical rethinking about external alchemy which began towards the end of the period of the Six Dynasties (420–589 CE). It did not, however, save a horrifying catalogue of T'ang emperors who fell victim to premature death after swallowing regular doses of 'immortality pills'.

MONKS PRAYING AT SENCHAITANG MONASTERY IN TAIWAN.

meditation, the practice of Yin-Yang (see p.180), a form of sexual alchemy, and non-sexual discipline, would provide the key to immortality when used in the right combination. Tradition has it that Wei Po Yang, his assistant and his dog all achieved the sought-after result!

Another major figure in external alchemy was Ko Hung who lived during the period of the Eastern Chin Dynasty (317–420 CE) and who compiled a major work, the *P'ao P'u Tzu*, including detailed advice on the formulation of immortality pills which he advocated should be used in conjunction with physical exercise and mental discipline.

The doubts which became increasingly voiced about the efficacy of external alchemy swung the balance of interest towards internal alchemy. A number of Taoist sects subscribe to the theory of the Singular Path in that the alchemy leading to longevity can be worked by an individual alone through meditation and physical exercise and requires neither a sexual component nor the ingestion of pills. These sects are not necessarily celibate in their practices but advise against sexual activity. Some regard physical exercise as the preferred route, others emphasize exercise of the mental powers, whilst a number of sects involve both disciplines.

Chang San Feng Sect

Founded during the Ming Dynasty (1368–1644 CE) by the hermit from whom it takes its name, the sect was patronized by a number of Ming emperors although it subsequently declined. A master of the arts of internal alchemy and herbalism, Chang San Feng's interest lay in techniques of 'meditation through movement' and in the physical health of the body through slow, carefully prescribed exercise. These exercises, known as *t'ai chi ch'uan* are still practised today by students of Taoism and are also an aspect of so-called 'internal martial arts'.

After the death of Chang San Feng, his students developed the principles of internal alchemy that he had founded and formed the Wu Tang Shan Sect which is still active today in parts of central China. In the cultivation of the body, the sect differs from others, including Lung Men.

The masters of external alchemy were to be found amongst the members of the Fang Shih priesthood. They did not found sects as such but enjoyed popular followings of a sectarian nature. The most significant was undoubtedly Wei Po Yang who lived during the Eastern Han Dynasty (25–220 CE) and who wrote the archetypal text of alchemy, the *Tsan Tung Chi* (The Tripartite Unity). Wei Po Yang and his successors subscribed to the belief that a magical elixir, coupled with

DEVOTEES IN SHANGHAI PRACTISE *T'AI CHI CH'UAN*, ONE OF THE 'INTERNAL MARTIAL ARTS'.

Lung Men Sect (Dragon Gate)

Founded contemporaneously with the Chang San Feng Sect and under the aegis of the Complete Reality School (see below), its members concentrated on the cultivation of the mind through a combination of Taoism, Zen Buddhism, Confucianism and ritual in which it followed the practices of the Complete Reality School. Towards the end of the Ming Dynasty a splinter group arose within the sect which became known as the Wu Liu branch.

Wu Liu

This is a non-monastic alchemical sect which has rejected sexual aids to longevity but has not insisted on celibacy. It arose late in the Ming dynastic period out of divisions within the Lung Men sect. Its founders, Wu Chung Hsu and his student, Liu Hua Yang, both disaffected members of the Lung Men, followed the Singular Path and adopted so-called Action and Karma Taoism which is generally an amalgam of Confucian, Buddhist and Taoist theories. Wu Liu adapted this for lay membership by abandoning ritual and the Confucian aspects of Lung Men but incorporating elements of Zen Buddhism combined with Taoist practices.

Wu Liu uses a method of meditation which requires the adoption of a demanding posture for long periods of time and focuses on the internal cavities of the body as a means of disciplining the mind into a controlled state. Seven of these cavities are listed, commencing with the Life Gate or *ming men* cavity which is positioned in the lumbar region of the backbone. This cavity is considered a comparatively straightforward focus of attention and is particularly favoured by members of Wu Lui which is one of the most accessible sects for the layman in terms of the ease of its discipline. During meditation it is necessary to empty the mind of all thoughts and stimuli and the mental powers are then concentrated on the area of the cavity.

Hsien Tien Tao Sect

This sect also focuses on the internal cavities but in a more rigorous and thorough way than that of Wu Liu since it uses all seven cavities, some of which are extremely difficult areas on which to meditate and are not suitable for novice practitioners. Its meditation practice, in seven stages equating to concentration on the seven cavities, is known as Returning to the Earlier Heaven, and is unique amongst Chinese sects.

In physical terms it requires that the body adopts some rigorously difficult attitudes, generally versions of the lotus position, and that the hands are placed into specific *mudra* positions, reminiscent of those found in Hinduism and Buddhism, on each of seven areas of the body which become transformed. These include the Lower Cavity immediately above the navel, the Front Cavity which lies just below the navel, the Life Gate, the Central Palace in the region of the solar plexus, the Upper Cavity between the eyes, the Lowest Cavity in the sole of the foot and the formless Earlier Heaven Gate which is the ultimate achievement of the practitioner. A sensation of weightlessness is experienced as the energy of Tao is directed inwards and is merged with both mind and body of the practitioner. The sect therefore practises a combination of strenuous physical and mental disciplines in order to maintain body and mind in a high degree of health which is believed to be the key to longevity.

Tzu Yang Sect (Purple Yang)

Emanating from southern China, this sect was founded by Chang Po Tuan out of another division within the Complete Reality School. Tzu Yang, unlike Lung Men, found an advantage in steering away from the Singular Path. The emphasis lay on cultivation of bodily strength and fitness as a way to longevity before that of the mind, and it used sexual Yin-Yang alchemy as a means of replenishing bodily vitality and preparing the way for effective mental techniques.

The Complete Reality School

Not so much a sect as a movement subscribing to an ecumenical approach, it was founded by Wang Ch'ung Yang during the northern Sung Dynasty (960–1126 CE). He believed that the fundamental reality of everything is Tao, or pure energy, the ultimate reality of the universe, which can be experienced only when the mind is empty. The idea of Complete Reality involved the fusion of Taoist alchemical arts promoting health and longevity, Confucian ethics and the Buddhist concept of ridding the mind of unnecessary thoughts, desires and stimuli. It was the addition of certain aspects of Buddhism and Confucianism to Taoism, separately focusing on disciplines of the mind and body, which Wang Ch'ung Yang believed would offer complete enlightenment and would encourage goodness.

Subsequent divisions arose amongst students of Wang Ch'ung Yang, the so-called Seven Masters, some of whom established splinter sects detailed above and including most notably the sects founded by Ch'iu Ch'ang Ch'un and Ch'ang Po Tuan, known respectively as the Lung Men (Dragon Gate) Sect in northern China and the Tzu Yang (Purple Yang) Sect in the south.

OTHER SECTS

At least two other significant sects should be mentioned, neither of which necessarily fits with any degree of ease into the groupings already mentioned.

Ling Pao Sect (Sacred Jewel)

Founded in south-east China early in the fourth century CE as an essentially magical Taoist movement, this sect developed in the aftermath of the so-called Yellow Turban Rebellion which took place, in effect as a Taoist peasant revolt, towards the end of the Han Dynasty in the third century. Its members advocated peaceful principles and developed significant rituals of Taoism which were subsequently adopted by the Heavenly Master sect. It relies considerably on magic and ritual, including the use of talismans and carefully prescribed dances in order to control malevolent spirits, and its practices are based on the religious text known as the *Ling Pao Wu Liang Tu Jen Shang Ching Ta Fa* (Limitless Highest Writings and Great Method of Deliverance). It is in these scriptures that the deified name of Lao Tzu, T'ai Shang Lao Chun, is first used, from where it extended to the other orthodox sects.

Shang Ch'ing Mao Shan Sect

This orthodox order developed from the tradition allegedly begun by Lady Wei Hua T'sun, the daughter of a high-ranking priest amongst the Celestial Teachers during the Western Chin Dynasty (265–316 CE). She is supposed to have received the teachings in revelations and to have recorded them in a text known as the *Shang Ch'ing Huang T'ing Nei Ching Yu Ching*. The

MONKS AT RUERGEI MONASTERY IN SZECHUAN PROVINCE.

sect was allegedly formalized in the first century CE by the Taoist hermit T'ao Hung Ching (see p.156). These origins, however, have no historical foundation and the true founder may well have been a member of the same aristocratic family named Yang Shih. He is attributed with the authorship of most of the Shang Ch'ing texts and it was in his era that the sect enjoyed its first real following. In modern China it is based on Mount Mao or Mao Shan where T'ao Hung Ching lived his reclusive existence after leaving the political stage.

The sect used talismans to invoke deities and as vehicles with which they carried themselves into other non-temporal planes. Above all its members believed that Tao, the 'Way' and the all-pervading force in the universe, resides within the human body. The force is also known as the Sacred Foetus of Immortality, and it is believed that it must be nourished and preserved within each and every individual in order to maintain the spiritual link with Tao and to achieve the status of an immortal.

THE FIVE BUSHELS OF RICE SOCIETY

This movement, also known as the Way of the Five Bushels of Rice, arose early in the second century CE during the period of the Eastern Han Dynasty (25–219 CE). It stood halfway between a political body and a religious sect and was, arguably, the forerunner of the Taoist religious organization. By then Taoist philosophy was well established in China and was benefiting from large numbers of followers, but the Society began as a revolt against the conditions suffered by the peasant classes under the Han emperors.

HISTORICAL BACKGROUND

China had been bedevilled by almost constant unrest and fighting between rival power bases for several centuries. Under the Han Dynasty the country at last experienced unified government, with the warlords stripped of much of their power. The bloodshed was destined to re-emerge under the Three Kingdoms which followed and to continue for many decades thereafter, but in the comparative peace of the Han period ordinary people of the working classes continued to be neglected by government. They became increasingly interested in finding alternative ways and means of preserving their crops from drought and blight and protecting themselves from disease and infirmity. It was in this climate that the people began to turn to the religious aspects of Taoism and to the Fang Shih priests for comfort and protection.

Founded in the Shu area (modern Szechuan province) in western China by Chang Tao Ling (35–157 CE), also known as

THE SOCIETY'S PHILOSOPHY WAS BASED ON THE TEACHINGS OF LAO TZU, WHO INSPIRED ITS FOUNDER, CHANG TAO LING.

Chang T'ien Shih, the Five Bushels of Rice Society gained widespread support amongst illiterate country people living in a particularly remote and culturally independent region surrounded by mountains. The old ways of the Wu religion, magic and shamanism were still a firmly entrenched part of the

RICE HAS ALWAYS BEEN PART OF CHINA'S STAPLE DIET, HENCE ITS HISTORICAL IMPORTANCE AS A MONETARY UNIT.

traditions of this rice-farming area and provided an ideal climate for the religious hierarchy in setting up a quasi-autonomous political administration. The Society was operated on the basis of the teachings of Lao Tzu (see p.152). He was said to have inspired Chang Tao Ling when he visited him in spirit in a mountain retreat and conferred on him the title of T'ien Shih, Celestial Teacher or Heavenly Master. According to differing reports, the title was either self-declared by Chang Tao Ling, or subsequently awarded to the heads of the sect after the death of the founder by Chin Emperor T'ai Wu (424–52 CE). But the term was revoked subsequently by Emperor T'ai Tsu (1368–99 CE), the first ruler of the Ming Dynasty, who argued, logically, that mortal men could not also be masters of heaven.

FROM POLITICAL BODY TO RELIGIOUS SECT

The reverence of the Society to the teachings of Lao Tzu was highly instrumental in its being allowed to function with a degree of autonomy. The Eastern Han emperor was a strong supporter of Taoism and during the second century CE is known to have established a number of shrines where official ceremonies were conducted in honour of Lao Tzu. This imperial patronage was continued under the troubled aegis of the Wei Kingdom, one of three factions which waged war on each other more or less continuously for about 40 years following the ending of the Han Dynasty. By this time Lao Tzu had been elevated to the rank of deity by Chang Tao Ling who accorded him the title of T'ai Shang Lao Chun (The Illustrious Lord on High) and the Society was effectively transformed into a religious sect. The move paved the way for the establishment

of the Celestial Teacher, or Heavenly Master, Sect which evolved from the Five Bushels of Rice Society.

Chang Tao Ling was trained in the Confucian classics and was a master of talismanic magic and a respected alchemist. It was only in later life, however, that he turned to the teachings of Lao Tzu. The curious title given to the Society of 'Five Bushels of Rice' originates, according to differing traditions, either from the initiation 'fee' for membership, or from the high charges Chang Tao Ling is said to have levied on clients seeking the magical elixir and on other patients anxious to obtain cures for their ills. He specialized in preparing talismanic water concocted by writing talismans which were then burnt and the ashes mixed with water. The mixture was then either drunk by the patient or was sprinkled over them. The levies that Chang Tao Ling extracted were typical of the payment-in-kind system that existed in southern China at the time and they also earned him the nickname of 'Rice Thief'.

Chang Tao Ling and his sons nevertheless used the proceeds from the sale of the 'rice revenue' to found an establishment approaching the style of a non-secular state in the area now known as Szechuan. The Society engaged in a number of significant public-works projects in which its members built roads, erected hostels and were encouraged to care for the sick and infirm as well as offering food and hospitality to travellers. Chang Tao Ling adhered to the conviction that it was necessary to restore the true Way of Tao amongst the peasant population. The political organization existed for only a few decades but the Society survived for much longer and in the fifth century CE it became officially recognized as a branch of Taoism. The descendants of Chang Tao Ling were empowered to take on the leadership of the movement and its priesthood eventually became regarded as the representatives of orthodoxy in religious Taoism.

TAOIST RELIGIOUS RITUALS

Ceremonial Taoism represents its most devotional aspect and requires an emphasis on the celebration of religious festivals to reinforce the links between deities and the human population. These festivals, supervised by Masters of Rituals, include readings of sacred texts, chanting, dancing and the presentation of offerings.

Religious ritual was suppressed in mainland China at the time of the cultural revolution in the 1960s when Mao Tse Tung used his Red Guards to persecute the priesthood. Most of the Taoist traditions have, therefore, survived not in mainland China but on the nationalist island of Taiwan. Three types of ceremonial are practised by modern orthodox Taoist priests, each of which combines ritual with meditation. These religious events are conducted before an altar which represents the spiritual focus of the Tao.

In Taiwan Taoist priests are distinguished according to whether they follow orthodox or heterodox Taoist doctrine and the two categories are identified by different coloured headbands. Those wearing black, and so termed Blackheads, are the Tao Shih (Masters of Tao) who follow the orthodox canon. They are initiated by the Heavenly Master, the head of orthodox Taoism who descends from Chang Tao Ling, the founder of the Five Bushels of Rice Society. These priests are permitted to minister to the needs of both the living and the dead and their ritual is normally conducted away from the public gaze. In contrast, the heterodox priests, known as Fang Shih (Masters of the Methods), wear a red headband and adopt a more liberal style of devotion to which the lay public have open access.

SYMBOLISM

On the Tao altar stands a lamp, its flame representing both the sacred wisdom of Tao and the elixir of immortality. In front of the lamp are placed a number of objects, all of which reflect Taoist ideas. Three bowls provide a reminder of the emphasis on sexual energy in Taoism. One containing tea symbolizes the female *yin* principle, the second with water symbolizes the male *yang* and the third containing rice represents the generative outcome of the union between *yin* and *yang*. Five plates contain differently coloured fruits which symbolize the elements of earth (yellow), fire (red), water (black), metal (white) and wood (green), each of which acts upon the others in either constructive or destructive fashion. For example, wood generates fire which is generative, but water quenches fire in a destructive action. When the elements within the body, either the human frame, the corporate body of society, or the body of the universe, are seen to be in a constructive harmony, the body is healthy, when they are not, it becomes weakened.

A PRIEST USES INCENSE STICKS AS PART OF A RELIGIOUS RITUAL.

THE TEMPLE OF HEAVEN IN BEIJING HAS A LONG HISTORY AS A
CENTRE FOR TAOIST CEREMONIAL WORSHIP.

includes consultation with deities, prostration and invocations before their images and altars, requests for absolution and chants of praise. The Jade Ceremony follows a similar pattern. All three place considerable reliance on the value of meditational practices.

ANCESTRAL SPIRITS

Prior to the Communist take-over many of the most ancient traditions had survived with remarkable tenacity and, to the last days of the Ch'ing Dynasty in 1911, the Temple of Heaven in the Forbidden City of Beijing still witnessed imperial sacrifice. Although this style of ceremony was abandoned Taoists continue to lay considerable emphasis on other kinds of ritual, including ancestor worship. Great religious importance is attached to funerals and this focus is also supported by aspects of Confucian philosophy which dictates that ancestral spirits have a profound effect on the secular world. Funerals, supervised by orthodox Taoist priests, are important rites of passage, when effigies of philosophers and deified masters of Taoism are called upon to watch over the ceremony. Because it is implicit that the soul is setting out on a journey it must be provided with the necessities and with proper insurance against the influence of evil spirits. Mourners therefore bring gifts of food and paper models representing all the requirements that the deceased may need, often vastly exceeding anything he or she experienced in life. Gifts are also presented to propitiate any adverse influences or evil spirits which may be present. Houses, boats, cars, aeroplanes and money, all carefully modelled out of paper, are burnt in a sacrificial fire which both purifies and transports them in its smoke to heaven. The belief persists that the soul of the departed relative becomes divided at death, whereby one part ascends to heaven, one remains in the grave where it is entitled to receive offerings from the living, and a third inhabits the ancestral shrine which is maintained in the home of the eldest male heir.

The lamp is framed by candles to its left and right which symbolize both the eyes, the windows of the mind, and the celestial orbs of the sun and moon. The altar also includes an incense burner symbolizing the refining and purifying of the internal energies.

Of the three rituals the most elaborate is that known as the Yellow Register Ceremony. Its detailed and complex rites were not widely understood until they were gathered together and published by the eighteenth-century Ch'ing emperor Ch'ien Lung. The ceremony places strong emphasis on the links between the living and the dead, so that the souls of the departed are honoured and given comfort whilst the living are offered spiritual guidance. Prayers and chants are delivered to free the dead from torment in the underworld and the living from earthly misfortunes.

The other two rites, the Golden and Jade Ceremonies, are simpler and of more ancient origin than the Yellow Register, based on some of the oldest rituals of Taoism which can be traced back to the time of the Chou Dynasty. The Golden Ceremony

Because of the significance placed upon the grave, its location and after-care are also of major importance and to allow it to fall into disrepair affords considerable dishonour to the living relatives. The services of a Fang Shih are purchased to advise on the most expedient siting, and when the funeral is over, the grave is carefully tended and its occupant supplied with offerings. Within a limit of 100 days it is also necessary to dedicate an ancestral shrine in the form of a tablet which includes a portrait of the deceased and details of his or her status in life. This shrine is kept in the home and reverenced on a regular basis, and on certain occasions, such as a family wedding, the newly married couple will be expected to pay their respects to the shrine.

I CHING
AND OTHER
EARLY TEXTS

Taoism is not a single system but is separated into its philosophical school and the religious sects which in turn rely on the philosophy as a means of access to the Tao, the all-pervading essence of the universe. Consequently the texts of philosophical and religious Taoism can sometimes be better separated according to purpose rather than content.

THE TAOIST CLASSICS

The major texts of Taoist philosophy include the *Tao Te Ching* of Lao Tzu and the classical writings named after his successors, the *Chuang Tzu* and the *Lieh Tzu*. The *Tao Te Ching* is a product of the period of Chinese history known as the Spring and Autumn which extended from 770–476 BCE under the Chou Dynasty and was characterized by the rise of a large number of semi-independent fiefdoms operated by powerful nobles. Some of these feudal overlords had the pragmatism to realize that maintenance of power lay not merely in military strength and clannish conquest but also required sound political philosophy. It was in their quest for suitable advisers that the new breed of thinkers and their writings arose.

The *Tao Te Ching*, also known as the *Lao Tzu*, identifies Tao not as a spirit being living somewhere in the skies but as a benevolent force, impersonal and anonymous, to which everything in nature contributes so as to generate an homogenous power in the universe. Tao is the 'Way', the nature of reality and the means by which the universe operates through a regulated and positive mechanism. In this respect the new philosophy has moved on significantly from the diverse

world of shamanistic spirits, although its roots show clear evidence of having arisen from the old Wu religion. There is still, for example, considerable emphasis on the role of the shaman, or Taoist sage as he becomes recognized, and he may be seen, therefore, as representing something of a halfway house between the old-style shamanism and the masters of the philosophies which were to emerge later in China, stimulated by Buddhism and Confucianism.

The *Tao Te Ching* advocates a form of non-intrusive participation in the affairs of society known as *wu wei* (see p.154) although it defines this in a manner accountably different from that of its literary successors, the *Chuang Tzu* and *Lieh Tzu*. The maxim is 'do the work required and then leave well alone' but it also endorses the concept of princely sages being intimately involved in government. The *Tao Te Ching* requires that its disciples practise physical and mental techniques in the pursuit of health and longevity. The physical demands include adopting rigorous postures for periods of time, breath control and control of orgasm during sexual intercourse. The mental aspects include meditation.

The two major works of Classical Taoism which followed the *Tao Te Ching* were compiled during the next political phase of the Chou Dynasty known as the Warring States Period which extended from 475–221 BCE. As its name suggests, this era was marked by considerable bloodshed and brutality with larger and more powerful fiefdoms conquering and swallowing up smaller ones. It also marked a change in the attitude of many of the more influential thinkers of the day. They looked at the world around them and found it difficult to accept that Tao was a benign force or that participation in the political affairs of society was desirable. For them *wu wei* became, literally, a principle of 'do nothing' and the attitudes towards *wu wei* proclaimed in the texts of the *Chuang Tzu* and *Lieh Tzu* are at strong variance with that of the *Tao Te Ching*. These new

LAO TZU, REGARDED AS THE FOUNDER OF TAOISM AND AUTHOR OF THE *TAO TE CHING*.

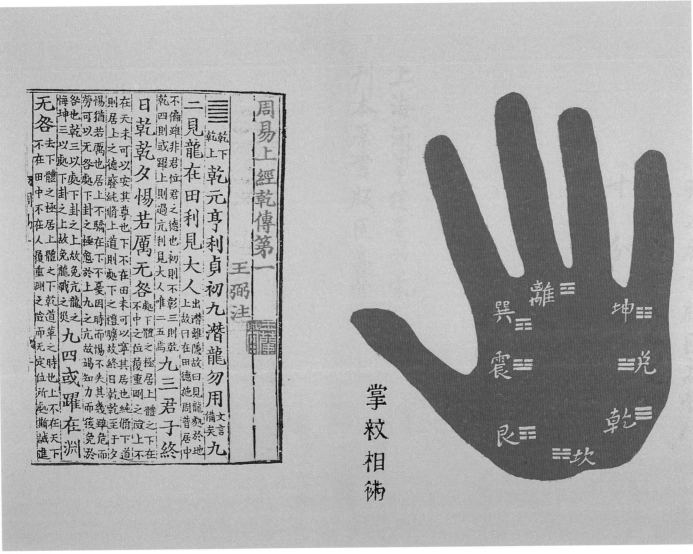

A DIAGRAM FROM THE *I CHING*, SHOWING THE EIGHT TRIGRAMS IN RELATION TO THE PALM OF THE HAND.

Taoist philosophies abandon the idea of Tao as a benign force with some measure of control over events and, for them, there is no such thing as the benevolent ruler. They argue that Tao is strictly neutral and that what will be will be. They decry politics as essentially corrupt and advocate complete non-interference in the affairs of society. Their objection is that the pursuit of health and longevity cannot be achieved whilst the student is also involved in politics or government and that he must distance himself from all worldly affairs.

I CHING

There are, in addition to the three Taoist classics, the so-called 'Five Confucian Classics' on which the teachings of Confucius are based. Originally six, these include the *I Ching* (Changes), *Shi Ching* (Odes), *Shu Ching* (History), *Ch'un Ch'iu* (Annals of Spring and Autumn) and *Li Ching* (Rites and Ceremonies). The sixth, the *Yue Ching* (Music) has been lost. (See The Confucian Canon, p.176.)

The *I Ching* (Book of Changes), however, represents much more than an element of the Confucian canon. The *I Ching* is one of the most ancient and important literary works of China. It constitutes a manual of divinatory techniques, consisting of 64 sections, each part being prefaced by a hexagram. This takes the form of a diagram of lines or *hsaio* created by the arrangement of stems, conventionally those of the yarrow or milfoil plant, into 64 different mathematically based patterns, representing all the structures and changes in the universe. It is from the perceived changes that the work takes its title. The hexagrams are followed by a mystical verse and a text made up of short commentaries or essays, sometimes only a few words in length and often enigmatic in their meaning, which relate to the interpretation of the hexagram.

There is no clear information on who wrote the work and some traditions place its authorship in the hands of the first emperor, Fu Hsi, as early as 3322 BCE. Mythology records that Fu Hsi, who taught the human race much of its early knowledge, discovered a tortoise on whose back were a series of esoteric markings. Fu Hsi is attributed with having constructed eight diagrams or trigrams known as *kua* from these patterns and it is on the basis of the trigrams that the hexagrams and the entire system of *I Ching* evolved.

In terms of its more probable chronology, the text is considered to have been compiled sometime during the Chou Dynasty which ended in 221 BCE and it is notable that the *I Ching* is first mentioned in the Official Book of the Chou Dynasty. Tradition claims that Wen Wang, the founder of the dynasty in 1122 BCE, composed the titles and brief explanatory verses towards the end of the preceding Shang Dynasty and that his son, Wu Wang or Tan, wrote the rest of the explanatory text. It is known from archaeology that various forms of it existed during the first and second centuries BCE and it appears not to have been standardized into one edition until many centuries later during the Han Dynasty.

Each of the 64 hexagrams is made up of six horizontal lines, equally spaced and of similar length, which are counted from the bottom to the top and which are either continuous, known as 'nines', or broken and known as 'sixes'. The first is the *Ch'ien Hexagram* which consists of six unbroken lines or 'nines'. The brief verse beneath the hexagram constitutes Wen Wang's limited explanation: *Ch'ien represents what is great and originating, penetrating, advantageous, correct and firm.* His son's more detailed commentary follows:

In the first or lowest Nine, undivided, the dragon lies concealed in the depths. It is not the time for active doing. In the second Nine the dragon emerges in the open field. It will be advantageous to meet with the great man. In the third Nine the superior man is active and watchful all day, and in the evening is still guarded and apprehensive. The position is dangerous but there will be no mistake. In the fourth Nine the dragon is still in the depths but looking up as if about to leap. There will be no mistake. In the fifth Nine the dragon flies in the sky. It will be advantageous to meet with the great man. In the sixth and uppermost Nine the dragon exceeds proper limits and there will be occasion for remorse.

The lines are all strong and undivided and if the dragons thus emerging were to lose their heads there would be good fortune.

Confucius refers to the *I Ching* in glowing terms, including the much quoted cry from his final years: 'If some years were added to my life, I would give fifty to the study of the *I Ching* and might then escape falling into great errors.' It is claimed that he read his copy of the text so extensively that its bindings wore out on no less than three occasions. A number of sections and appendices were added by Confucius and were further enlarged upon by later Confucian scholars, an aspect which has added to the difficulties of accurately dating the work.

OTHER TAOIST WORKS

Although Taoism began as a philosophy it became modified into a religion which functioned in parallel with the philosophical movement. The first of the religious texts is known as the *T'ai P'ing Ching*, the Book of Peace and Balance, whose authorship is unknown but which, according to tradition, was revealed by deities. This work became the basis of the religious beliefs expounded by Chang Tao Ling during the Eastern Han Dynasty (25–219 CE). It includes a 'Genesis' section explaining the origins of the universe and elevating Lao Tzu to the ranks of deities, describing him as T'ai Shang Lao Chun, the Great Lord on High, akin to a creator god. It also places the route to health and longevity firmly with correct religious ritual and observation, as well as emphasizing a strong moral and ethical code.

In the wake of this work, the so-called *Ling Pao* or Sacred Spirit scriptures appeared, based on the writings of Chang Tao Ling and including texts revealed by celestial sources to the Heavenly Masters (see p.164). The most important of these is a work entitled *T'ai Shang Ling Pao Wu Fu Ching*, the Highest Revelation of the Five Talismans of the Sacred Spirit. Chang Tao Ling also compiled a biographical reference work, the *Auspicious Alliance Canonical Register*, which includes a substantial number of deities and spirits whom he listed by name and function.

From the fifth century CE onwards the number of Taoist texts multiplied rapidly, beginning to focus on different specialized aspects including alchemy and mysticism, whilst other texts emulating the *I Ching* explored divination theory and techniques. In 471 CE the first Taoist canon appeared, edited by a highly respected scholar and alchemist from southeast China, Lu Hsiu Ching.

Mystical Taoism was detailed in several early texts, including the *Huang T'ing Nei Ching Yu Ching* or Yellow Court Jade Classic of Internal Images of the High Pure Realm, compiled by Lady Wei in about 288 CE, which became part of the standard writings of Shang Ch'ing Taoism.

A number of important works on alchemical Taoism include its oldest recognized text, the *Tsan Tung Chi* (Unity of Three). This work, detailing both internal and external alchemy, was compiled at some time around the middle of the second century CE by Wei Po Yang (see p.159). Named with reference to the master, his apprentice and his dog, all of whom according to tradition took the elixir of immortality, the text places considerable emphasis on the Yin-Yang theory of generating sexual energy, together with discourses on nonsexual techniques and the value of meditation practices. The *Tsan Tung Chi* takes a more or less classical approach to Taoism, quoting extensively from the *Tao Te Ching* and *I Ching*, and accepting Tao as the source of all life. It offers considerable practical detail, including the preparation of the alchemical furnace which generates the *yang* energy and the use of the other ingredients and apparatus.

CONFUCIUS

Confucius, the name by which this extraordinary personality is more commonly known, is a westernized corruption of K'ung Fu Tzu (Master Kung), its Latinization having been coined by Jesuit missionaries in the sixteenth century. Accurate biographical details about Confucius are sparse. He was born in 551 BCE during the Spring and Autumn Period of the Chou Dynasty in the small principality of Lu, which constitutes part of the modern province of Shantung, and he was probably the greatest and most influential thinker in Chinese history.

ELEMENTS OF CONFUCIUS' LIFE

Confucius was a near contemporary of Lao Tzu, the founder of philosophical Taoism, and in common with Lao Tzu who lived in the southern state of Ch'u, his father was a member of the educated upper class. The earliest work recording discontinuous elements of his life is the *Historical Records* which was compiled in the first century BCE, some 400 years after his death. There is also mention of him in the contemporary chronicles of the state of Lu.

It is stated that Confucius' family had fallen on hard times and that his first recorded employment was as a granary supervisor. Tradition has it that he rose from these inauspicious beginnings to become either Prime Minister or Minister of Justice in Lu in 501 BCE, resigning the post some four years later having become disillusioned with the brutal administrative conduct and political intrigues of the local overlord. This experience probably did much to fashion both his abhorrence of improper behaviour, particularly amongst the nobility, and his philosophy of a peaceful and harmonious society where the correct codes of conduct were rigorously applied. For some thirteen years after abandoning his post in government he became an itinerant, wandering though northern China, and during this phase of his life he was steadfast in his attempts to persuade petty Chinese rulers in favour of greater benevolence

and moral integrity. Apparently he was largely unsuccessful in his endeavours but whilst on his travels he gained a small band of followers who became the nucleus of a teaching centre when he eventually returned to Lu.

Confucius, by all accounts, was an unassuming and modest man who made few claims for himself but insisted that his contribution to society lay not in his abilities as an originator but in learning from others and passing on that which he had been taught. He was also a pragmatist, expecting perfection neither from society as a whole nor from his individual students whom he required only to do their best. A man of profound emotions, he is said to have shown ecstatic heights of pleasure in things which he discovered to be of beauty, but also great sorrow when he encountered loss or suffering. He had simple tastes, enjoying walking in the countryside, music and reading.

IDEOLOGY AND INFLUENCE

Confucius established his philosophical school, known as the *Ru*, in his home state and his students, all from the local region, irrespective of social background, came to be known as the Gentlemen of Lu. The size of his eventual following is unclear because only a limited number of his students' names have been recorded for posterity, but even during his lifetime they may have amounted to several hundreds. The most significant amongst the disciples was Mencius, Meng Tzu, who took on the mantle of Confucius' appointed successor after the death of the Master (see p.178).

The most important and reliable source of original Confucian ideology is the text known as the *Analects*, the *Lun Yu* or Selected Sayings, which comprises a somewhat disjointed collation of his conversations, put together by students shortly after his death. This work became a staple textbook for Confucian students and was used to export Confucian philosophy to other parts of South-East Asia.

Confucius pioneered the education of students from all social ranks – a courageous step because, hitherto, the aristocracy had benefited exclusively from the only education available. This formal schooling of the nobility required mastery of the so-called Six Arts, comprising ceremonial conduct, archery, charioteering, music, writing and mathematics. Confucius refused to acknowledge class distinctions in his students and the term which normally identified a person of noble birth in China, *chun tzu,* was applied by him to all who adopted modesty and benevolence in their behaviour towards others.

The philosophy he taught was at variance with that of Taoism in so much as he believed that the forces pervading the universe were fundamentally benevolent, whilst Taoists were, by then, arguing their neutrality. He insisted, nonetheless, that the establishment of a good society was not determined by these universal forces but by proper conduct between individuals and the correct observation of rituals. He drew strong links between ethics and government, insisting that the political institution could not exist simply as an apparatus with which to wield power, but in order to be effective had to adopt a moral responsibility in its administration.

Confucius died in 479 BCE. In spite of self-effacing comments about his own talents, his philosophies are widely regarded in the west as having been innovative, and it is undeniable that he originated many fundamentals of Chinese civilized society. When he did convey the ideas and teachings of others, he did so in an extremely effective manner, adapting and redefining where he believed necessary along ethical and humanitarian lines, and it was his ability to teach and to transmit ideas that earned Confucius his outstanding place in world history.

It is worthy of note that his philosophies were revitalized by the Neo-Confucian movement, begun in about the tenth century CE as the School of Li. They were observed by imperial rulers of China as an orthodox secular doctrine and a basis of formal education until the collapse of the Ch'ing Dynasty in 1911. The Communists who came in the wake of imperial rule suppressed Confucian principles, claiming that they were reactionary and designed to impede progress towards a modern socialist society. Today, however, in the more liberalized climate of post-Mao ideology, Confucianism is again beginning to find favour.

FOR 13 YEARS CONFUCIUS LIVED AS AN ITINERANT IN NORTHERN CHINA, A PHASE OF HIS LIFE DEPICTED IN THIS NINETEENTH-CENTURY ENGRAVING.

CONFUCIAN RITUALS

TEACHER DAY CELEBRATIONS AT A TEMPLE IN TAIWAN HONOUR THE BIRTH OF CONFUCIUS.

Confucius maintained a fundamental belief in the importance of ritual in the secular world, a view upheld by his students. He argued that this was essential at all levels of society and was not only the key to civilized behaviour but linked the society of the present with that of the revered ancestors who had first performed the various rites.

The Chinese psyche has always placed a high regard on *li* or righteous, proper behaviour and during the period of the Chou Dynasty in which Confucius lived the so-called Five Relationships determining this behaviour were an established part of Chinese tradition. The Five Relationships focus on the formal conduct of respect that is required between civilized people whereby it is necessary to maintain a proper and prescribed association between ruler and subject, husband and wife, father and son, the old and the young, and between friends of equal standing. Confucius stressed in his teaching that adherence to the principles was the mark of a gentleman and of his quality of life. He also subscribed firmly to the principle of *jen* as a prerequisite to *li*. In its original sense *jen* is a Chinese term which probably meant virile or manly but which, in Confucian philosophy, came to describe a moral quality – that of perfect manly virtue, in other words goodness. Confucius believed that *jen* stood as the sum total of all human integrity, including steadfastness, simplicity and courteous reserve, and was the supreme virtue. It is, he claimed, only through *jen* that a man is able correctly to perform *li*.

Confucius taught that, in practice, *jen* required love of one's fellow beings and he maintained the principle of doing to others what you would have them do to you. In this he placed great emphasis on the importance of ritual, which served to reinforce moral conduct, especially through ancestor worship, the offering of sacrifices and administration of funerary rites, and through devotion to music. It particularly applied to the emperor whose power on earth was sent from heaven and was maintained through the proper performance of ceremonials, but ritual also extended to all other areas of secular society. It supported rigid distinctions of class so that, for example, the courteous rites and ceremonies to which an emperor was entitled could not be extended to a state minister. It influenced the manner in which such matters as Filial Piety from subjects to emperor and children to parents were conducted, the style in which combatants engaged each other, and the way that business deals were effected.

Predictably, ritual extended to honouring Confucius himself. Serious claims were made after the collapse of the Chou Dynasty that subsequent emperors of the Ch'in and Han Dynasties did not have the mandate of heaven to govern. This authority, it was claimed, had been conferred on Confucius by the gods, including one known as the Black Emperor. It was alleged that Confucius possessed all kinds of miraculous powers of magic and divination and that he was entitled to worship as a divinity in his own right. For many centuries temples dedicated to the Master were erected throughout China and this ultimate level of devotion was later extended to other areas of South-East Asia, where it persists to the present day.

Ritual probably became more greatly emphasized in Confucian circles after the death of the Master, when Confucians came to envisage themselves as the honoured custodians of rites in Chinese society. It is suggested that Book 10 of the *Analects*, which elevates *li* to the level of a sacred rite in a manner which is not encountered in the other volumes, was added at a later date in order to meet the demands of a society that had become obsessed with ritual down to the smallest detail. Nonetheless a theme which occurs constantly in the books of the *Analects* attributable directly to Confucius' own view is one of scrupulous attention to matters of conduct, even down to correct facial expressions and body language when dealing with those of comparable or of different social

CONFUCIUS EMPHASIZED THE IMPORTANCE OF RITUAL
AS THE KEY TO CIVILIZED BEHAVIOUR.

station. He believed that propriety must be demonstrated at all times by public expression. This sometimes reached levels that the western mind might find fussy or over-meticulous. He would, for example, adopt a cringing position when entering the imperial grounds, not necessarily because he held the emperor as an individual in particular reverence but because he believed in the authority and status of the imperial office to which it was necessary to adopt proper decorum.

Not all schools of thought in China subscribed to the Confucian emphasis on ritual. The followers of Mo Tzu's doctrine of universal love found it repugnant and detrimental to the Chinese way of life. They rejected Confucian rites of mourning which, amongst others, they proclaimed wasteful and excessive. They also objected to the Confucian's slavish devotion to music as an adjunct to *li* which they saw as having taken on more or less ritual dimensions.

Generally, however, the Confucianists have been seen to be the custodians of a tradition of ritual which is deeply embedded in the Chinese psyche. In earlier centuries, imperial sages would call upon them as experts in matters of ritual procedure much as they called on other philosophical Masters for advice on spiritual, legal or military matters. Little has changed amongst Confucian society today wherein the principles of *li* and the rituals which sustain it are still rigorously applied.

THE CONFUCIAN CANON

*T*he principles of Confucianism are contained in a library of philosophical texts known collectively as the Confucian Canon. The canon recognized today, however, has changed over time and is not as it was originally written. In part this is because it fell victim to an intellectual purge during the third century BCE and in part because differences arose subsequently between Confucian reformers and traditionalists over the style of script to be followed.

During the Ch'in Dynasty (221–207 BCE) the emperor Ch'in Shih Huang Ti instigated an intellectual persecution which resulted in the burning of large numbers of books in 213 BCE. This tragic destruction was the outcome of advice rendered to the emperor by his prime minister, Li Si, that all the old books should be consigned to the flames with the exception of those that dealt with 'medicine, divination and husbandry'. The situation arose because the emperor, having managed to unify the political and military factions whose squabbling had bedevilled China for so long, was concerned to suppress any movement back towards devolution. This required the control of potentially subversive organizations and their propaganda material and such groups included the Confucians.

It is known that the *I Ching* escaped because it was held to be a book of divination and it was also claimed that some of the original Confucian texts had survived the assault. The story goes that they were discovered many years later where they had been immured in a wall cavity in Confucius' old house.

With the *I Ching*, these salvaged works were adopted as standard during the succeeding Western Han Dynasty (206 BCE–8 CE) by a Confucian school known as Ku Wen Chia,

the Old Character School. However, another contemporary faction, the Chin Wen Chia or New Character School, contested the authenticity of some of these texts and stood by the editions which had been rewritten.

As Taoism and Buddhism increased in popularity in China, the fortunes of Confucianism waned. A scholarly interest was reawakened during the Tang Dynasty (618–906 CE) but it was not until the time of the Sung Dynasty (960–1279 CE) under the emperor Chu Hsi that the make-up of the present canon was agreed and formalized. Chu Hsi, who ruled from 1130–1200 CE, is regarded as being the greatest of the neo-Confucian philosophers. He promoted the revitalized Confucian school of *Li* with the incorporation of Buddhist and Taoist elements.

THE MAJOR BOOKS

In its present form the canon includes the Five Classics and the Four Books agreed under the aegis of Chu Hsi. Parts of the Classics date from earlier times but incorporate material added by Confucius and his scholars. The most notable is the *I Ching* or Book of Changes which has been discussed on p.168. The *Shu Ching* or Book of History is a largely invented collection of early documents, speeches and other conversations to which Confucius refers in passing in his *Analects*. The content is claimed to stem from very ancient times in the pre-Chou dynastic era and from the early decades of the Chou Dynasty. Some is probably authentic but in many instances the material is thought to have been compiled by writers living under the Eastern Han Dynasty (25–220 CE).

The *Shi Ching* or Book of Poetry and Odes includes 300 or more poems, hymns and folk songs gathered from various local regions and put together in a single collection during the early part of the Chou Dynasty in about 1000 BCE or shortly after. The songs, often on the subject of love, were performed at the Chou imperial court and they were greatly admired by

A GRAPHIC INTERPRETATION OF THE EMPEROR CH'IN SHIH HUANG TI BURNING BOOKS AND EXECUTING SCHOLARS.

Confucius who carried the book with him. He quotes from it fondly a number of times in the *Analect* conversations.

The *Ch'un Ch'iu* or Annals of Spring and Autumn are historical records drawn from the Chronicles relating to Confucius' home state of Lu and covering the period between 722 and 484 BCE. It is claimed that much of the material was written by Confucius himself, although there is no substantive evidence for this. Certainly the original text was added to in the form of other commentaries compiled over the following two to three hundred years.

The *Li Ching* or Book of Rites and Ceremonies incorporates three volumes on the subject of the Li, the so-called Rites of Propriety, covering a wide range of ritual practice. The first of these is the *Chou Li* (Rites of Chou) followed by the *I Li* (Rites of Ceremonials) and the *Li Chi* (Record of Rites). The dating of these

works is unclear. Some of the material cannot be providenced but is thought to have come down from ancient times, whilst other sections were added during the Western Han Dynasty.

There was at one time a sixth Classic, the *Yue Ching* or Book of Music, but this was lost at some time before the second century BCE and has never been recovered.

The Four Books, which stand alongside the Five Classics, form the basic texts of neo-Confucianism. All originate from Confucian writers and include commentaries added by Chu Hsi. The *Lun Yu* or *Analects* is a collection of speeches and conversations of Confucius himself; the *Chung Yung* or Doctrine of the Mean and the *Ta Hsueh* or Great Learning are volumes drawn from the old Classic Book of Rites; the fourth, the *Meng Tzu* or Book of Mencius, purports to include some of the writings of Confucius' successor but was compiled after the death of Mencius.

MENCIUS

Meng Tzu (371–289 BCE), whose westernized name is Mencius, was the recognized successor to Confucius as the great champion of social order and virtue in ancient China. In the aftermath of Confucius' death, the philosophical movement which he had founded entered a period of disarray with various ideological factions squabbling for supremacy. In spite of this confusion, however, Confucianism dominated philosophical debate in China in company with the philosophy of Mohism, or self-sacrifice and 'universal love', advanced by Mo Tzu, another of the great contemporaries of Mencius during the Warring States Period.

The intellectual stage also included another influential although poorly recorded philosopher, Yang Chu, who first expounded the radical idea that 'human nature' or *hsing* might be in conflict with the needs of society as a whole. He pointed out that we have an inborn disposition to look after our own interests and well-being before looking after those of others.

Little is known of the background of Mencius himself other than that his birthplace was in Tsou, a small dependent region within the state of Lu where Confucius had lived and worked, and that he grew up during the Warring States Period of the Chou Dynasty. As a young man he took a position in the neighbouring state of Ch'i in the court of King Hsuan, employed as a *shih*, a man of service in the lower ranks of government.

Mencius followed the Confucian conviction that the nobility carried a deep moral obligation and that it was necessary to maintain a correct and virtuous propriety in the relationship between ruler and ministers. At the time Ch'i represented a powerful and influential principality and Hsuan was, by tradition, the founder of the famous philosophical academy of Chi Hsia. At the Ch'i court, Mencius devoted considerable energies to attempting to convert Hsuan to Confucian values, although apparently with little success. Hsuan was generous in salary and was prepared to listen to his arguments with magnanimity, but do little more to change the conservative order of things. Notwithstanding Hsuan's relative tolerance, this was in a period of Chinese history when power politics had become increasingly brutal and when the dignity and virtue of the aristocracy had increasingly given way to baser instincts. Mencius believed that the trend away from virtue in the nobility was in danger of destroying the objectives of Tao. He saw the 'Way' as being in rapid decline through the personal greed and ambition of petty rulers who acted in a tyrannical fashion against the interests of the population at large. This had led to a distortion of ethics and the emergence of all kinds of heretical view. The restoration of Tao was, therefore, dependent on the return to proper and morally driven conduct amongst the nobility.

Frustrated by the lack of positive response from Hsuan, Mencius travelled extensively from state to state attempting to persuade other rulers of the value of Confucian ethics and morality but largely with the same lack of success experienced by his venerated forebear. This promotional activity was a courageous exercise on the part of Mencius since it flew in the face of the political vogue. By and large the local princes, such as King Hui, the ruler of the neighbouring state of Liang, were more interested in expanding their own power bases regardless of ethical niceties. Only with Duke Wang, the overlord of the tiny principality of T'eng, too small to harbour expansionist hopes, did he apparently gain a sympathetic ear.

TEACHING AND PHILOSOPHY

The philosophy and work of Mencius is contained in the so-called *Book of Mencius*, a compilation of his teaching, and his arguments with other philosophers and local rulers, which was produced probably by his students after his death. During his lifetime he devoted his energies to extolling the Confucian ethics of goodness, or *jen*, and righteousness, *i*, which he believed to be innate qualities in all human nature. He argued that people of every disposition and background can be persuaded to act out of purely moral motives once they realize that they possess an inborn natural tendency, *hsing*, towards moral conduct. But he also believed in the notion that there is an overall power which governs the cosmos and to whose conditions of morality rulers of earthly kingdoms should that conduct — general interests of humanity set beside personal self-interests. He argued that the conventional theory of the interest of the individual being best served by meeting the interests of society as a whole fell apart whenever the objective was utilitarian or material. He pointed out that, in practice, the pursuit of general interest invariably descended into one of self-interest when administrators, or those in positions of power, had personal ambition, material gain and prestige in mind. Put in another way, as long as the attention of power-brokers is focused on material results, they are unlikely to be convinced that self-interest is best served when the general interest of the greatest number is being pursued. It is recorded, for example, that when Mencius first met King Hui of Liang, the ruler suggested that there must be some way that Mencius could 'serve the interests of the state'. Mencius' response was to point out that this interest did not lie truthfully in the objective of peace, which would have served all of humanity, but in increasing the material wealth and power of Liang and its ministers. The alleged interest of the state was, in reality, self-interest because the objective was a utilitarian one.

Mencius also followed some religious convictions. His view, though, was deeply bound up with his belief that the salvation of the world lay in the hands of noble men and that their defence of morality was the key to the Will of Heaven being effected on earth. He argued that it is essential for society to maintain contact with its own

MENG TZU, OR MENCIUS, IS REGARDED AS A PHILOSOPHICAL LEADER AND THE SUCCESSOR TO CONFUCIUS.

properly conform. These conditions were summed up as the *T'ien Ming*, the 'Will of Heaven'.

Mencius subscribed firmly to the Confucian principle of *li*, the correct spirit of ritual and social behaviour, but one of his preoccupations was with the interests which were served by

human nature and that this nature is an embodiment of Heaven no less than the stars in the sky. The belief is summed up in Mencius' famous statement: 'He who fully realizes the potentialities of his heart knows his nature. He who knows his nature knows Heaven.'

YIN-YANG

The image of sexual opposites working as complementary forces in the cosmos must be one of the oldest philosophies in the history of humankind. It is essentially a dramatic extension of the strongest drive we experience in life's reality, that of coupling between male and female protagonists in order to regenerate not only our own species but also the life which exists around us in nature. The Chinese philosophy of Yin-Yang subscribes to this concept, whereby the Yin force is associated with that which is perceived to be feminine in nature, including the earth, the moon, passivity, cold, darkness and night, and the Yang reflects the masculinity of the heavens, the sun, dynamic activity, heat, light and day.

The Chinese agriculturalists of ancient times, like many others at a comparable stage of cultural development, believed that the seasonal cycle on which they depended lay in the hands of male and female celestial forces but they extended this to the notion that changes of the seasons were a result of progression and alteration in the balance between Yin and Yang. Because of their constitution, these forces were closely linked with the notion of the five primordial elements — water, fire, wood, earth and metal — given that wood and metal were essentials required by a pioneering agricultural society rather than cosmic entities.

It is unclear where and when the concept of Yin and Yang first developed in China and it was probably not the product of a single mind or time but rather a reflection of the collective subconscious of the agricultural pioneers the world over which appealed especially to the Chinese mentality.

Although the origins of the doctrine remain vague it is therefore likely that they stem from a much earlier period of China's prehistory than the date of the first literature on the subject. During the Han Dynasty (206 BCE –219 CE) the Yin-Yang school, Yin-Yang Chia, became recognized as one of six schools promoting reputable philosophies in China. These schools represented centres of wisdom with sufficient credibility that emperors would call upon them for advice whenever their particular services were required. The Yin-Yang school drew heavily on the teachings of the Confucian master Tsou Yen who lived in the province of Ch'i and was allegedly a member of the influential Chi Hsia Academy.

LINKS BETWEEN THE COSMOS AND HUMANKIND

Yin-Yang ranked alongside Taoism, Confucianism, Mohism and others, and it was part of a broad belief that the activities of heaven and the activities of humankind exert a strong effect on one another. The concept of Yin-Yang was thus extended and applied to changes which took place in history, politics and social conditions. It became firmly accepted that Yin-Yang phenomena could have a profound effect on the fortunes of dynasties and individuals alike.

Tsou Yen was amongst a number of Han Dynasty theorists who proposed the existence of the links between events taking place in the human population and changes in the cosmos. He developed a theory of correlation between the Five Elements, which he believed ran in cycles of dominance, and the cyclical patterns which he claimed could be observed in human history. He also believed that the forces of Yin and Yang, through their waxing and waning, could disrupt the elemental rhythms of

ABOVE: A PENDANT MADE FROM BOXWOOD DISPLAYS THE
YIN-YANG SYMBOL AND THE SACRED TRIGRAMS.

nature and therefore of history. His theory suggested that various Chinese dynasties had shown, predominantly, either Yin or Yang characteristics which had not necessarily corresponded with the natural cycle of the elements. This idea of conflict was amplified in the words of a fellow philosopher, Tung Chung Shu, who stated that 'the human order often fails to resonate with the natural order'.

The theory of Yin-Yang is touched on, to a greater or lesser extent, in a number of Chinese philosophical works from the Classical Period, although it is sometimes interpreted in different ways and as part of various groupings of elements. So, for example, in one physician's textbook Yin and Yang are included as components of the so-called 'Six Ch'i' including Yin, Yang, wind, rain, light and dark.

In the *Tao Te Ching* of Lao Tzu, the father of Taoism, there is a strong interest in the opposites of nature whereby he draws contrasts between the weak and the strong, soft and hard, passive and active, each of which are characteristics of Yin and Yang. Lao Tzu, however, also draws some provocative comparisons. 'Man,' he states, 'when born is soft and weak but when he dies is hard and solid'. Lao Tzu thus infers that the human lifespan witnesses a rhythm by which, from cradle to grave, Yin is transposed gradually by Yang. The analogy is extended to other aspects of nature and suggests that Yin is more powerful and vital than Yang: 'The ten thousand things – grass and trees – are born soft and supple but when they die they are withered and hard. Therefore the hard and strong are the companions of death; the soft and weak are the companions of life.'

Amongst the Five Classics (see p.176) both the *Spring and Autumn Annals* and the *I Ching* (Book of Changes) expound on the Yin-Yang theory. The *Annals* attributes the decline of the Chou Dynasty to excessive cultural complexity, known as *wen,* which it allies firmly with Yin, and to an absence of simplicity or *chih.* It is inferred that this bias in favour of one protagonist threw the natural Yin-Yang cycle out of rhythm and caused dislocation in the earthly order.

In the *I Ching*, the lines of the trigrams and hexagrams which form the basis of its discussion, are considered to reflect Yin and Yang. The link between changes in the universe and human activity is emphasized in the descriptions of the hexagrams' lines which include terms like fortitude or indecision. Those which are undivided, the 'nines', are to be thought of as Yang lines, whilst the broken 'sixes' are Yin lines. If in proper conjunction the Yin and Yang lines should alternate, but often in the hexagrams they do not. Where a Yin

ADULTS AND CHILDREN ARE SHOWN STUDYING THE YIN-YANG SYMBOL, IN A SEVENTEENTH-CENTURY CHINESE PAINTING.

line appears in what should be a Yang position or vice versa there is an indication in the text of some kind of disruption.

The *Hang Hexagram*, number 32 in the series, begins (from the bottom) with a Yang 'six' which although it correlates correctly with the fourth line, a Yin 'nine', nonetheless opens the hexagram on a weak note. Much better were the first to be a Yin 'nine' and the fourth a Yang 'six'. Between the first and the fourth there are also two strong 'nines' which, even though the third is in its proper place, together throw the balance out. The weak fifth can be seen to correlate with a strong second but then the sixth is also weak, throwing the balance still further and ending the hexagram on a sombre note: 'The topmost six, divided, shows its subject exciting himself to long continuance. There will be evil.'

THE INTRODUCTION OF BUDDHISM IN CHINA

Mahayana Buddhism probably reached China by way of Nepal and Tibet during the first century BCE, in the period of the Western Han Dynasty, although some authors claim that its arrival did not take place until as late as the second century CE. The missionary monks brought with them the Amitabha BUDDHA and a heavenly retinue of DHYANIBUDDHAS, BODHISATTVAS, ARHATS and others (see p.70). They came armed with Buddhist scriptures and, because at the time religious Taoism was still at little more than a fledgling stage of development beside an outmoded Wu religion, they found a country that was potentially receptive to new influences for its spiritual needs.

A CARVING IN A TEMPLE IN TAIWAN SHOWS ONE OF THE MONKS RESPONSIBLE FOR SPREADING BUDDHISM FROM INDIA TO CHINA.

Certain aspects of the alien religion, however, received a lukewarm reception. The celibacy of the Buddhist monks and their abhorrence of ordinary work was wholly foreign to the Chinese mentality. These things went against the deep-rooted Chinese character of maintaining family ties and working for a living. There were also common themes to be discovered, at least on the surface. The nothingness, *wu,* of Taoism is approximately paralleled in *sunyata,* the importance of reaching a state of emptiness stressed in Buddhist *sutras,* particularly the *Prajnaparamita,* which was amongst the first of the Buddhist texts to be translated into Chinese language. This apparently shared concept, however, revealed differences because the definition of 'nothingness' was one over which the two philosophies in fact diverged markedly, The idea of other abstract principles such as *karma* was also perhaps extremely difficult to grasp for a people not possessing a background of Hinduism. Nonetheless, in spite of the negative aspects, much in Buddhist theory and practice came to attract the Chinese and they showed themselves willing to adapt and modify the indigenous form of religious Taoism. For their part the proselytizing Buddhist monks were also amenable to incorporating the teachings of Lao Tzu and Chuang Tao Ling into their own religious ideologies.

BUDDHIST MONKS IN THEIR SAFFRON ROBES ARE A FAMILIAR SIGHT
IN THE STREETS OF TAIWAN.

AMALGAMATION OF BELIEFS

The actual synthesis was a protracted process. For a long period of time the two religions did not actually meld and it was more a matter of tolerant 'live and let live'. Amongst the outstanding pioneers of promoting Mahayana Buddhism in China during this formative phase was the Buddhist monk Kumarajiva, who arrived in the country from northern India in 401 CE. He and his students were responsible for translating and, in some respects, adapting to suit the Chinese mind more than 30 of the most important Buddhist scriptures. Later, in the sixth, seventh and eighth centuries, during the time of the Sui and T'ang Dynasties, Chinese scholars began to render their own interpretations of the Buddhist works and to make important contributions to the ideologies of Indian Buddhism. These writers included, most notably, Chi I and Chi Tsang, founders of the T'ien Tai and Sanlun schools, followed by Fa Tsang who founded the Avatamsaka school.

It was in this cultural climate that a number of varieties of Mahayana evolved, including Ch'an (Zen) and it was this branch which paved the way to a true synthesis with Taoism and Confucianism. Ch'an already amalgamated aspects of Taoist *wu wei*, 'doing nothing', with more practical notions of Confucianism and features of Mahayana mysticism.

The change in Taoism came about in the climate of an increasing disillusionment with the old style of alchemical magic which many sceptics came to regard as operated by charlatans who delivered esoteric jargon and indulged in outmoded practices that regularly did not work. The promise of immortality to be gained from pills and potions no longer rang with any conviction and although the quest for longevity still ranked high amongst people's priorities it was increasingly fashionable to look for alternative routes.

The amalgamation of the three beliefs was begun during the early part of the T'ang Dynasty and was pioneered by several notable Chinese scholars and philosophers, including the Confucian-schooled Lu Tung Pin, Wang Ch'ung Yang and Chen Hsi Yi. Lu Tung Pin is one of the eight Chinese immortals (see p.146) under whom Wang Ch'ung Yang was a student, having first studied T'ien Tai and Ch'an before coming to Taoism. Chen Hsi Yi was a sage who developed a system of internal martial arts. These three and others realized that spiritual and physical benefits lay in combining the eclectic aspects of each religion and by the eleventh century the synthesis was completed, gaining a widespread popular following in the Sung Dynasty (960–1279 CE). It resulted in the production of the Taoist canon which was based on the Buddhist canon, the *Tripitaka* or 'Three Baskets of Sacred Writings', and in the establishment of a Buddhist-style priesthood and monasteries. Old Buddhist rituals and festivals were adapted and their names changed to suit Chinese preferences.

The period also saw the development of other forms of Buddhism in China, including T'ien Tai and Ching Tu, through the inspiration of Indian Mahayana. T'ien Tai, which focuses particularly on the teachings contained in the *Padmasutra* (*Lotus sutra*) stressing the importance of emptiness, compassion and morality, involves Tantric Buddhism and meditation and is essentially another monastic branch of Buddhism. In Japan it becomes Tendai. Ching Tu, closely allied to Zen, is more accessible to the lay person and focuses on the Amitabha *buddha* as an icon of worship through whom the paradise may be reached where rebirth takes place. Known as the doctrine of the Pure Land, the realm of Amitabha, it was first promoted through the White Lotus Society founded in Lohan late in the fourth century CE by Hui Yuan and rejects both monastic life and celibacy. In Japan it becomes Jodo.

The fusion of Taoist, Confucian and Buddhist ideals has proved highly durable and it characterizes at least two of the modern Taoist branches, Hsien T'ien Tao (Way of the Earlier Heaven) and Ch'uan Chen (Complete Reality School).

ZEN IN CHINA

*A*lthough in modern times Zen Buddhism is most closely associated with Japan and Korea, it began in China as Ch'an. Its architects included such eminent minds as that of the Sixth Zen Patriarch, Hui Neng. These masters were attracted to the meditational aspects of Mahayana Buddhism but felt it was necessary to arrive at an eclectic combination, integrating the influence of Indian culture with the needs of the Chinese mind and involving elements of Confucianism.

AN IMPOSING STATUE OF THE *BUDDHA*, 71 METRES HIGH, STANDS AT LESHAN IN SZECHUAN PROVINCE.

BODHIDHARMA

Tradition has it that the Zen school was brought to China by a monk named Bodhidharma at some time between the fifth and sixth centuries CE, several hundred years after the Chinese were introduced to Buddhism. Bodhidharma is almost certainly a figure of mythology whose story in literature can be traced back no earlier then the eighth century, although the name of Bodhidharma appears in one text, the *Lo Yang Ch'ieh Chi,* compiled in the mid sixth century. The mythology suggests that he grew up in a Brahmin family in southern India and migrated to China during the reign of Emperor Wu Ti (502–550 CE) in the period of the so-called Six Dynasties. There he met the Emperor and entered the Shao Lin Ssu monastery where he meditated, without interruption and facing a blank wall, for nine years. His famed technique of wall-gazing, *pi kuan,* was destined to become a fundamental aspect of Zen meditation and the miraculous stories of his life and death became incorporated into the Zen chronicles of later centuries as if authentic parts of history. In truth it is more likely that several Indian and Chinese Buddhist monks were involved in the development of Zen metaphysics and meditative techniques over a period of time, but the figure of Bodhidharma is so central to the traditions of Zen that his historical credibility is made almost immaterial.

The successors to Bodhidharma in sustaining the Zen movement and its traditions in China became known as the Zen Patriarchs, equating, in effect, with the *bodhisattvas* of Mahayana Buddhism (see p.88). The first of these masters to emerge with any degree of certainty as an historical figure is the Sixth Patriarch, Hui Neng.

HUI NENG

Born in 638 CE, Hui Neng grew up at a time of disaffection between two schools of Zen that had become established in the north and the south of China with rival ambitions. The Northern school, originally known as the Lankavatara school after the Buddhist *Lankavatara sutra,* was led by Shen Hsiu, who is claimed to have been a student of the Fifth Patriarch, Hung

THIS WOOD AND GILT LACQUER IMAGE DATING FROM THE MING DYNASTY REPRESENTS AMITABHA, ONE OF THE FIVE *DHYANIBUDDHAS*.

Jen. Shen Hsiu claimed that the attainment of enlightenment could be properly achieved only by a gradual contemplative process. The Southern school was that of Hui Neng who argued in favour of techniques that resulted in sudden enlightenment. Hui Neng allegedly impressed Hung Jen to such an extent when they met at the patriarch's monastery of Wang Mei, that he conferred on Hui Neng the title of Sixth Patriarch.

For some time there was considerable hostility between the two schools and their ideologies. Shen Hsiu also claimed to have inherited the succession from the Fifth Patriarch and at one stage instigated a purge, attempting to have his rival exiled. The Southern school, however, was more vigorously defended and received the backing of some influential Zen followers. Hui Neng retired meanwhile to a reclusive existence in a remote part of southern China for the remainder of his life and is said to have died, seated in the lotus position, in about 713 CE.

After the deaths of both Hui Neng and Shen Hsiu the Northern school was effectively eclipsed and Hui Neng became regarded as the founder of all subsequent Zen schools and successions. His most significant work, the *Sutra of the Sixth Patriarch,* is unusual in being the only religious text from a Chinese hand to be denoted as a *sutra*, although in reality much of it was probably written by his students after his death.

Hui Neng extended the Mahayana idea of nothingness, inherent in the Indian Buddhist theme of *sunyata,* into the necessity for irrationality to be allowed free rein in acquiring enlightenment. He said: 'fundamentally not one thing exists', confirming his belief that the temporal life is an illusion: the only means of escaping this impermanent material deception is through enlightenment which reveals the real nature of the universe and results in transcendence. The radical elements in his teaching included the notion that, in order to acquire enlightenment, the rational consciousness must be discarded and replaced by supra-rationality. This, he argued, is an ability which is innate in every human being, deep in the human subconscious, but can only be developed by way of correct mental discipline and physical practice in conjunction with each other. In his argument, enlightenment and practice are inseparable if not identical, although by practice he refers to inner as well as outer regimes. The adoption of the lotus position for the body, the meditation posture in which he placed great store, is therefore as important as the proper exercise of the mind. His belief in the necessity for irrational enquiry also brought him into conflict with the upholders of academic scholarship since he regarded this as a hindrance to enlightenment.

LATER DEVELOPMENTS

Hui Neng's most notable student was Shen Hui, but he did not appoint a successor to the patriarchy and after the death of Shen Hui there was a vacuum for two or three generations until two outstanding Zen masters emerged during the Tang dynastic period, Shih T'ou Hsi Ch'ien (700–790 CE) and Ma Tsu Tao I (709–788 CE). Based in the provinces to the west and south of the Yangtse River – modern Kiangsi and Yunan – their influence on the evolution and spread of the philosophy was considerable and the lineage of Zen Patriarchs more properly stems from these two. They subscribed strongly to Hui Neng's philosophy, condoning a degree of liberalization amongst the schools of Zen whilst retaining the basic principles of discarding rational thought and academic-style enquiry.

The number of Zen schools expanded steadily in China until the period of the Five Dynasties (907–960 CE) when they became streamlined into the so-called Five Houses, all essentially following the doctrine laid down by Hui Neng but with minor idiosyncrasies distinguishing one from another. It was from amongst these schools that Zen philosophy was destined to be transported to Japan where it evolved into the great and enduring sects of Rinzai and Soto.

JAPANESE BELIEFS

🐚🐚🐚🐚🐚🐚🐚🐚🐚🐚🐚🐚🐚🐚🐚🐚🐚🐚🐚🐚🐚🐚🐚

The ancient religion of Japan is Shinto, the 'Way of the Gods', although the name was given in comparatively late times. Shinto originated in the prehistoric period but still commands a considerable following beside the other great strands of philosophical belief in Japan, Buddhism and Confucianism. In spite of its antiquity Shinto is a dynamic living religion and its endurance is attributable largely to the fact that it has been prepared to live in harmony with, and adapt to, other faiths and philosophies. It is a pantheistic belief although in its worship of a multitude of divinities or *kamis* it recognizes a supreme figure, the national patron deity, Amaterasu, the sun goddess. Its focus is on the benefits of life in the present world which it regards as divine gifts from deities who expect, in return, purity of mind and body coupled with devotional practices. It is not a religion of mass congregation, but more one of individual practice and ritual through occasional visits to shrines and temples staffed by a professional priesthood.

Shintoism has been greatly influenced during the course of its evolution by Mahayana Buddhism which was brought to Japan mainly from Korea and China, and by the Chinese secular philosophy of Confucianism. It was these alien factors which were responsible for the moulding and reforming of ancient shamanistic rites into the Shinto faith and practice that is recognizable today. Some of the earliest aspects are, however, also still clearly evidenced and may be seen in the construction of the more ancient national shrines including Ise-*jingu* and Izumo.

The principles of Buddhism proved attractive to the Japanese mind and the two religions became partly assimilated, though still retaining their individual identities. It is not unusual today to find people taking part in both Shinto and Buddhist rituals to mark the key moments in their lives.

EARLY JAPANESE RELIGION

*T*he ancient prehistoric beliefs and religious traditions from which Shinto developed in Japan are probably little different from those of countless other primitive societies around the globe. Japanese religion evolved out of the beliefs of scattered tribes of nomadic hunters, who subsequently became the first settled communities with an existence based on agriculture and fishing.

ANIMISM

The beliefs of such societies are invariably animistic, recognizing that all things in nature, animate or inanimate, are controlled by unseen spirits. The intercessors who invoke these spirits and are temporarily invaded by them for purposes benevolent or otherwise are the shamans or magician-priests. Early beliefs also tend to recognize the existence of ancestral spirits whose presence can strongly affect the fortunes of the living.

In the Japanese islands and the neighbouring mainland peninsula of Korea these animistic beliefs took the form of a host of differing and localized folk traditions which were only later combined to constitute the basis for more formalized philosophy. Japanese religion, however, is perhaps unusual in that archaic elements have persisted into modern times, particularly in social and family life. Numerous festivals and rites are still observed which closely follow magical and superstitious beliefs and which, to a western mind, may seem quaint and anachronistic.

There is evidence of two distinctly different types of belief in the prehistoric agrarian society of Japan, known as *uji-gami* and *hito-gami*. *Uji-gami* focuses on ancestral spirits and their shrines within family groups, whilst *hito-gami* is concerned with the relationship established between a specific *kami* and the shaman through whom the deity operates. It is probable that ancestor worship is the older of the two types and that its popularity slowly waned as family clans or *dozoku* became more attracted to the protection afforded by a guardian deity. It was almost certainly from amongst the powerful shamans of these *kamis* that the imperial dynasty was founded.

The most ancient traditions have continued to the present day in folk religion and this endurance, seemingly incongruous when set in the context of a modern industrial nation leading the way in such areas as computer technology, is an integral part of the Japanese mentality. Some have argued that it has actually hindered the modernization of Japan.

The old religion of Japan was probably based on a seasonal round of festivals and rites. Because the economy of land-based clans was primarily a rice-growing one, the guardian deities of the earth and its fruits were particularly revered. There is evidence of belief in a Great Rice Mother, the rice-soul or spirit of the rice, who, in the guise of a shamaness, was ritually wedded to the emperor to produce a sacred Rice Child. In comparatively modern times there have been rice harvest ceremonies in which the priest selects bunches of rice ears which are then tied together and adorned with flowers to represent a Rice-bride and Rice-groom. A wedding feast is enacted in their honour and the cutting of the rice harvest can then begin. In some parts of the Far East, in a continuation of the theme, when the last two sheaves of rice are cut they are carried to the barn, decorated as the husband and wife, and laid together on a small platform to encourage the rice stored in the granary to increase in quantity.

There have also existed rites of passage associated with the seasons of the human lifespan. These include birth, puberty, marriage, child-bearing and death. Those associated with puberty, particularly amongst male children, may have involved tuition about the traditions of the clan and physical ordeals to mark initiation into adult society. For girls, initiation often involved tattooing on the hand or face. Some of these rites have persisted and those amongst noble classes are known as *ui-koburi* or 'wearing the crown', whilst within the lower social groups they are *eboshi-gi* which derive from a *samurai* ritual of donning the warrior headgear known as *eboshi*.

The landscape itself took on a spiritual significance and mountains and lakes became sacred places, either the homes of gods or the actual embodiment of deities. Hence such landmarks as the volcanic Mount Fuji, with its connotations of a god either at peace or angered, have been prayed to, as *kamis*, since time immemorial.

SHAMANS AND MAGICIANS

The earliest priest-magicians arose as two distinct types, with shamanesses probably more in demand than male shamans. One type has affinities with the shamans of tribal societies in eastern Siberia, including those living in the Kamchatka Archipeligo which extends down towards the Japanese Kurile islands. The other shows links with the religious customs of Polynesia. Today those of the Arctic tradition are found mainly in Hokkaido, the northernmost of the main islands, whilst those of Polynesian tradition are concentrated in Honshu to the south.

Out of the assortment of rather vague animistic spirits invoked by village shamans there emerged divinities or *kamis* who possess names and, to a greater or lesser extent, human characteristics. These formed the cast of the Shinto pantheon. The creation account in the *Kojiki* chronicle indicates that after the primordial trio of gods created themselves out of nothing on the Plain of High Heaven (see p.190), subsequent deities, known as the Seven Divine Generations, emerged from reed-like growth in muddy swamps: 'from a thing that sprouted up like a reed-shoot when the earth, young and like floating oil, drifted about medusa-like'. It suggests that the originators of the myth may have

been lowland agriculturalists planting the first of the rice paddies and it was not until the seventh of the generations, Izanagi and Izanami, that sexual procreation and death were introduced.

There is an indication in the chronicles that the traditions and authority of a single tribe, the Yamato clan, out of which the imperial dynasty arose, slowly became dominant and took on special credentials. The genealogy of the deities listed in the 'run up' provides the first earthly Yamato emperor, and the priests who attended him, with divine origins.

Towards the end of the eighth century CE there was a notable shift in certain aspects of folk religion. The *hito-gami* beliefs in tutelary *kamis* and their shamans were transformed into *goryo-shin*. The term translates into a view that the spirits or *kamis* are of essentially malevolent or angry disposition and that shamanistic magic is needed to counter their effects. In response three magical traditions arose during the ninth and tenth centuries – Nembutsu, Shugen-do and Onmyo-do – which in differing ways sought to protect humanity against the activities of these spirits. Nembutsu, the most widespread, meaning 'a prayer for the *buddha*', invokes the Amida *buddha* as the saviour and protector of human souls and offers a negative magic that sends the evil spirits to the 'Pure Land' of the *buddha*. The magic of the other two traditions is more positive in its defence against the activities of the *kamis*.

Folk religion became largely lost in the cities and amongst Japanese intellectuals, replaced first by the imperial religion of Shinto and then by Buddhism and Confucianism, but it has persisted in many parts of rural Japan, more or less unchanged, and it still an active force at a domestic level.

A NINETEENTH-CENTURY PAINTING OF MOUNT FUJI, ONE OF JAPAN'S SACRED PLACES.

THE SHINTO PANTHEON

THE 'WEDDED ROCKS' IN ISE BAY ARE REPUTED TO HAVE SHELTERED THE PRIMORDIAL DEITIES IZANAGI AND HIS CONSORT IZANAMI.

Shinto, meaning the 'Way of the Gods', is strongly focused on the worship and invocation of the Japanese celestial pantheon but the word itself is a corruption of the Chinese SHIN TAO and Shinto creation theories include much that can be traced to Chinese sources. The term Shinto came into use only after the introduction of Buddhism in about the eighth century CE in order to distinguish between the two religions.

Some of the older indigenous belief of Japan originates from very ancient times and this archaic religion was probably first called *Kami-no-michi*, a term which relates to the *kami* or gods. *Kami* may be interpreted, literally, to mean 'above'. Though it refers to named divinities which now form the pantheon of Shintoism, additionally the old nature spirits are similarly identified and, in Japan, features of the landscape are often endowed with powerful spirituality. This means that a mountain, a cave, a spring, a tree or an animal may be termed a *kami*. Animals, in particular, may be possessed by spirits and accused of bewitching people.

The *Kojiki* and *Nihongi* chronicles discuss theories of creation and identify various celestial, earthly and subterranean realms. The cosmos is perceived to resemble the two halves of a giant eggshell, above which lies the highest or ninth heaven, Taka-maga-hara, the High Plain of Heaven. Below this is Nakatsu-kuni, the Middle Land, which is seen as the 'Eight Island Country', the Japanese realm. At the lowest level lies Yomi-no-kuni, a dark underground kingdom to which the recently deceased must go and are prevented from leaving, until permitted, by hideous monsters. The celestial realms also include a mysterious spirit country, Tokoyo-no-kuni, which is neither a paradise nor a hell.

THE DIVINE HIERARCHY

At the apex of the pantheon, in the ninth heaven, is an ethereal and distant divine principle, also termed Kami, which pervades the universe. More precisely this essence is called Ame-no-minaka-nushi-no-kami, translating as the Deity Master of the August Centre of Heaven, the sole purpose of whom has been to engender the pantheon and to propagate the earth below.

He emerged on the Plain of High Heaven, was born alone, and has always remained hidden from mortal eyes. He has no cult following, no images are created in his likeness and he is mentioned by name once only in the *Kojiki*.

Ame-no-minaka-nushi-no-kami heads a trio of primordial creators in the cosmos which includes two subordinate figures – Taka-mi-musubi-no-kami (High August Producing Wondrous

AMATERASU, THE SUN GODDESS, IS DEPICTED HOLDING AN ORB CONTAINING A CROUCHING HARE, A MYTHOLOGICAL ANIMAL COMMON TO BOTH CHINESE AND JAPANESE EARLY BELIEFS.

191

the island of Onogoro, believed to be the island of Nu-Shima off the southern coast of Awagi. Following this act they created the remaining fourteen islands which make up Japan, the so-called 'Eight Island Country', in similar manner.

Izanagi and Izanami also embody the introduction of sexuality and death. They are the parents of the rest of the Shinto *kami* pantheon of whom the most significant members are Amaterasu, the sun goddess, and her brother Susano-wo, the storm god, who became the joint rulers of the universe. Izanami suffered a violent demise when she was fatally burned whilst giving birth to the god of fire, Hi-no-kagu-tsuchi, and it was this incident that first introduced the phenomenon of death to the world and the notion that, through the cleansing power of fire, comes purification and rebirth. It is said that Izanagi tried, without success, to rescue his consort from the flames. Having failed, he went and cleansed himself with water, the other great agent of purification. Although the other deities of the pantheon were conceived 'normally', it was only after the loss of Izanami that Amaterasu and her brother were born from the body of Izanagi.

THE SUN GODDESS

Amaterasu-o-mi-kami (She who makes the Heavens Brilliant), the sun goddess, is the central figure of Shinto worship and lends her image to the national symbolism of Japan as the ancestral mother of the imperial lineage. The birth of her generation of deities marked the transition from cosmic to material genesis. Mythology records that she was born from the left eye of Izanagi and was ordered to ascend to heaven as its queen because her parents were blinded by her brilliance on earth. Susano-wo, one of three siblings, took dominion over the earth as the storm god whilst another, Tsuki-yomi, became god of the moon.

It was probably the disappearance and subsequent reappearance of the sun in the sky that led to the central myth of Amaterasu. She found that, in order to survive, she had to live in cosmic harmony with her brothers. At one time she was betrothed to the moon god Tsuki-yomi whom she later banished to the night sky in order to avoid seeing his face, but she was then joined in the heavens by Susano-wo. He outraged her by entering her house uninvited in order to attempt sexual impropriety and, in response, Amaterasu hid herself away in a cave, shutting the entrance with a boulder.

KOTOHIRA-*GU* SHRINE, DEDICATED TO THE GUARDIAN OF SEAFARERS.

Deity) and Kami-misubi-no-kami (Divine Producing Wondrous Deity). These two are equally remote and vaguely defined and all three were possibly moulded from Chinese influence.

The most significant of the primordial divinities born of the creator source include a pair, Izanagi-no-kami (His Augustness the One who Invites) and his consort Izanami-no-kami, said to represent the seven generations following Ame-no-minaka-nushi-no-kami. They are listed amongst seventeen beings involved in creation and were given the responsibility, according to the text of the *Kojiki*, of creating the islands of Japan from the primeval waters. They were instructed to 'make, consolidate and give birth to this drifting land'. In order to perform the task, the pair were given a heavenly jewelled spear. Using this, they stood upon the floating bridge of heaven to stir up the waters beneath. Tradition tells that when the spear was withdrawn, drops of brine falling from its tip created

At first she refused all entreaties by the other deities of the pantheon to come out. With the world plunged into darkness and chaos, various devices were employed in an attempt to persuade her to change her mind. None of these met with any response until the power of flattery and the services of Ama-tsu-mara, the smith god, were called upon to fashion a perfect mirror called the Jata-kagami in which Amaterasu could see her immaculate reflection. Through concerted action a dazzling spectacular of song and dance was mounted in the area in front of the cave and an assortment of gifts was laid out, including a glorious string of jewels. After some time the sun goddess was persuaded to move the boulder just enough to catch sight of her own image and subsequently she returned to her rightful place in the heavens.

Amaterasu is venerated in the Amaterasu shrine at Ise-*jingu*, revered as the Omi-kami, the 'Great and Exalted Divinity'. She is believed to be the divine ancestor of the Japanese emperors and it was her grandson, Prince Ninigi-no-mikoto, who descended to earth and founded the imperial Nippon Dynasty, bringing with him as his most sacred symbols the divine mirror, a magic sword, Kusanagi-no-tsurugi, which Susano-wo was forced to yield to Amaterasu (see below), and a jewel of fertility called the Magatama.

THE STORM GOD AND OTHER DEITIES

Susano-wo was born from the nose of Izanagi shortly after the birth of Amaterasu and in many respects he is viewed as her antithesis, the personification of evil. His powers over the clouds had allowed him to ascend into the heavens and attempt the violation of his sister. But after the incident, when she had re-emerged from the darkness of her cave, he was banished forever to the earthly realm.

At first he was forced to live as a vagrant, requesting food from a minor goddess, O-ge-tsu-hime. He was also challenged by an eight-headed dragon which was marauding in a small town, Izumo, on the west coast. He killed this adversary and claimed its magic sword but was then forced to hand it over to Amaterasu in acknowledgement of her superiority as effective head of the pantheon. He married an Izumo princess and this union is said to have been the catalyst for a power struggle between the Yamato and Izumo tribes which took place during the early historical period of Japan.

As god of thunder, Susano-wo is also associated with snakes, seen as representing lightning strikes, and is ruler of the ocean where his storms are most keenly felt.

Okininushi-no-mikoto (the Master of the Great Land) occupies a significant place in Shinto worship. One of the descendants of Susano-wo, he was the patron god of agriculture, fishing and marriage, but he also became a guardian deity of the royal Yamato tribe. Myth relates that his consort was a Yamato princess and that his condition for taking her as his bride was that he was worshipped from henceforth at the Izumo Taisha shrine near the hill of Yakumo. This arguably aided the emerging dominance of the Yamato clan over that of Izumo.

Hachiman stands as the god of war, the apotheosis of a questionably historical warrior overlord, the Emperor Ojin. There are also 'Seven Lucky Gods', the Shichifukujin, who equate with the Ba Hsien of Chinese mythology. They include two *kamis* of wealth – Daikokuten who is drawn with a sack slung over his shoulder, and Ebisu who carries a fishing rod and a fish tucked under his arm. The other members of the seven are Benten, involved with music and the arts, Hotei, who represents magnanimity, Jurojin the *kami* of longevity, Fukurokuju representing popularity and Bishamonten, who stands for benevolent authority.

Amongst the clear Buddhist introductions to the pantheon is Emma O, the lord of the dead, who derives from the Hindu Vedic god Yama. He is considered to reside by the Yellow Springs in the underworld kingdom of Yomi and sits in judgement of dead souls when they reach Gakido, the so-called Demon Road which represents a kind of purgatory. Before this encounter they must cross the dried-up river of the dead, the Sanzu-no-kawa, which is controlled by an old woman known as Sodzu Baba. Emma O hurls those who have been sinful in life into a vat of molten metal.

On the side of mercy stands another Buddhist deity, Kwannon or Guan Yin, who is modelled on the *bodhisattva* Avalokitesvara. She may intercede to allow the soul to rise into a perfect and peaceful afterlife particularly if, in earthly existence, the person has paid the proper devotions to her shrines. Kwannon has a male counterpart named Jizo who is the benevolent guardian of cemeteries and is modelled on the *bodhisattva* Ksitigarbha. By hiding them in his clothing he keeps souls away from the worst excesses of Emma O and from the *oni*, the monstrous inhabitants of Yomi, each of which possesses three eyes, horns and talons.

The Ryijin or storm gods hold a significant place in the pantheon of an island nation surrounded by ocean which relies heavily on fishing. Near the islands of Ryu Kyu is a mythical undersea palace built of coral and occupied by a dragon king. He controls thunder and rain and is the most powerful of the Ryijin deities. In his realm a single day is equal to the span of a hundred earthly years and on each side of his palace stand the Halls of the Seasons which not only reflect the seasons of the year but also the span of human life from spring to winter.

Outside of these clearly defined figures the Japanese Shinto worshipper recognizes a vast number of local *kamis* whose influence may extend only to the boundaries of a village or a small region. This diversification has become more apparent since Shinto ceased to be the state religion.

DIVINE EMPERORS

S *hintoism recognizes that in mythical times there took place a transition from godly to earthly rule and that the transformed individual, representing the head of the Japanese imperial dynasty, was bestowed with the divine right to govern. The emperor was, literally, the divine presence on earth and he became known as* ARAMI-KAMI, *meaning 'visible god'.*

The mythology of imperial origins recounts that whilst in the heavens Prince Ninigi-no-mikoto stood as the deification of the rising sun, Kushi-dama-nigi-haya-hi. His parents were Taka-mi-musubi and Ame-no-oshi-ho-mimi and his paternal grandmother was Amaterasu, the sun goddess. She sent him to earth after various other envoys had been dispatched to bring order to the world but had failed to return or send messages of progress back to the gods.

Prince Ninigi and his retainers, a guard of warrior deities amongst whom were the Ryijin or storm gods, descended through the clouds accompanied by his sister, Ame-no-uzume, the goddess of dancers and keeper of the floating bridge of heaven. The party landed on the summit of Mount Takachihiat in the northern part of Kyushu. By tradition this is a place from which eight earthly roads are believed to lead away in every direction, but the party was immediately challenged by the guardian of the ways. After negotiations mediated by Ame-no-uzume, the guardian agreed to show Prince Ninigi the kingdoms of the earth in return for the hand of the celestial dancer in marriage.

The Prince and his cohorts advanced from this southerly point in the Japanese islands, fighting their way towards the Yamato Plain on Honshu. There he established himself as the head of the Yamato tribe and the first earthly emperor of the royal dynasty, becoming known as Jimmu-tenno. In mythology Prince Ninigi married the goddess of the sacred Mount Fuji, Ko-no-hana (Sengen), who is also the guardian of the elixir of immortality and goddess of flowers. She bore him three sons, but Ninigi's increasing jealousy over her fragile beauty led her to commit suicide by self-immolation.

LITERATURE OF MYTHOLOGY

In order to explain the transition, to validate the status of the emperor, and to record the details of imperial shrines and rituals, it was deemed necessary by the royal Yamato court to develop a literary 'evidence' which would properly establish the mythological history. This was produced from the seventh century CE onwards under the authorship of the orthodox priesthood, the Nakatomi. They compiled a library of sacred books of which two volumes are of outstanding importance in understanding the nature of the pantheon and its chronology. The first of these books, the *Kojiki* or Records of Ancient Matters, was completed and submitted to the imperial court in 712 CE. This was followed by a sister work, the *Nihongi* or *Nihon Shoki*, the Chronicles of Japan, finalized in 720 CE.

The early sections of the books encompass the mythological period but in the eighth century they also played their part in the politicization of Shinto. In political terms, the various ancient tribes which rivalled each other for supremacy in the Japanese islands each claimed their own divine ancestors amongst the celestial ranks. Gradually, however, the Yamato (Sun) tribe gained military and political supremacy and, allied with this, their patron deity Amaterasu increased in prominence. By the end of the century the chroniclers employed by the Yamato emperor had effectively 'confirmed' his divine status and given the rule its legitimacy.

RESTORATION AND DECLINE

For many hundreds of years, during the era of the Tokugawa shoguns (feudal overlords) between the twelfth and nineteenth centuries, the imperial dynasty represented little more than a symbolic figurehead presence and the devotional

EMPEROR HIROHITO, LAST IN THE LINE OF EMPERORS INVESTED WITH THE DIVINE RIGHT TO GOVERN.

cult waned. But in 1868 the Meiji Restoration ended the Shogunate and set the emperor back in a position of administrative power. Three years later Shinto was re-established as the state religion.

From the moment of his birth the emperor was treated as a living god and the spirits of his deceased forebears provided with honoured places of residence in the imperial shrines of Ise situated on the Shima Peninsula of Honshu. This politicization of the religion became known as Kokutai Shinto and it continued unchallenged until the end of the Second World War. In spite of its relative decline during the period of the Shogunate, the status of the imperial court and the head of the ruling family has also been reinforced by the impact of Confucianism in Japan which places considerable emphasis on unswerving loyalty to the emperor.

Shinto lost its status as the official state religion of Japan in 1945 only after Hirohito broadcast his message of surrender to the Japanese people. Such was the subsequent catharsis between religion and state, a bond which has been identified as one of the causes of more extreme Japanese imperialism and militaristic aspiration, that the emperor was obliged to renounce all claims to divinity and the 1947 post-war constitution of Japan included a ban on any involvement by the state in religious matters.

SHINTO SHRINES AND SACRED PLACES

One of the most noticeable features of the Japanese landscape lies in the profusion of small shrines and sacred places to be found throughout the country. Generally situated in groves of evergreen trees known as SAKAKI, they often follow the Chinese Buddhist tradition of being constructed on mountain and hill tops. The shrines or JINJA are generally dedicated to a particular KAMI, which may be a widely recognized deity of the pantheon, such as the sun goddess Amaterasu, or a KAMI of more localized rural interest, like Uga-no-mitama, the goddess of agriculture.

DESIGN AND CONSTRUCTION

In very ancient times the sacred places probably took the simple form that exists the world over in animistic cultures — a space with a crude altar in the form of a rock or tree trunk, its upper face carved to a flat surface. Over centuries these open-air shrines became enclosed by unpainted wooden buildings constructed with raised floors, like old-fashioned storehouses, and dedicated to the *kamis* of rice and other crops. The most famous of the Shinto shrines are located on the largest island of Honshu and they include the Ise-*jingu*. Of national importance, it is dedicated jointly to the sun goddess, Amaterasu, and the rice goddess, Toyouke, and is built in this ancient style. Second only to Ise-*jingu* is the shrine at Izumo where Prince Ninigi, Amaterasu's grandson, is said to have descended from heaven to begin godly rule on earth and where tradition has it that all the *kami*s of Japan return once a year.

The *kami*s are often linked with certain animals that may form an important aspect of their mythology and the roofs and forecourts of shrines may frequently be decorated with sculptures of these animals. Hence shrines dedicated to Amaterasu may include stone cockerels since these birds, with their dawn crowing, were amongst the enticements used to lure the sun goddess from her cave. Other shrines popularly include stone lions, indicating Buddhist and Chinese influences.

Amongst those animals most frequently encountered are foxes. They decorate *Inari* or 'fox shrines', readily distinguished because they usually possess carvings of foxes at the entrances.

DEVOTIONAL MESSAGES ARE HUNG AROUND THE WALLS OF A SHRINE AT AMANOHASIDOTE.

The most venerated, dating from the eighth century CE, is the Fushimi *Inari* in Kyoto. The fox is regarded as an animal which can do considerable damage to crops and poultry and the *Inari* reflect an ancient rural cult which was directed towards appeasing the guardian spirits of agriculture and fertility and, in particular, the foxes which are employed to do their bidding.

Most Shinto shrines which include buildings possess a number of common features in the arrangement. Each shrine has a sacred gate or *torii* which delimits it from the secular surroundings and which is often decorated with strips of coloured paper, or *gohei*, announcing the presence of gods, much as a flag flying above a building with a royal personage in residence. The shrine is also usually marked off by straw ropes known as *shimenawa*. Larger shrines may include another gate-like building known as a *heiden* which marks the limit beyond which lay devotees do not pass and which functions as a place for offerings to be deposited.

THE STRIKING FORM OF THE GREAT TORII GATE AT HEIAN-*JINGU*.

They may also include a hall for public ritual. Beyond the gate-house stand buildings into which only the Shinto priests venture – an oratory or *haiden,* and the central hall of the shrine, the *honden*, in which the image or symbol of the deity stands. This may be an icon representing the *kami* or some sacred object of a more widely recognized status.

THE ISE SHRINES

The grandest of all Shinto shrines are those at Ise, the Ise-*jingu,* which lie either side of the Isuku river in the Mie region. One, the inner shrine or *naiku*, is dedicated to Amaterasu and houses the holiest of all symbols, the Divine Mirror of Amaterasu, which was allegedly placed there in the fourth century CE by its original builder, by tradition the Emperor Suinin. The other, the outer shrine or *geku*, founded in the fifth century CE by the Emperor Yurkaku, is dedicated to the rice goddess Toyouke, and the two shrines are considered to reflect the union of earth and sky deities.

The Ise-*jingu* is unusual amongst Japanese sacred places in that the wooden building complex is demolished and restored on an adjacent site once every 20 years by carpenters who carry on a family tradition from generation to generation. The ceremony, known as the Sengushiki, is designed not only to maintain the unprotected wooden buildings in a reasonable state of repair but to symbolize the spiritual refreshing of the *kamis*. At the time of renewal the images or 'god bodies', the *go-shintai*, are ritually transported from old to new sanctuaries. The practice at Ise-*jingu* was initiated in the eighth century CE and was most recently accomplished in 1993.

The Shinto shrine may also be portable, suitable for carrying in procession in a festival, in which case it is known as a *mikoshi*. Shinto, however, recognizes many features of the landscape – mountains and hills, waterfalls and springs – to be sacred places since these are regarded as the embodiment of *kamis*. So Mount Fuji, Fuji-*san*, is seen as both mountain and *kami*, and those devotees who ascend its slopes are performing an act of worship in doing so. At the domestic level each traditional Japanese household maintains its own small shrine known as the *kamidana*, which includes a miniature ceramic replica of the main hall of the *jinja*.

SHINTO PRIESTS AND RITUALS

*A*n indication of the extent to which religion permeates secular life in Japan may be gained from the fact that, prior to the abandonment of state Shintoism, each time a new government was formed the prime minister would make a formal report on the make-up of his new cabinet to the sun goddess, Amaterasu, in her shrine of Ise-*JINGU*.

WORSHIPPERS PERFORM RITUAL WASHING IN THE SHRINE AT HEIAN.

SHRINE-CENTRED RITUAL

Many thousands of ordinary Japanese visit sacred shrines each year to pay their respects, although devotions made at the great national shrines of Ise-*jingu* and Izumo are the subject of present-day controversy since some critics fear it might stimulate a Shinto-inspired nationalist revival. These national festivals are nowadays observed by the emperor in private, although before the 1947 constitutional reforms he conducted them publicly as head of the Shinto state religion, and the Shinto priesthood was employed by the imperial government under the aegis of a state department, the Bureau of Shrines in Tokyo.

Shinto shrines may be of a general nature or may be dedicated more specifically. The Meiji shrine in Tokyo is dedicated to the great nineteenth-century reformist emperor Meiji, whilst the Yasukuni shrine, also in Tokyo and a subject of regular political controversy, is dedicated to the spirits of the Japanese war dead. Smaller militaristic shrines of a different kind are scattered throughout the country. These are known as Hachiman-*gu* and are dedicated to Hachiman, the patron god of war and the martial arts.

There is much less formalized ritual involving large gatherings of worshippers than in congregational religions like Christianity. Much of the devotion is an individual matter and is directed for some specific purpose, perhaps an appeal to the *kami* for protection, restoration of health or wealth, or for guidance in some impending action. The devotee may have undergone a voluntary fast or some other form of abstinence known as *imi* and will leave offerings at the shrine to appease the *kami*. Nowadays, however, the practice of *imi* is normally carried out on behalf of the lay devotees by the priests attached to the shrine.

The *Inari* 'fox' shrines (see p.196) are usually attended by people who are seeking to secure a favourable business

SYMBOLIC MATERIALS

A Shinto priest is carried across the sand in a symbolic parade at the festival of Karatsu Okunchi.

Visitors to shrines hang the *gohei* from the gates and rope barriers as votive offerings which also symbolize the presence of the *kami*. They buy an assortment of talismans and charms, including *fuda* which are papers bearing the name of the shrine. These papers are kept in the sacred area at home until the following year when they are returned to the shrine and burnt. Small wooden arrows are also sold for the purpose of warding off evil spirits.

The stalls selling religious materials are managed by altar girls known as *miko*. Originally these were vestal virgins believed to possess strong shamanistic powers and the role of a *miko* is a highly respected occupation that has been followed by generations of daughters from the same families. The *miko* girls can be readily distinguished by their costumes of red skirts and white surplices. In addition to work on the market stalls they perform special dances during the religious festivals and generally assist the priests.

Buddhist shrines sell similar talismans and prayer banners but also market papier mâché images of the *buddha* which are, as with the *fuda* strips, kept at home for a year and then returned to the shrine for ritual burning.

FESTIVALS

On a more public scale of devotion there are many seasonal festivals in Shinto known as *matsuri*, which probably started in ancient times as rites associated with key moments in the agricultural year. These include a procession to the shrine, headed by priests, and the parading of the portable shrines or *mikoshi*, thus symbolizing an annual journey of the *kami* around the region or locality. They are sometimes extremely elaborate affairs which take on the atmosphere of a fair, including decorated floats, side-shows and market stalls. When the main shrine is reached the lay followers attach *gohei* to the *shimenawa* ropes and to the *sakaki* trees to symbolize the presence of the *kami*. The priests pass the boundary gate of the *heiden* to place offerings on the altar or before the 'god body', often including *sakaki* branches accompanied by gifts of rice and *sake* for the refreshment of the *kami*. They then invoke the *kami* on behalf of the lay pilgrims.

transaction. Others may be visited before commencing a journey or facing an academic test or when the birth of a child is due. Many pilgrimages are made on an annual basis and Japan follows a religious calendar of visits to various shrines. The rites of passage through a person's life – in particular, those of birth, marriage and death – are usually divided amicably between Buddhist and Shinto establishments. For instance, Shinto priests, of both sexes, tend to conduct wedding ceremonies, whilst male Buddhist clergy supervise funerals.

The visit to a shrine may also involve a request for purification or exorcism from evil influences and the ritual, performed by the priests, is known as *harae*. This is based on an ancient mythology that the primordial *kami* Izanagi was beset by demonic spirits whilst attempting to rescue his consort Izanami from the underworld after she had been burnt to death giving birth to the fire god. To rid himself of these spirits he bathed in a river. *Harae* involves the blessing and purification of the supplicant with holy water from a spring and the waving of a *gohei* or paper strip on which is written an invocation. The supplicant is required to wash his or her hands in a basin situated within the sacred area, using a wooden dipper, and to rinse out the mouth, in this way symbolizing both outer and inner purification. The person thus freed from the potential of future disaster, usually anticipated as illness, the risk of accident on a journey, problems in childbirth or merely failure in a business deal, then makes his or her obeisance towards the *go-shintai* or 'god body' resting in the sanctuary.

BUDDHISM AND SHINTOISM

The old religions of China and Japan, on the one hand the Wu religion and early Taoism, and on the other Shinto, share much in common. They compare with the more western-style beliefs in the powers of iconic divinities living in some form of celestial dimension and of whom mortal men and women are imperfect copies.

Shinto is typical of such beliefs, being strictly a religion based on the invocation of gods. It exhibits an archaic outlook in as much as it is based on a set of old seasonal festivals and rites without any clear philosophical or moralistic doctrine. The more intelligent oriental minds, however, became disenchanted with this style of spirituality and were quickly receptive to Buddhism which represents much more a philosophy and way of life based on ethics.

Buddhism extended from India, its birthplace, by way of Tibet and northern China, eventually reaching the peninsula of land that became known as Korea. Japan was therefore the last of the major cultural areas of the Far East to receive its wisdom, but Buddhism became amicably combined with the old indigenous Japanese beliefs much as it had done with Tao in China and with the early folk religion of Korea.

In Japan the two schools of thought have never actually merged but a partial assimilation has taken place, helped by the Shinto emphasis on the essential purity of all things and the notion that what is good for a society is morally correct. This has provided fertile ground and made the introduction of Buddhist principles attractive to the Japanese, the majority of whom subscribe to both Buddhism and Shintoism. The marriage of the two faiths is visible in many of the Buddhist temples of Japan which include, or are set close by, Shinto shrines. It also permeates Japanese homes, within which Shinto, Buddhist and Christian sacred objects may stand together, side by side, and people use Buddhist and Shinto rituals to an equal degree. A person may be married by a Shinto priest, for example, and buried by means of a Buddhist funeral ceremony.

INTRODUCTION AND EXTENSION OF BUDDHISM

It is not altogether clear how Buddhism first arrived in Japan. Mahayana is held to have come originally by way of China in the sixth or seventh century CE, brought by a sage named Shotoku Daichi (572–621 CE), and it was under his missionary guidance that many of the followers of traditional Shinto were said to have been converted. Some of his details may, however, be mythical. He is said to have been the second son of the emperor Yomei, born in the imperial stables after his mother developed labour pains whilst walking in the imperial gardens. He is alleged to have founded the oldest temple of Japan, the Horyu-*ji* in Nara.

There is a firm report contained in the *Nihongi* chronicles, however, that Buddhist schools were formally introduced from Korea in 552 CE, and included the gift of various Buddhist sacred objects to the emperor Kimmei, whilst other texts suggest that the year was 538 CE. In any event it seems that Korean scholars first taught the Japanese to read the *sutras* in Chinese and it has been the tradition to apply Chinese as the basic lingua franca for Buddhist terminology with Japanese phonetic equivalents.

Early in the ninth century CE the teaching of the T'ien Tai sect arrived from China with another missionary monk named Saicho and was developed as Tendai. Zen, however, did not appear until the Kamakura period between 1185 and 1336 CE which marked a time of intense religious fervour in Japan. It was introduced by Eisai, a former Tendai priest who had studied the Ch'an religious doctrine in China, during two separate visits.

Kobo Daichi, also known as Kukai (774–835 CE), one of the great architects of Tantric Buddhism in Japan, was responsible for another significant advance in establishing the

DECORATED STATUES AMONGST THE TOMBS IN KOYA-*SAN* CEMETERY, A CENTRE OF BUDDHISM IN JAPAN.

Shingon sect. In 806 CE he founded a small meditation centre on Mount Koya in the Wakayama region of Honshu. Today it lies some two hours by train from modern Osaka. On this cloud-wreathed summit the monastery complex now includes more than a hundred buildings and shrines interspersed with gardens of white gravel, all of which was hewn out of solid rock. The complex is centred on the grave of Kobo Daichi which is venerated each year by thousands of monks and pilgrims, particularly on the anniversary of his death, 15th March. The tomb is sited in a simple wooden shrine which is renewed by monks at regular intervals over the years.

For more than a thousand years Koya-*san* has also been a place of burial where the faithful have been interred so as to remain close to their saint. More than 100,000 graves are sited in the surrounding forest in a vast sprawling cemetery.

Three main branches of Buddhism became established in the centuries which followed its introduction – Jodo, Zen, and a philosophical division based on the teachings of the *Avatamsaka sutra* which had become known as Fa-Yen in China, but which evolved in Japan as Kegon.

In general the Buddhist priesthood took a very liberal attitude towards Shinto shrines and often built Buddhist temples on adjacent land. They put forward the popular notion that the Shinto *kami* and the Buddhist *bodhisattva*, who became renamed *bosatsu*, were more or less synonymous. It was out of this melding that the branch of Shinto known as Ryobo Shinto developed. Literally meaning 'Two Aspect Shinto', it resulted in a combined priesthood and a situation whereby Buddhist monks supervised Shinto shrines and vice versa. The Tendai sects, which follow the teachings of the *Lotus sutra*, were particularly attracted to the concept of Ryobo Shinto.

JAPANESE SECTS

*J*apan is a nation of sects without equal. There has long been a sectarian interest, particularly in respect of Buddhism, brought about to no small extent because different Buddhist schools arose to concentrate on the interpretation of various SUTRAS or religious texts as they were imported from India, Korea and China. This, however, does not account for the modern explosion of sects.

Much of the recent proliferation has come about in the aftermath of the Second World War, largely encouraged when state Shintoism was disallowed through the 1947 constitution. Its rejection encouraged a fragmentation of religion into small local cults, some of which have since grown into significant movements and even begun to infiltrate the political scene again.

As an indication of the trend, by 1912, at the close of the Meiji era, some 13 Shinto-oriented sects were officially recognized by the government. Currently, however, more than 180,000 sects are registered in Japan, ranging from tiny insignificant cells with a few hundred members to large organizations claiming membership running into millions. Some of these are Shinto-based, some Buddhist-based, and, of the overall total, about 10 per cent proclaim fairly extreme religious views. Some of the more prominent ones are covered here.

TENDAI

This is one of the largest and most successful of the Buddhist sects and its name is derived from the T'ien Tai sect in China. It was introduced by a missionary monk, Saicho, who had spent time studying in China and returned to Japan in about 805 CE. Based on the philosophical teachings of the *Padma* (Lotus) *sutra*, which became the *Hokkekyo*, and other influential works such as the *Mahaparinirvana sutra*, the reverence of the sect is focused on the Yakushi *buddha*. This figure derives from Bhaisajyaguru, the 'Supreme Physician', reputed to have been an earthly healer who became deified as the first of the *sMan-bla* or 'medicine Buddhas' of Tibet. In Tendai he becomes the counterpart of the Amida *buddha*.

Tendai also incorporates an amalgam of meditative techniques akin to that of Ch'an (Zen) and Tantric magic. Tantrism was introduced to Japan by a pupil of Saicho named Ennin, who became the chief priest of Tendai in 854 CE and was known after his death by the title Jikaku Daishi. It was Ennin who introduced the Tantric *mandalas* and other esoteric rituals and promoted the technique of *nembutsu*, repeated chanting of the name of the Amida *buddha* with the mind fixed on the *buddha* image (see also p.92).

Tendai first explored and promoted the notion in Japan that all things, both animate and inanimate, including mankind, exist as part of the *buddha*-nature within the eternal cycle of birth and death, *samsara*. The sect claims about 30 per cent of practising Japanese Buddhists and is centred on Ichijoshikan-*in*, a monastic and teaching complex at Mount Hiei, north-east of Kyoto on the main island of Honshu. At the centre of its devotions is the Enryaku-*ji* temple which was formally recognized in 823 CE, razed by fire during a sixteenth-century purge and rebuilt as three separate temples. It was at Ichijoshikan-*in* that Dogen, the main architect of Zen in Japan, studied Buddhist scriptures as a student and the main Kamakura schools of Buddhism, Zen and Nichiren, are generally staffed by monks trained in Tendai.

SHINGON

Derived from the Chinese Chen Yen, meaning 'True Word', Shingon is a Tantric Buddhist sect, the philosophy of which was introduced into Japan in 806 CE by a missionary named Kobo Daichi or Kukai. Having spent two years in China he returned and founded a small meditation centre on Mount Koya in the Wakayama region of Honshu. When Kukai died he was buried on Mount Koya which became the spiritual headquarters, Kongobu-*ji*, of the sect.

The spiritual devotion in Shingon is focused on the Mahavairocana *buddha* who became translated into the Dainichi *buddha* in Japan. The philosophy is based on a massive 10-volume teaching manual completed by Kukai in 822 CE, the *Juju Shinron*. This was subsequently revised into three shorter volumes known as the *Hizoboyaku*, the 'Jewelled Key to the Store of Mysteries', but the original principles of the path to enlightenment, separated into 10 steps, remained. These were graded from basic animal desires, through essays in morality, aspects of Mahayana teaching, the principles of Tendai and Kegon (see p.201), and finally the more esoteric aspects of worship and ritual.

JODO-SHIN

The sect of the 'Pure Land', which derives from the Chinese Ching Tu, was founded in Japan during the Kamakura era by Honen (1133–1212), formerly a Tendai priest who built the Chion-*in* temple in Kyoto. Jodo, however, came to fruition in the hands of a contemporary Mahayana Buddhist monk and a student of Honen's named Shinran (1173–1262). Also a former Tendai priest, he was converted to Amida Buddhism and came to believe that faith in the power and magnanimity of the Amida *buddha,* a Japanese synthesis of the closely related Amitabha and Amitayus *buddhas,* was the only ingredient needed to achieve spiritual salvation and the rebirth of the soul in the Pure Land. Belief in Jodo, therefore, is effectively synonymous with the cult of Amidism.

Jodo no longer has the widespread following and authority that it enjoyed during the medieval period but still retains substantial membership in Japan. Like many other religious sects, including Tendai, whose spiritual focus is on the Amida *buddha*, it incorporates the technique of *nembutsu* (see p. 202). It is not, however, a monastic sect and celibacy is not required of its priests, who can marry and raise families. Furthermore the concept of Jodo-shin, although of Buddhist origin, is purely Japanese and has no equivalents elsewhere.

NICHIREN

Also known as Hokke-shu, this sect was founded by a priest of the same name who was born in the Chiba region and lived from 1222–82. He studied Tendai before founding the first of Japan's wholly native sects in 1253. He based his teachings on the Buddhist *Lotus sutra* and was passionately opposed to what he saw as the social evils of the Kamakura era. On two occasions he

A BRONZE STATUE OF ENNIN, CHIEF PRIEST OF THE TENDAI SECT IN THE NINTH CENTURY, AT YAMADERA TEMPLE IN YAMAGATA.

was banished for his extreme and outspoken views and on the second occasion was sentenced to death, but he returned to continue his exhortations about returns to morality. Eventually he retired to the temple of Kuon-*ji* in the Yamanashi region where he died and where his tomb is located. Over a period of time some 40 divisions of the Nichiren sect were founded.

TENRI-KYO (THE SECT OF THE HEAVENLY TRUTH)

Probably the most significant of an accountable number of sects which arose at the time of the Meiji Restoration in the nineteenth century, Tenri-kyo was founded in 1838 by Miki Nakayama, the wife of a farmer, and follows a strictly Shintoist path. Its headquarters are in Tenri which lies in the heart of the Yamato region of Honshu, south of the old regional capital of Nara. It was effectively developed as a sect by Iburi Izo who is regarded as the co-founder and it claims a membership of about 2 million located wholly within the Japanese islands. Its subsequent leaders have all been descendants of Miki Nakayama.

Essentially a faith-healing and missionary organization, its spiritual focus lies in devotion to the pantheon of Shinto deities, the powers of whom it channels for its healing work. At the head of this pantheon it recognizes a creator deity, Tenri-o-no-mikoto, and it claims to know the spot where creation first took place. It also follows the Buddhist-style philosophy of Jodo, the doctrine of the Pure Land, and believes that through work and service, reincarnation can be achieved in a more perfect state. Its doctrine is effectively contained in a revealed prose poem of 1711 verses named the *Ofudesaki* or 'Tip of the Divine Writing Brush'. Tradition has it that this revelation, extending to the nature of the cosmos, the celestial hierarchy and the proper relationship between gods and mortals, was given to Miki Nakayama by a spirit named Tentaishogun, 'The Great Heavenly Shogun', who claimed that he and a further nine spirit beings represented the only genuine *kami* pantheon.

THE ENRYAKU-*JI* TEMPLE ON MOUNT HIEI IS THE MONASTIC
AND TEACHING CENTRE OF THE TENDAI SECT.

OTHER SIGNIFICANT SECTS

Amongst other comparatively modern sects are various groups with wide-ranging devotional interests. They include mountain-worshipping ascetics such as the Jikko-kyo and Fuso-kyo on Mount Fuji, and Mitake-kyo based on Mount Ontake in the Nagano region. Others of significance are the Konko-kyo or Golden Light Sect founded by Bunjiro Kawate, and Kurozumi-kyo named after its founder, Munetada Kurozumi. Most movements of this type were founded by disaffected Shinto priests, or landowners who had fallen on hard times, or poor peasant farmers, all of whom were seeking some form of spiritual liberation from their impoverished or failed secular lives.

Bunjiro Kawate (1814–83) lived near Okayama where magico-religious beliefs were still strong amongst the peasant population and where the influence of a malevolent *kami* known as Konjin was widely felt. Various members of his family apparently fell victim to Konjin and eventually Bunjiro himself was 'possessed'. However, in various revelatory experiences, he was converted to the view that Konjin was, in fact, a spirit of more benign disposition and this formed the basis of his teaching. He appointed himself the Ikigami-Konko-daijin (Great Living Kami Light) and, through his sect, promoted the notion that Konjin was a true guardian deity.

Munetada Kurozumi was born in 1780 in the Okayama area, the child of a Shinto priest, and grew up in the twilight period of the Tokugawa Shogunate. He became deeply devoted to the worship of Amaterasu, having made a pilgrimage to her shrine at Ise-*jingu* as a young man. Shortly afterwards his parents died of tuberculosis and, having contracted the disease himself, he became critically ill. He eventually recovered and devoted the remainder of his life to leading a sect based on reverence for Amaterasu.

Between the end of the First World War and 1931, the year of the Manchurian Incident, two significant magico-religious sects emerged which became popular amongst people in urban areas. These included the Omoto Sect (Great Foundation) founded by Nao Deguchi, and the Hitonomichi Sect (Way of Mankind) which derived from Mitake-kyo. Both were the subject of an official ban in the years immediately before the Second World War but have since been revived. Omoto emerged under new colours as Omoto-aizen-en (the Great Foundation Love of Goodness Garden), whilst Hitonomichi was renamed the Perfect Liberty Sect.

A number of movements sprang up following the traditions of the Nichiren Shoshu Buddhist sect, of which two or three became particularly noteworthy. Soka Gakkai (the Creating Value School) is, today, the largest Japanese cult, which came into existence in 1930 as the secular lay division of the Nichiren Buddhists and which now claims about 10 million members worldwide. It maintained a comparatively low profile until the early 1960s when its leadership changed. Under a cultic chief named Daisaku the membership expanded rapidly and the style of leadership became more autocratic. Considerable wealth was amassed through donations earned by members renouncing worldly and material possessions and the cult promoted an association with the peace movement in Japan. It has developed a political wing named the Clean Government Party and this group benefits from about 60 members of parliament; this has permitted the sect to exercise a balance of power within the main opposition New Frontier Party with which it merged in 1994.

Less well-reported, but with substantial numbers of devotees, are the Rissho-kosei-kai sect, or Integrative Becoming, and the Reiyu-kai sect which also subscribe to the teachings of the Nichiren Buddhists.

KOREAN BUDDHISM

Z en Buddhism was formally introduced into Korea from China and it now forms one of the few surviving links with the ancient philosophy of Ch'an from which it developed. It is also from Korea that Zen has largely been exported to the west and particularly into the United States.

It is generally accepted by historians that Buddhism arrived in the Korean peninsula in 372 CE when a mission ordered by one of the emperors of the Eastern Ch'in Dynasty (317–420), Fu Chien, was sent to Koguryo, the southernmost of three ancient kingdoms prior to Korean unification. The mission was led by a Buddhist monk named Shun Tao, but the ease with which he was able, more or less immediately, to disseminate his teaching confirms that Buddhist ideology had probably been recognized in Korea for some time. It is well documented that for many decades Korean monks had been visiting China and returning armed with its philosophies.

WORSHIPPERS PAYING HOMAGE TO THE AMIDA *BUDDHA* AT A TEMPLE IN SOUTH KOREA.

The preliminary expedition was followed some twelve years later by one made by an Indian Buddhist named Marantara who came to the neighbouring kingdom of Paekche, and from there Buddhism was subsequently introduced to Japan.

The doctrinal approach on which, at first, Buddhism in Korea was largely based is contained in the teachings of the *Avatamsaka sutra* which became known as the *Hua Yen sutra*. Out of these beginnings the Zen meditational philosophy found a natural breeding ground in Korea although it has never been a part of mainstream culture. It has always retained a fairly exclusive presence and has evolved as an accountably different style of Zen compared to that witnessed in Japan. Whilst, in common with Japanese Zen, it is a movement focusing on the meditative aspects of Mahayana Buddhism, it possesses a less scholarly or pretentious ideology and has largely followed a route of celibacy in its monastic life. In Japan Zen recruitment has been more or less limited to the aristocracy and ranks of the military but the Korean style has appealed to a far broader spectrum of people. Nor is Korean Zen split into sects and, whilst it possesses sectarian distinctions beside other aspects of Korean Buddhism, it exists as an homogenous philosophy.

For much of its history a large proportion of its monks have been illiterate and so there has been less of an interest in reading the *sutras* and greater emphasis on a down-to-earth mixture of meditation, worship and work — mostly farming — embellished by a rich store of anecdotal folklore about past Zen masters and fortunes.

EARLY PROPONENTS OF ZEN

One of the most outstanding figures involved in the early groundwork prior to the establishment of Korean Zen was a monk named Won Hyo (617–86 CE). Born in Zainmyon in the third kingdom of Silla, whose dynastic rulers effectively unified Korea from the seventh century, he was the founder of the Popsong school of Buddhism. This school sought to adopt an ecumenical approach to religious practice in Korea rather than the sectarian stance found in China and Japan. To this end he strove to meld all the different aspects of Buddhism into one eclectic whole. Although himself a formidable scholar, he was also a populist in his attitude to religion, believing strongly that Buddhism should not be an exclusive or necessarily monastic faith but that its quintessence should be accessible to the common people irrespective of scholarship or social position. For them he pursued an 'Awakening of Faith', *kishinnon,* on which he wrote two major surviving works, today combined as the *Kishinnon Haedong Sogi.* Although not recognized as a Master of Zen, Won Hyo nonetheless probably stimulated the development of Zen Buddhism in Korea more than any other of its early luminaries.

The person to whom the founding of Korean Zen is officially credited is an eighth- and ninth-century Scillan monk named Toui, who spent thirty years in China studying Ch'an at a time when Buddhism had entered a period of waning popularity in Korea. He returned to the country in 818 CE and began to challenge the heavy doctrinal slant of Buddhism, a stance which led, ironically, to the kind of sectarian schism that Toui's predecessor had abhorred. Zen, the meditative pursuit, became represented by the school of Son, as distinct from the more doctrinal and scholarly aspect of Buddhism which was staunchly defended by the school of Kyo (also sometimes referred to as the Sutra school).

Toui retired from public life and died in obscurity in 825 CE, but his work was faithfully carried on through a lineage of Masters. One of these, a monk named Pojo Chejung (803–80), the third Master of Korean Zen after Toui, founded the temple of Porim on Mount Kaji, regarded as the nucleus from which the popularity of the Korean Zen philosophy spread. His pioneering mission stimulated the development of the so-called Nine Mountain Schools of Son which emerged during the next hundred years.

The most significant figure from later centuries was probably Pojo Chinul (1158–1210). He was arguably the counterpart of Hui Neng, the Sixth Zen Patriarch in China (see p.184), in his development of a truly native tradition of Zen in Korea and his writings are still the standard reference texts of Son.

IDEOLOGICAL INTEGRATION

For a long time the various schools of Son were autonomous one from another which tended to foster ideological conflict. In 1356, however, the Nine Mountain schools were

PART OF TONGDO-SA TEMPLE, NORTH OF PUSAN
IN SOUTH KOREA.

amalgamated as the Chogye Order by the Zen Master Taego Pou (1301–82) and from that time they managed to exist comfortably alongside one another. The two main ideological divisions of Korean Buddhism, those of the Son and Kyo schools, persisted until as recently as 1928, when a move was instigated to amalgamate, and in 1935 unity was achieved, joining the two into the single Chogyejong sect whose headquarters were constructed in Seoul. Today Kyo and Son adherents may still pursue different practices but commonly they rest under the same temple roof without conflict.

Buddhism has been the main religion of Korea for most of its recorded history, although for more than five hundred years Korean Buddhists have been persecuted to a greater or lesser extent. This occurred first under the Yi Dynasty (1392–1910) when there was a concerted effort to replace it with Confucianism, and then under Japanese occupation. During the 1930s and 1940s, Japanese elements were increasingly introduced to Korean Buddhism which caused considerable adverse reaction. After the country was liberated in 1945, the Chogyejong sect instigated a purge which eliminated much of the Japanese influence.

Korean Buddhism has remained steadfastly a philosophy of the common people and, even today, it is largely ignored by the Korean political administration.

THE NINE MOUNTAIN SCHOOLS

THE SORAK MOUNTAINS, HOME OF THE SONGJU SCHOOL.

*E*stablished, as their name implies, on mountain tops in the ancient kingdom of Silla which existed before Korea was unified, the nine schools represent the quintessence of Korean Son (Zen). All are of more or less similar persuasion and doctrine and differ only in terms of the stamp placed upon them through the personalities of their founders – a feature which often assumed mythical proportions, particularly in the tendency to romanticize the circumstances of their births.

The schools arose in the ninth and tenth centuries, coinciding with the period of the Tang Dynasty in China and all of their founders received training in Chinese monastery schools of Ch'an, most in the Hui Neng tradition of 'sudden enlightenment' (see pp.184–5). At first they came into serious conflict with the more conservative Buddhist establishment in Korea which viewed them as being unacceptably liberal because they did not follow the intellectual path of Kyo, the doctrinal Buddhism. This was represented chiefly by the school of Uisang Hwaom, dedicated to the study of the *Avatamsaka* and other *sutras* and the pursuit of *dharmadhatu*, the 'roots' of *buddha* teaching.

The Mountain Schools, in contrast, shunned scholarship and logic, emphasized freedom of thought implicit in Son and defended the 'mind-to-mind' transmission of the philosophy which bypasses words and speech. In addition, they were all agreed on the need to adopt a simple, unassuming lifestyle.

Kaji

The founder, the Buddhist monk Toui, trained in China under Hsi Tang Chih Tsang, whose Ch'an school followed the teachings of the Patriarch Ma Tsu (709–88 CE). Versed in the techniques of 'sudden enlightenment' achieved through non-logic or irrational thought, Toui challenged the validity of the doctrinal tradition, but the Kaji school achieved little success during his administration and recruited few students. Toui subsequently transferred his authority to a pupil, Uksung Yumku, who, in turn, passed the leadership to Pojo Chejung (803–80). The latter built the Porim temple on Mount Kaji and popularized Son to the extent that the school developed considerable national fame and as a result recruited large numbers of students.

Tongni

This school was founded by Hyechol (785–861) who was initiated at the Pusok-sa temple of Uisang Hwaom at the age of 15. He went on to study in China under Hsi Tang Chih Tsang, travelling as a passenger aboard a convict ship, though his teacher died shortly after his arrival. When Hyechol returned to Silla in 839 he founded the Son Tae-an temple on Mount Tongni before temporarily taking up a position as monk to the royal court. His most influential pupil was Master Toson who, having studied the *I Ching* in China, popularized divinatory techniques in Korea. Hyechol is said to have made the enduring statement: 'Mind of no-mind is the true mind'.

Songju

The founder of this school was Mu Yom (799–888) whose ancestry traces back through various high-ranking government officials to the Sillan royal clan. Having entered the Osaek-sok temple in the Sorak Mountains at the age of 12, he later studied Ch'an techniques in China for 24 years under the tutelage of the Patriarch Ma Ku Po Che, a former student of Ma Tsu. Mu Yom also ran into ideological conflict with the Kyo schools, proclaiming their doctrinal approach to be intellectually inferior to that of Son. He followed the maxim of one of his Ch'an teachers, 'no tongue in two mouths is the essence of our school', and achieved a burgeoning popularity for Son methods. In old age he was rewarded with the title 'National Teacher'.

Silsang

It is known that the school was founded by Hongjik, a Buddhist monk, but little detail about him is recorded. He built the school on Mount Chiri in 828 after a period of study in China under Hsi Tang Chih Tsang, and is claimed to have been the first to establish a traditional Son teaching programme in Korea.

Pongni

The school was established in memory of Hyon Uk (787–869) who entered a Buddhist monastery at 21, studied in China and returned to Silla in 837. There he became head of the Silsang temple, possibly having been appointed by the royal court as a successor to Hongjik. Some 30 years after his death the school on Mount Pongni was founded by one of his disciples, Chingyong Simhui, and rose to considerable success as a centre of Son teaching.

Sagul

Pomil (810–89), the founder, was the son of a regional governor. He entered monastic life at 15, followed by a protracted training period in China under the Ch'an Master Yen Kuan Chi An and others. At one stage he was caught up in anti-Buddhist polemics instigated by the emperor Wu Tsang, but after 15 years he returned to Silla, staying first in a monastery on Mount Paekdal before taking a government commission to build the Sagul mountain school where he remained until his death.

Saja

This school was established by the son a noble family, Toyun (797–868), who entered monastic life aged 18 in the doctrinally orientated Kwisin temple, before becoming an itinerant. Later he studied in China under Nan Chuan Piu Yuan, a celebrated and gifted student of Ma Tsu. On his return to Silla he built a small temple in the Diamond Mountains which was subsequently expanded by his student Chunghyo Cholchung as the Hungyong school. At a later date the school was moved to Mount Saja from which it gained its name.

Huiyang

The school, which technically predates any of the others, was founded by the Buddhist monk Pomnang, who brought Chinese Ch'an to Silla at sometime during the seventh century. He is not, however, credited with introducing authentic Son because he did not study the 'sudden enlightenment' tradition of Hui Neng, the Sixth Chinese Patriarch from whose teachings it is agreed that Korean Son stems. Pomnang studied under the Fourth Ch'an Patriarch of China, Tao Hsin Hsi, and his school is therefore unusual amongst the majority of the nine in that it originated in the earlier Bodhidharma tradition.

Sumi

This school shares with Huiyang the distinction that it does not derive from the Hui Neng tradition. Its founder, Iom (870–936), studied under Ch'ing Yuan Hsing Su in China from whom the Ts'ao Tung school was to evolve. The Sumi school was established in 936 under the royal patronage of Wang Kong, the first of the Koryo Dynasty, who was also responsible for funding the building of the Kwang-jo temple on Mount Sumi.

ZEN SECTS

Although there are a substantial number of sects in Japan with Buddhist leanings, only some are specifically concerned with Zen Buddhism, which is primarily a monastic tradition. The ethics and meditational practices of Zen were effectively transplanted from China from the twelfth century CE onwards, many hundreds of years after the more Indian-styled Mahayana Buddhism had arrived by way of Tibet.

Zen appeared in Japan as a distinct philosophy during the ninth century CE but for many decades it remained sidelined by the more established Buddhist sects. It was introduced in company with neo-Confucianism, ethics of which have always been deeply ingrained in Zen teaching. It came through the Chinese Zen schools of Lin Chi and Ts'ao Tung from which the major Japanese Zen sects of Rinzai and Soto derive. The Chinese schools, which had themselves evolved during the Sung Dynasty (960–1279 CE), both subscribed to the teachings of one of the most remarkable figures in the history of Zen. This scholar was the Sixth Chinese Zen Patriarch, Hui Neng, who lived during the eighth century and who was instrumental in the popularity which Zen philosophy achieved under the T'ang emperors. There were many other eminent Zen masters in China during this period but the influence on more or less all of them can be traced back to Hui Neng.

Zen eventually appealed to the Japanese mind not least because it had already taken on a truly oriental flavour through its development in China, a country whose culture Japan had long revered and emulated. It evolved as a formal philosophy in Japan under the aegis of two sects, Rinzai and Soto, which became established during the medieval period. There is little difference in the teaching of the two and those distinctions which have arisen are accounted for by style and administration. Rinzai and Soto still account for mainstream Zen Buddhism in Japan and have expanded to include universities and schools, publishing organizations and charitable work in the community, apart from their powerful monastic institutions.

THE RINZAI SECT

The founder of Japanese Zen is regarded as being Eisai (1141–1215), a Buddhist priest who visited China on two separate occasions and learned the philosophy of Lin Chi. When he returned to Japan for the second time in 1191 he first settled in Kyushu but was obliged to leave because of doctrinal opposition. Eventually he found his way to one of the old regional capitals, Kyoto, and set up a small school there

EIHEI-*JI* TEMPLE, FORMERLY CALLED DAIBUTSU-*JI*, IS THE MONASTIC HEADQUARTERS OF THE SOTO SECT.

where he taught the philosophy which translated as Rinzai. It was this which became incorporated as the Rinzai sect.

Eisai was first granted permission to occupy the Kennin-*ji* monastery at Kyoto in 1202 and from there the movement expanded to Kamakura, where he gained the patronage of a local military overlord and received the resources to build the Jufuku-*ji* temple. Three other major Zen monasteries were established in the Kyoto and Kamakura area and these scholarly institutions became known as the *gozan*, the 'Five Mountains'. For a long period they represented the focuses of cultural excellence in medieval Japan. Rinzai particularly appealed to the ruling classes of nobles and *samurai* warriors and was destined to become the dominant Zen sect not only throughout the Kamakura period but also in the Muromachi era which followed (1336–1568).

Amongst the most outstanding Rinzai masters of later generations was Hakuin Ekaku (1685–1768) whose scholarship and artistry were matched only by his exceptional personality. Hakuin was responsible for the further development and promotion of one of the fundamental

SYMBOLIC PAPERS IN SOFOKU-*JI* TEMPLE, A PLACE OF WORSHIP BELONGING TO THE OBAKU SECT.

practices of Rinzai known as *koan*, the application of the mind to conundrums, through which the practitioner may achieve perfect enlightenment. Today there are 14 registered schools of Rinzai in Japan known as *ha*, and an indeterminate number of independently run establishments pursuing Rinzai Zen ideals.

THE SOTO SECT

This sect was founded as a modest school when compared with Rinzai but subsequently became the more popular of the two. Whilst Rinzai was attractive to the minds of the intellectual aristocracy, Soto offered a more broad-based appeal to the common man. It incorporates, with other meditative techniques, the practice of *zazen* which relies on the adoption of a difficult physical posture for long periods as an aid to freeing the mind.

The philosophy was first promoted by another Buddhist priest named Dogen (1200–53), a former pupil of Eisai, who also studied in China and became wedded to the philosophy of Ts'ao Tung. When he returned to Kyoto in 1227 Dogen established his Zen school, but this lasted for only a brief period until a reactionary group of Tendai monks, who

disagreed with the radicalism of the philosophy he was promoting, obliged him to leave. By 1244 he found himself in the Fukui province and established his school in the more liberal climate of the Daibutsu-*ji* temple which became renamed as the Eihei-*ji*. After the time of Dogen the Soto sect was further reformed and developed under the tutelage of Suzuki Shosan (1579–1653). Today its administration is shared between the monastic headquarters at the Eihei-*ji* and the Soji-*ji* temple in Yokohama.

THE OBAKU SECT

Obaku represents a third Zen movement in Japan, though one enjoying considerably less influence. In common with Rinzai and Soto it was imported from China, although not until much later, during the seventeenth century. The Chinese Buddhist priest Yin Yuan (1594–1673) emigrated to Japan, where he became known as Ingen, bringing with him the philosophy of Huang-po. He settled near Uji and built an administrative centre and school known as the Mampuku-*ji* which was constructed along the architectural lines of a Chinese temple.

TECHNIQUES IN ZEN MEDITATION

The two great masters who founded Zen schools in medieval Japan, Dogen and Eisai, were students of the philosophical and ethical teachings of the Sixth Chinese Zen Patriarch, Hui Neng. Both Japanese masters promoted monastic practices amongst their disciples which would result in SATORI, the gaining of true enlightenment, and their respective schools of Soto and Rinzai were developed towards this objective, though with distinct administrative bodies, temples and styles.

Both schools adopted comparable practices in their spiritual training which, whilst originating amongst masters of Chinese Zen and tracing back to the teachings of Hui Neng, came to long-lasting fruition in Japan. The schools applied, on the one hand, a mental discipline of conundrums known as *koan,* and on the other, the practice of *zazen* or 'sitting meditation' which requires the adoption of a certain physical position known as the lotus posture during prolonged periods of intense mental control. Whilst the two schools continue to use both practices, *koan* has become more identifiable with the Rinzai school whilst Soto followers have focused on *zazen.*

KOAN

The *koan* style of meditation, dynamic and vocal, stands in sharp contrast to the silent and essentially passive contemplation favoured by other Buddhist philosophical schools, including some of those devoted to Zen. It derives originally from the Chinese technique of *Kung An* which translates, literally, as 'public announcement' and the title is an indication that it constitutes part of an open schooling programme.

Koan is an unusual route to enlightenment which was begun in China during the Tang Dynasty (618–906 CE) and seems to have been first recognized as an effective device to aid meditation in the tenth century CE by the Zen Master Nan Yuan Hui Yung. He developed the technique as part of the routine question-and-answer exchanges that took place between master and disciples in his school and it has always been recognized that the most essential prerequisite in the successful use of *koan* is a very close one-to-one relationship between teacher and pupil. Over a period of time the questioning became more and more obscure and was such that, in order to obtain a satisfactory answer, the student was obliged to abandon thoughts which conform to any rationale. The only way to secure an answer to the 'unanswerable' was to transcend beyond rationality into the realms of the supra-rational. By this means the student was carried into the transcendent realm of enlightenment.

In practice the technique requires the student to focus his mind wholly on the problem posed by the conundrum. All other thoughts are banished as he works through the riddle for as many days or weeks or months that it takes. Sometimes this mental process may involve reducing the conundrum to an all-encompassing sentence or even a single word which the student repeats over and over, in his head or aloud, in the style of a *mantra*, examining the task from every angle. The final elucidation may come as an unexpected and shocking revelation and, as more and more of the conundrums are unravelled, provides the key to total spiritual enlightenment. The underlying intention is to release the mind into an advanced state of consciousness and it is said that this state is reached when each *koan* riddle is resolved.

The earliest-known written compilation of *koans* is that of Fen Yang Shan Chao (947 –1024). This work includes some 300 *koans* which are separated into three groups. Each group includes responses, or poems and responses, written by Fen Yang, to *koans* which were originated either by himself or by other Zen masters. *Koan* has been poorly reported in the west, not least because its principles may seem illogical and paradoxical to the western mind and yet it is these same principles which provide such an appeal in terms of eastern wisdom.

The Rinzai school in Japan developed a particular affinity for *koans* and this route to enlightenment became one of the mainstays of its teaching which has been upheld to the present day. Amongst the Zen masters who were subsequently responsible for elaborating on *koan* practice within the school were Yuan Wu K'o Ch'in (1063–1135) and Ta Hui Tsung Kao (1089–1163). Other similar collations of *koans* which have remained in use include the collection of 100 known as the *Hekinganroku* compiled by Yuan Wu K'o Ch'in. To each *koan* he has added a commentary and explanation and these have been embellished further with a collection of songs on the *koans* composed by another master, Hsuch Tan Ch'ung Hsien (980–1052).

The outstanding teacher of this discipline of mind puzzles, however, was Hakuin Ekaku who represents a later generation of scholars, since he was born in 1685. He was a major influence on the Rinzai school as consummate teacher

AN ARTIST'S INTERPRETATION OF THE KOAN MEDITATION TECHNIQUE.

213

A Painting in Chogyesa temple, Seoul, symbolizes the importance of meditation in Zen Buddhism.

and artist and he developed the *koan* riddle exercises to a sophisticated level, believing that it was necessary and valuable to arouse *taigi*, the 'Great Doubt', in the minds of his students. He argued this on the grounds that the greater the doubt, the more intense the enlightenment which followed. The conundrums effectively have no answer in the material or logical sense and, by way of illustration, Hakuin was responsible for one of the most famous and oft-quoted *koan* utterances: 'If someone claps their hands, there arises a noise. Listen to the noise of the single hand!' Hakuin Ekaku died in 1768, leaving a flourishing and enduring school in his wake.

ZAZEN

This was developed as another important meditation technique amongst Zen devotees but is a much more passive technique than *koan* relying on the adoption of a particular and physically demanding posture, the lotus position, for long periods of time. *Zazen*, as in the case of *koan*, originated in China and was brought back to Japan by Zen Buddhist monks who had gone there to be schooled by Chinese Ch'an masters. Once established in Japan *zazen* became most closely identified with the Soto school of Zen.

The most important figure in the promotion of *zazen* is Dogen (1200–53), the founder of the Japanese Soto school. An extraordinary personality in the history of Japanese Buddhism, Dogen was born into an aristocratic family, but both his parents died whilst he was still a young child and as an orphan he was raised by relatives. He first entered a Buddhist Tendai monastery at the age of 12 and, after a noviciate period in the Tendai school on Mount Hiei, he moved to the Kennin-*ji* monastery in Kyoto where Eisai, the founder of the Rinzai school, had taught. However he became disillusioned with his masters and their involvement with the imperial court and government, believing that this conflicted with the true spirit of the Buddhist philosophy. He decided to travel to China, during the period of the Southern Sung Dynasty, in search of enlightenment. He was admitted to the Zen monastic complex on Mount Ti'en Tsung where he studied under the master Ju Ching (1163–1268) and gained enlightenment in what he later described as 'a sudden and shocking experience'.

On his return to Japan, Dogen established his own monastic school at Koshohorin-*ji* near Kyoto, still shunning the influential imperial and government circles. There he was to remain for eleven years until he uprooted once more and made his way to the remote province of Echiren where he founded the Temple of Eternal Peace, the Eihei-*ji*, that was to become the permanent home of the Soto school.

Whilst in China he had been impressed by the importance of correct positioning of the body, by tradition the posture once adopted by Shakyamuni *buddha,* as an aid to meditation and as a route towards perfect enlightenment. The approach and attitude of the Chinese Ch'an practitioners was one which he found to be in stark contrast with that of the Japanese monks, whom he considered had more or less abandoned the pursuit of enlightenment through control of the mind. He believed that practice, involving the abandonment of the body and mind, was the key to enlightenment or *satori*. This, he argued, was the 'correct way to enter *buddha dharma*'. He therefore developed his own version of the lotus position which he adopted during long sessions of personal meditation and this posture was to become the cornerstone of *zazen*. It is promoted constantly in his writings, beside his other chief concerns – the scrupulous adherence to monastic rules and ethics, and the need to develop compassion towards all living things.

He claimed that the suddenness of revelation, akin to that which he had experienced in China, was a characteristic result of practising *zazen* through which the practitioner would experience a rapid release from normal consciousness into transcendence. In this respect both *koan* and *zazen* appear to offer similar results, one through intense application of mental stimulus in the form of a puzzle, the other through a rigorous and physically demanding posture.

Dogen's writings make no claims that *zazen* and enlightenment are synonymous but that *zazen*, as a combination of physical control, conscious mental resolve and focused devotion, provides an effective route towards a level of spirituality wherein the mind and body are detached from the impermanence of the material world and its delusions. Dogen's earliest literary work is the *Fukanzazengi* (Universal Advancement of the Principles of Zazen) but his teachings are more comprehensively encompassed by a massive work in 95 chapters called the *Shobogenzo*. He provided detailed instructions on the physical and mental aspects of the technique and exhorted his pupils to:

> ... *cast aside all involvement and cease all affairs. Do not think good or bad. Do not administer pros and cons. Cease all movement of the conscious mind, the gauging of all thoughts and views. Have no designs on becoming a buddha. This has nothing to do with sitting or lying down.* (Extracted from Abe and Waddell, *Dogen's Fukanzazengi*)

After the death of Dogen the centre of *zazen* practice and teaching remained at the Eihei-*ji* monastery and was further promoted by a succession of Soto masters. The greatest of these was undoubtedly Suzuki Shosan who lived from 1579 until 1653, his death coming some thirty years before the birth of the great Rinzai reformer and promoter of *koan*, Hakuin Ekaku.

THE
ZEN ARTS
AND SKILLS

*P*art of the quest for Zen enlightenment has been devoted to the arts and artistic skills. These were first developed by Zen masters in China but they found their real and enduring home when Zen was transported to Japan. These arts are not necessarily products of enlightenment but are considered to be allied to meditation techniques and, in this, the talents and inspiration they require may arise out of the deep concentration demanded in meditation.

Although Chinese in their original form, to a great extent they are a product of the quintessential Japanese psyche and the needs of Japan's nobility who largely staffed the ranks of Zen devotees during the Classical Period between approximately the twelfth and sixteenth centuries CE. There is a Japanese intellectual desire not only to be in intimate contact and understanding with the natural order of things, but also to express this intimacy through excellence in the arts.

The Japanese mentality is one of correctness. It places great store on the proper and ritualized manner of conducting all sorts of activities from preparing tea and arranging flowers, to gardening and to the martial arts of swordsmanship, archery and self defence. Anyone who has taken part in a *judo* class or visited a Zen garden will understand that the precise arrangement of actions or objects is both formalized and underpinned by more esoteric philosophical concepts. There exists an intimate relationship between Zen philosophy and the arts whereby, in the latter, a sense of spirituality is always present. The artistic aspect of Zen has also led to a broadening of the movement beyond the purely monastic and into more secular activity.

One of the earliest proponents of Zen art was Muso

Sosecki (1275–1351), also known as Muso Kokushi, who lived during the Muromachi period or Ashikaga Shogunate (1333–1573). This was a time characterized in Japan by the awkward combination of militarism in secular life and intense artistic flowering in the monasteries. Muso sought to bridge the gap between the two extremes and for much of his life was strongly influential in politics. An indication of this influence lies in the construction, on his behalf, of the Tenryu-*ji* monastery sponsored out of government funds by the *shogun* Ashikaga. He was also instrumental in arranging the first official mission in more than 500 years to China and it was from China that much of the Zen artistic inspiration came during the Ashikaga period. Zen priests became advisers to the *shoguns* on all matters artistic and were responsible for instructing trade missions to China on which artworks should be sought for decorating the residences of the Ashikaga court.

INK PAINTING

Known as *sumi-e,* inspired by Zen philosophy, ink painting became fashionable early in the fourteenth century and, whilst it was losing its vogue in China, it was destined to achieve an enduring popularity in Japan. Wealthy Japanese patrons were inspired to assemble great collections of Chinese-style ink paintings, whilst Zen artists in the monasteries around Kyoto were taught the techniques. Many of the Japanese artists who created early paintings remain anonymous, but those whose names are recorded include Mokuan and Kao who are thought to have been active during the early part of the fourteenth century. One of the most famous surviving works attributed to Mokuan is the scroll known as the 'Four Sleepers', a humorous composition which depicts three rather corpulent figures reposing idly across the torso of a dozing tiger.

The fifteenth century witnessed the rise of several other great Zen painters, including Josetsu and Shubun, who came from the Shokoku-*ji* monastery in Kyoto, and a student of

Shubun named Sesshu who studied at monasteries in China. These artists painted typical Japanese landscapes in the classical Zen style that is familiar today – jagged mountains clothed with gnarled pine trees providing a backdrop to various more immediate human activities from everyday life.

Amongst the best-known painters of later generations was the Zen Master Hakuin (1685–1768) who was closely involved with the development of the Rinzai school. His favoured subjects were themes from the Buddhist scriptures and paintings of other great Zen masters, which include at least one amusing and caricatured self-portrait.

POETRY

The 'Way of Poetry' or *kado* was closely allied with Zen-inspired painting. Amongst its greatest exponents were Sesshu and a seventeenth-century monk named Basho (1644–94) who, like Sesshu, was also an accomplished ink painter. Unlike the paintings, which are 'readable' in any language, the beauty of Japanese poetry is often lost in translation. Much is composed in a form known as the *haiku* which is characterized by its brevity and which reminds the reader of the ancient enigmatic poetry of the Hindu *Veda*. The *haiku* consists of three lines, the first with five syllables, the second with seven and the third

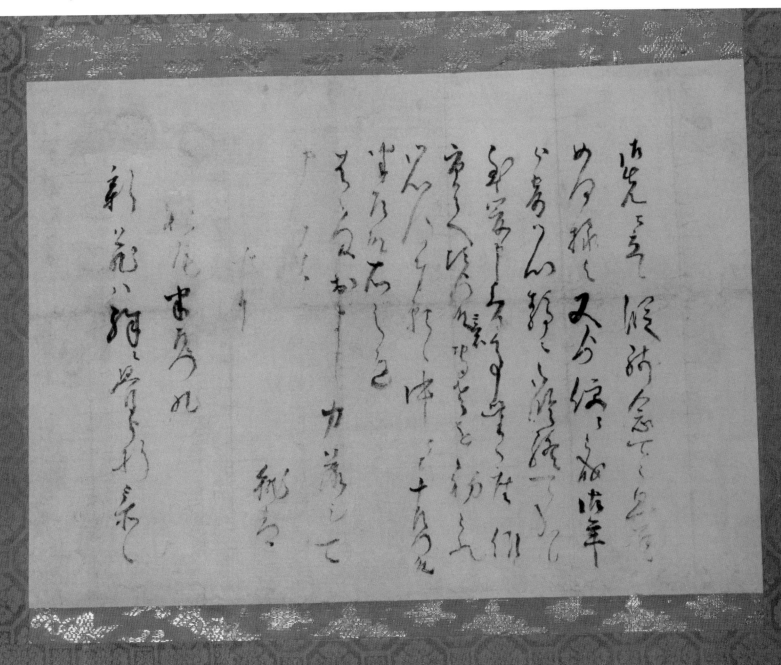

IN THIS MESSAGE, WRITTEN TWO DAYS BEFORE HIS DEATH, MATSUO BASHO APOLOGIZES TO HIS DISCIPLES FOR DYING BEFORE THEM.

reverting to five and it may be typified by one of Basho's most famous compositions:

The ancient pond —
A frog leaps in,
The sound of water.

THE TEA CEREMONY

Sado or the 'Way of Tea' is another Zen art which was introduced from China, where it became virtually obsolete, but which was then made intrinsically and enduringly Japanese. As with ink painting, the tea ceremony, known as *cha-no-yu*, which lies at the heart of the ritual of formal tea drinking, became firmly established in Japan during the time of the Ashikaga Shogunate. It was arguably first adopted there by Eisai (see p.210), but it was largely promoted to popularity by the Zen master Ikkyu (1394–1481) and his pupil Shuko who taught the art to the *shogun* Yoshimasa. Yoshimasa's personal tea-room or *chashitsu* in the grounds of the Higashiyama estate in Kyoto, where the Ginkaku-*ji* or Silver Pavilion stands, is preserved to this day and forms the model for many later tea-rooms.

Further refinement of the ceremony is attributed to a sixteenth-century monk named Rikyu who laid down rules governing not only the style of the tea-room, the garden in which it rested, and the utensils used for preparation, including the *cha-ire* or caddy and the *chawan* or tea bowl, but also the smallest details of movement and gesture employed by the participants.

LANDSCAPE GARDEN DESIGN

The creation of gardens in Japan has also been deeply influenced by the spirituality of Zen and the Zen garden has attracted many westerners to emulate its precisely arranged formalities. These creations owe their inspiration, as with so much in Japanese Zen, to China. They were created by Zen philosophers to embody a great spiritual symbolism, yet in China their value and beauty was discarded whilst in Japan it was nurtured. One of the most important of the classical Zen works on garden design is the *Emposho* (Book of Gardens) which was compiled during the Kamakura period before the era of the Ashikaga Shogunate. During the subsequent Ashikaga or Muromachi period, the design of the gardens became even more abstracted and esoteric to all but the initiated and their spirit is captured in another classic textbook known as the *Tsukiyama Teizo-den* (The Creation of Hill Gardens), compiled by a famous ink painter of the period, Soami.

The main architect of Zen gardening in Japan was Muso Sosecki (see p.216) and the designs which he created at the Tenryo-*ji* and the Saiho-*ji* temples are faithfully maintained to this day. Unlike the landscaped gardens of western culture

THE ART OF THE TEA CEREMONY, REPRESENTED IN A WATERCOLOUR PAINTING FROM THE TURN OF THE TWENTIETH CENTURY.

these were not designed as places of vicarious pleasure and relaxation. Although they may include beautiful components from nature – trees, mosses, grasses and shrubs sets amidst rocks and gravel and overlooked by pavilions – they stand primarily as embodiments of the spiritual truths of Zen. It has been said that, like ink painting, the Zen garden sets out to express nature in symbolic terms and many of the garden designs were inspired by the works of the *sumi-e* artists. In his instructions

ROCKS AND GRAVEL EXPRESS ZEN SPIRITUALITY AT DAITOKU-*JI* TEMPLE IN KYOTO.

for the creation of a Zen garden in *Tsukiyama Teizo-den*, Soami wrote: 'One's heart and mind should be concentrated on the profundity of nature, and there should not be any suspicion of frivolity in one's attitude towards it.'

One of the finest Zen gardens still in existence dating from the fifteenth century is that of the *shogun* Yoshimasa on his Higashiyama estate, in which the Silver Pavilion stands. It was laid out in 1480 and, after his death, was converted to a Buddhist temple and grounds, the Jisho-*ji*. It is built on a comparatively conventional style of ponds, islands, bridges, pavilions, trees and shrubs, which subscribe to the natural features of the landscape, and it includes a curiously shaped flat-topped hill which may have been used as a viewing platform.

Some of the gardens, however, became abstracted to such an extent that they dispensed with plants altogether and relied on the design and arrangement of inanimate materials. Amongst the most celebrated is the Stone Garden at the Ryoan-*ji* in Kyoto which consists of a 'lake' of immaculately raked lines of gravel from which arise fifteen 'islands' of rock, each surrounded by gravel swirls and eddies. Rather as the riddle of the *koan* it invites concentrated meditation in order to unravel its secrets. Traditionally attributed to Soami, its architecture is actually by an unknown hand, but such is its acclaim that, in recent times, it has inspired the works of artists including the western painter David Hockney.

Some of the Zen gardens, known as *roji*, were constructed around tea-rooms and are of a more natural design than others with paths leading the visitor from section to section and, in particular, a set of stepping stones linking the gate with the tea-room. Many of these were designed by the famous Zen master of the tea ceremony, Rikyu, who lived during the sixteenth century.

MARTIAL ARTS

In Japanese Zen martial arts came, predictably, from China, where they arose out of the philosophy of Tao and were articulated in a collection of texts known as the *Seven Military Classics*. These include most notably Sun Tzu's *The Art of War*. In ancient China it was considered that success in warfare depended on the development of mental skills and resources that took on a philosophical and spiritual dimension. It was said by Sun Tzu that 'When you mobilise the army and form strategic plans, you must be unfathomable', whilst another of the Chinese military strategists, T'ai Kung declared, 'One whose wisdom is the same as the masses is not a general for the state'. This led to the Chinese development of the psychology of warfare.

When these concepts were transported to Japan the military and strategic skills were developed into an art form so that in the Zen martial arts, which include *judo* or self-defence, *kendo* or swordsmanship and *kyudo* or archery, a dimension is introduced which goes far beyond the physical act of striking and defeating an opponent. These arts involve deep mental and spiritual discipline which takes them out of the arena of being merely aggressive or defensive accomplishments. The drawing and releasing of the *kyudo* bow string, the thrusts and strikes of the *kendo* sword, the precise bodily movements of *judo,* are regarded as spiritual as much as physical actions, their sounds, motions and vibrations taking on profound meaning. The Zen martial arts involve control not only of the processes of breathing and of the action of arm and leg muscles, but also of the mind which must be focused with great concentration so that the bow is drawn, the sword is wielded, and the limbs are directed using spiritually derived rather than purely physical strength.

BIBLIOGRAPHY

GENERAL

Cults, Michael Jordan, Carlton Books, 1996

Dictionary of Indian Philosophical Concepts, B. N. Singh, Asha Prakashan, 1988

Dictionary of Religions, J. R. Hinnells (ed.), Penguin, 1984

Encyclopedia of Gods, Michael Jordan, Kyle Cathie, 1992

Iconographic Dictionary of Indian Religions, Gosta Liebert, SRI Satguru, Delhi, 1976

Myths of the World, Michael Jordan, Kyle Cathie, 1993

HINDUISM

The Bhagavad Gita, Eknath Easwaran (trans.), Penguin Arkana, 1986

The Call of the Vedas, A. C. Bose, Bombay, 1988

Hindu Festivals and Ceremonies, Om Lata Bahadur, UPSPD, 1994

Hindu Gods and Goddesses, A. G. Mitchell, Victoria and Albert Museum, HMSO, 1982

Hinduism for Our Times, Arvind Sharma, Oxford University Press, Delhi, 1996

Hindu Myths, W. D. O'Flaherty (trans.), Penguin Classics, 1975

Mahabharata, C. Rajagopalachari (trans.), Bombay, 1990

Ramayana, C. Rajagopalachari (trans.), Bombay, 1983

Religions of the Hindukush, Karl Jettmar, Aris & Phillips, Warminster, 1986

The Rig Veda, W. D. O'Flaherty (trans.), Penguin Classics, 1981

A Survey of Hinduism, Klaus Klostermaier, State University of New York, 1994

Upanisads, Patrick Olivelle (trans.), World's Classics, 1996

Vaisnava Iconography, R. Champakalakshmi, Orient Longman, 1981

BUDDHISM

Buddhist Monastic Life, M. Wijayaratna, Cambridge University Press, 1990

Dharma Paths, K. K. Rinpoche, Snow Lion Publications, New York, 1992

Holy Places of the Buddha, Dharma Publishing, 1994

Mahayana Buddhism, B. L. Suzuki, Mandala, 1992

Mainstream Buddhism, Eric Cheetham, Eden Grove Publications, 1994

The Path to Enlightenment, The Dalai Lama, Snow Lion Publications, New York, 1982

Ritual and Devotion in Buddhism, Sangharakshita, Windhorse Publications, 1995

Shakyamuni Buddha, Nikkyo Niwano, Kosei Publishers, Tokyo, 1980

Stories of the Buddha, C. A. F. Rhys Davids (trans.), Dover New York, 1989

The Tibetan Book of Living and Dying, S. Rinpoche, Rider, 1992

JAINISM

A Comprehensive History of Jainism, A. K. Chatterjee, Firma KLM, Calcutta, 1984

The Jaina Theory of Perception, Pushpa Bothra, Motilal Banarsidass, Delhi, 1976

The Jains, Paul Dundas, Routledge, 1992

CHINESE PHILOSOPHY

Chinese Mythology, D. Walters, Aquarian Press, 1992

I Ching, J. Legge (trans.), Citadel Press, 1964

Taoism, Eva Wong, Shambhala, 1997

The World of Thought in Ancient China, B. I. Schwartz, Harvard University Press, 1985

The World's Religions, Lion Publishing, 1982

Zen Enlightenment – Origins and Meaning, H. Dumoulin, Weatherhill, 1979

JAPANESE BELIEFS

The Art of the Warrior, R. D. Sawyer (ed. and trans.), Shambala, 1996

Folk Religion in Japan, Ichiro Hori, University of Chicago Press, 1968

Thousand Peaks – Korean Zen, Mu Soeng Sunim, Primary Point Press, 1991

Zen and Oriental Art, H. Munsterberg, Charles Tuttle, 1965

Zen Enlightenment, H. Dumoulin, Weatherhill, New York, 1979

Zen in the Art of Archery, Eugen Herrigel, Penguin Arkana, 1985

INDEX

HARTFORD PUBLIC LIBRARY

3 2520 07585 6996

Eastern wisdom : the
philosophies and rituals of
the East

DOWNTOWN MAIN FLOOR
32520075856996

FORD PUBLIC LIBRARY
500 MAIN STREET
ARTFORD, CT 06103
(HPL)

ACK   GEMENTS

The publishers would like to thank the following sources for their kind permission to reproduce the pictures in this book:

AKG photo, London; Ancient Art & Architecture Collection; Axiom/Jim Holmes; Bridgeman Art Library: / *'Peach Blossom'*
Chinese painting, Lindley Library, RHS, London /35 *'The chariot fight between Drona, Bhima and Arjuna, from Indian Epic'* c.1542 (page from
paper manuscript), Tamil Nadu, Oriental Museum, Durham University /135 *Water Buffalo hand painted incantation C19th*, Oriental Museum,
Durham University /18 *"The Holy Family of Shiva Parvati on Mount Kailasa, Indian"*, Victoria & Albert Museum, London / *'Fuji from Nakahara'*
by Nishimura Eijudo, Victoria & Albert Museum, London; **Jean-Loup Charmet; Christie's Images; Corbis UK Ltd.:** /Arvind Garg
/Lindsay Hebberd /Angelo Hornack /Bettmann-UPI /Hulton-Deutsch Collection /Earl Kowall /Craig Lovell /Kevin Morris /John Noble
/Tim Page /Brian Vikander; **ET Archive:** Biblioteque Nationale, Paris /British Museum /Musee Guimet, Paris /Oriental Art Museum,
Genoa /Marco Polo Gallery, Paris /Victoria & Albert Museum, London; **Mary Evans Picture Library; Werner Forman Archive:**
/Basho Kenshokai, Ueno; **Robert Harding Picture Library:** /G & P Corrigan /Alain Evrard /Tony Waltham; **Image Select; Images
Colour Library; Panos Pictures:** /Sadhur Anwar /R Berriedale /Jean-Leo Dugast /Alain Le Garsmeur /C Stowers; **People's
Republic of China; Trip:**/B Anthony /T Bognar /C Caffrey /R Cracknell /Dinodia/F Good /T Nooritis /P Rauter /C Rennie /H
Rogers /Spinx /A Tovy /B Turner /R Vargas /J Wakelin /M Watson.

Every effort has been made to acknowledge correctly and contact the source and/copyright holder of each picture, and Carlton Books
Limited apologises for any unintentional errors or omissions which will be corrected in future editions of this book.

Date Due

AUG 1 2 1999
MAR 2 7 2000
APR 0 8 2000
DEC 1 2 2000